SAILING IN CIRCLES, GOIN' SOMEWHERE

SAILING IN CIRCLES, GOIN' SOMEWHERE

Not Your Typical Boat Story

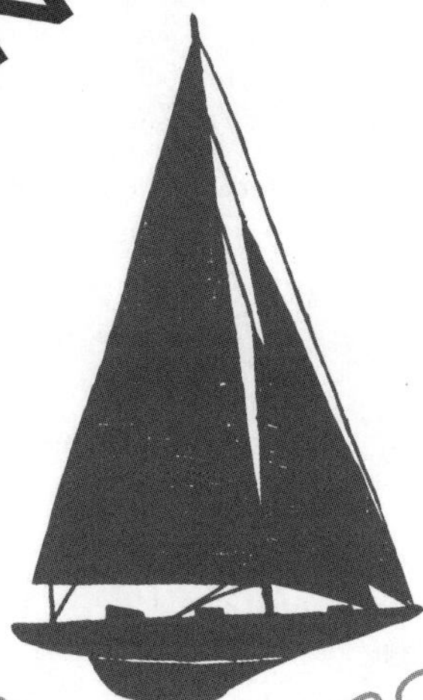

FINLEY MARTIN

a memoir

NIMBUS PUBLISHING
NIMBUS.CA

Nimbus Publishing Limited
3660 Strawberry Hill St, Halifax, NS, B3K 5A9
(902) 455-4286 nimbus.ca

Printed and bound in Canada
Cover & interior design: John van der Woude, JVDW Designs
NB1288

Library and Archives Canada Cataloguing in Publication
Martin, Finley, author
Sailing in circles, goin' somewhere : not your typical boat story / Finley Martin.

Issued in print and electronic formats.
ISBN 978-1-77108-633-2 (softcover).—ISBN 978-1-77108-634-9 (HTML)

1. Martin, Finley—Travel—Canada, Eastern. 2. Sailors—Prince Edward Island—Biography. 3. Sailing—Canada, Eastern. 4. Canada, Eastern—Description and travel. 5. Autobiographies. I. Title. II. Title: Sailing in circles, going somewhere.

GV810.92.M37A3 2018 797.124092 C2017-907961-1
C2019-907962-X

Canada | Canada Council for the Arts | Conseil des arts du Canada | NOVA SCOTIA

Nimbus Publishing acknowledges the financial support for its publishing activities from the Government of Canada through the Canada Book Fund (CBF) and the Canada Council for the Arts, and from the Province of Nova Scotia. We are pleased to work in partnership with the Province of Nova Scotia to develop and promote our creative industries for the benefit of all Nova Scotians.

FSC www.fsc.org MIX Paper from responsible sources FSC® C013916

Three cheers for my sons, Finley Martin and Robert Martin, Peter Grant, and my cousin, Bob Zack, who shared segments of my journey. All were able mates and good company.

TABLE OF CONTENTS

PART ONE

PART TWO

PART THREE

The author intended to sail this entire route, but only completed the section shown as a solid line.

PART ONE

Arja D. drying its sails in Murray Harbour, PEI.

Chapter 1

DREAM MAKER

I am perhaps five years old. Maybe seven, I don't recall. The day is summery and warm. The sun reddens as it lowers in late afternoon. I am on my sailboat; hand on the tiller, eyes on the sails, reclining against the cockpit coaming. The seas are broad, blue, and calm. The wind is fair. Oh...yes...and by my side is a beautiful girl. That was it, really. The dream. At the core of it lay romanticism, adventure, freedom—fascinations for every boy. However, the remarkable thing about it was that I had never seen the ocean or ridden in a boat. Nor would I until I was fourteen.

When I try to recollect where my love of sailing started, it always comes back to that dream. It was a night-sleep dream, not a daydream. It was the very first one that I clearly remember, and it was a dream that recurred in later years.

The ember of my odd dream may have been fanned by my love of poetry, for so much of the poetry we studied in those days had links to the sea and seafaring. During my senior year at high school I became delighted by Joseph Conrad's *Heart of Darkness* and *The Secret Sharer* and "Landfalls and Departures." His words moved with the rhythmic flow and ominous depth and mysteriousness of the ocean itself and fuelled my own desire to go to sea. After university, I received a commission as lieutenant in the US Marine Corps. There I managed to get a taste of life at sea—several months aboard the USS *Guam*, a helicopter carrier, and a bit of recreational sailing off Okinawa—but it was a decade later before I was on or even near the ocean again. Yet there was always, always, that tug inside, kindled in a dream and stoked by poetic words from so long ago. And eventually, twists of fate and quirks of life led me to work aboard commercial fishing vessels along Canada's east coast and as a seaman aboard a passenger ferry operating between Prince Edward Island and Nova Scotia.

During the mid-1970s, I took a boatbuilding course at the Marine and Fisheries Training Centre in Summerside, PEI. Until that time, I had never picked up a saw with any serious purpose in mind. In spite of dubious woodworking skills as a youngster, I found that, with proper training, I could square off a board without jamming the saw with four-letter expletives, and I could drive home a nail without curling it over like a staple. I grew more confident with my new-found abilities. I believed that I could indeed build a vessel. I was convinced that I would. In fact, I was determined to do so.

Before all that, however, I built a house for our family on a knoll overlooking the harbour in the pretty fishing village of Beach Point on the province of Prince Edward Island in the midst of Canada's Gulf of St. Lawrence. Later I added a large outbuilding, which my wife, Brenda, and I referred to as the "barn." And it was in that outbuilding that I would build a boat.

By this time in my life I had begun a career as a schoolteacher. Three children and a dog added to the busyness of our lives and, while visions of sailing boats coursed through my head, the expense of one limited any boat plans to those practical, build-able, and able to slide out of a thirty-foot barn with ten-foot doors.

In the end, I chose a design by William Atkin, naval architect and boat builder from Noroton, Connecticut. Atkin had drawn blueprints for this 26-foot knockabout sometime around 1936 and, while pondering what name it should carry, he thought of *Alice's Adventures in Wonderland* and *Through the Looking-Glass* and wrote, "While the ink was wet on the boom of the sail plan I remembered:

'Beware the Jabberwock, my son
The jaws that bite, the claws that catch!
Beware the Jubjub bird, and shun
The frumious Bandersnatch!'

And there was my sought-for name—*Jabberwock*," he concluded, borrowing from the Lewis Carroll poem.

Jabberwock was a decidedly odd and disturbingly cacophonous name to append to a boat. Still, even if Atkin had named it *Bandersnatch*, or something just as "frumious," it would have made no difference in my decision to build it. I just liked the look of his design.

Jabberwock was 26 feet of prettiness, I thought, and with seven-foot-six-inches of beam, nearly a four-to-one ratio if one added the rudder, which extends past the sternpost. Most of all, I admired the cross-section of the hull which, in the blueprints, showed the overlapping contours at each of the twelve stations from stem to stern. It revealed a gentle symmetry, a lovely gradual flow to all parts. It seemed the kind of vessel that would bear a wave nicely, not pound in a sea, and be relatively stable. *Jabberwock* had a straight keel too. It drew only two feet of water, which meant, of course, that I could take it into a cove with only a couple of teacups of water beneath me. Fifteen hundred pounds of lead blocks fitted beneath the floors gave it stability, and a sturdy oak centreboard reduced drift.

Jabberwock was a simple sloop rig. No back stays. Most unusual of all, though, was that it was a double-ender. Old-timers sometimes referred to such vessels as pink sterns or sharpies, all of which meant that the stern tapered to a fine, narrow end, just as the bow did. Such a design feature is uncommon. It reduces the space available aft for stowage, but it is useful in a following sea. When a boat is running downwind and waves overtake it from astern, a double-ender doesn't present a flat and, therefore, resistant surface to the wave. Instead, it parts the wave and lets it slip easily forward along both sides of the hull. As a result, there is less chance of a wave breaking into the cockpit.

I began construction in the summer of '86. My first step was lofting the plans full-length on the barn floor. This was accomplished by converting the table of offsets (a chart with lots of numbers) into the actual lines of the boat, which formed the patterns for wooden moulds that determined the shape of the boat. Accuracy was crucial. If I made a mistake at this stage, my future boat would likely resemble "the house that Jack built."

For a month or more, therefore, a visitor to my boat shop would find me crawling across the emerging design on my shop floor. I would have a pencil in one hand, a tape measure in the other. Howard Chapelle's *Boatbuilding* would be bent open to "Lofting, Chapter 2," a section so abstract and disagreeable that I must have read it twenty times over in order to impress its meaning on my unreceptive mind.

The keel was next. Most of my brothers-in-law had built their own lobster-fishing boats. One of them, Kevin MacLeod, had gathered lumber for his own new vessel, *Tyler's Choice*, including two squared-off maple logs. Kevin thought one of them might suit my boat. It did. I shaped it, bolted a curved stem to the keel, attached bed logs through which the driveshaft would pass, and added a sternpost. Then, with a mallet and chisel I cut a rabbet line, a recess along both sides of the keel, into which the first plank would fit.

After I set up the wood moulds and properly spaced them, the construction resembled the skeletal remains of some great creature, but I could now visualize what the hull would look like when completed. I studied it carefully. And I liked what I saw.

Planking was a slow but pleasant experience. The pine planking had been drying for a year or more. So it was easy to cut and plane. And I liked the smell of it. Each of the woods carried a different aroma: maple was sweet, but as pungent as burnt incense; oak was powerful and gingery; and the pine—it was clean, fresh and subtle. A fragrance I could enjoy throughout an entire day's work.

The steaming and nailing-in of the ribs was a day's work for a gang of relatives who showed up to help with that job. Deck installation, the cabin, and cockpit followed. Centreboard and centreboard housing, constructing the mast and spar, caulking seams, fitting hardware, painting, ordering sails, running electrical wires, searching for a diesel engine, fashioning bunks, building hatches, and smelting fifteen hundred pounds of lead ballast.

All of this occurred over seven summers, a long time it would seem, but I spent nearly as much time pondering how I should approach a task as I did carrying it out. So in 1992 the vessel touched the water for the first time. It was no longer *Jabberwock*. It had been rechristened the *Arja D.* after my daughter, Arja Denise Martin.

Arja D. under construction at Beach Point, PEI, in 1991.

I painted the hull a bold blue. The deck and cabin top were off-white. A short ladder led from cockpit to main cabin below deck. The centreboard housing separated the port side from starboard.

Everything below deck suited spartan living conditions. To port was a small washstand. Underneath was storage for food. To starboard were a tool chest, battery, fuse panels, and marine radio. Two bunks stretched forward on either side of the centreboard housing. A small fold-out chart table was at the foot of one bunk, a rack of nautical charts above it. Numerous storage cabinets separated main cabin from the forward compartment, in which one would find the freshwater tank, buoys, fenders, coils of rope, anchor line, and a chemical toilet. A bow hatch led to the deck above.

Years of sailing the Northumberland Strait and the lower Gulf of St. Lawrence followed until gradually I began to wish for more remote and exotic ports of call. The *Arja D.* is not a blue-water vessel. It was designed for coastal use. And that limitation began to shape the possibilities for me and my boat. Eventually, my imagination led me north and up the coast of New Brunswick, around the Gaspé Peninsula and along the St. Lawrence River. Before 1959, saltwater traffic from around the world could sail no farther than Montreal, and the Great Lakes freighters were limited to...well...the Great Lakes. Then, construction of the St. Lawrence Seaway opened a deepwater link to the very heart of the continent.

My daydreaming didn't stop there. It ventured beyond the St. Lawrence and beyond the Great Lakes. In fact, there seemed no limit to where it could go. I learned of a canal between Chicago on Lake Michigan and the Inland Waterways of the central United States, a thread of which led to the Gulf of Mexico. From there I dreamt of winding my way along the shores of Alabama and Florida, and up the Atlantic Coast. Georgia. The Carolinas. Virginia and Maryland. New England to the Bay of Fundy. A crossing to Nova Scotia. Cape Breton. Then a landfall on Prince Edward Island, the place from which my fantasy first took flight. Such a trip would be a great circumnavigation of the eastern North American continent. And it could be undertaken in a small coastal vessel like mine.

All of that was fantasy, of course. I only took it half seriously. And I'm sure that, if anyone thought it was more than that, they would have snorted in disapproval. It was unrealistic and whimsical, risky and unpredictable. *Seven thousand miles! Fer god-sake, man, what are ya thinkin'?* Such a venture smacked of silliness as well. A schoolboy's reverie, one might say, a Huck Finn scheme, delicious in its audacity only when safe in the arms of a fiction.

But people dream. Ordinary men and women cast themselves in starring roles in make-believe adventures. They quietly slip between the pages of tumultuous novels to spice dull lives. The humblest souls and the driest intellects occasionally hunger for a taste of the unknown, at least in the privacy of their minds. But dreaming is not always enough. And that is how I felt. At sixty-three. Retired. Knowing that dreams in the young are admired, while those in the old are humoured. And realizing that dreams not attempted become pathetic.

So, in the light of such sentiments, the expedition I had imagined became more and more desirable. It became a thrill too alluring to dismiss and a challenge too irresistible to forego. Finally, on Wednesday, June 23, 2004, my journey began. If all went smoothly, I could complete my venture in two summers, maybe three. The goal for my first season was Chicago and, on the day I left, that goal still seemed a pipe dream, half a world away.

Chapter 2

LIGHTS, CAMERA, ACTION

Steel and concrete breakwaters box in about two acres on the Beach Point waterfront. The wharves are broad enough for two trucks to pass when no lobster traps are stacked up for the start of the fishing season. Two of the wharves run perpendicular from the shore. Strings of fishing shanties line them. Each shanty holds fishermen's nets and bait tubs, anchors, and trawl line, and tanks for salting cod or hake or flounder. At least that was their use before the collapse of the groundfish stocks in the '80s. After that, little more than lobster remained to prop up an old way of life.

During the eight-week lobster season, sixty or seventy fishing boats, rafting two or three abreast, warp themselves to the quays and fill the compound. On the morning we departed, though, the harbour was empty except for my *Arja D.* Local fishermen set out before dawn to haul their traps.

My younger son, Robert, passed me the last few boxes and bags of supplies, and I stowed them below deck. Robert was a tall, wiry, athletic young man of twenty-eight, and his blond hair fell over his forehead as he worked. He laboured quietly, perhaps preoccupied, perhaps anxious about the week or so he would be with me at sea. He had always been ill at ease on the water. He could swim, but he did so with little self-assurance. So I was surprised when he asked if he could come along for the first week. And, though I did not say so, I was proud of him for staring down an old fear.

Robert let go the fore and aft lines. The weather was cool; the wind was brisk; the sun shone dully; and a tidal chop greeted us as we cleared Poverty Beach and the lighthouse on Old Store Point. A few inshore lobster boats passed us on their return; others still dotted the coast.

As we steamed further out the channel toward Cape Bear, the chop increased and the punt in tow behind us tugged on its painter, nosed into the waves, and then bravely leapt above a crest and dropped into a trough with a jerk. I shortened the tow-line to take up the slack.

The author, his wife, Brenda, and their son Robert on Day One in 2004.

I was not in the habit of having the boat in tow. Only once before had I ventured out with it, and that was on a trip to Charlottetown some fifty nautical miles away. It had been an annoyance. At the marina it drifted into awkward places or nudged and chafed our hull with each passing vessel's wake. On the return trip a nasty sou'easter kicked up seas, and the punt took spray and swamped. Three of us were aboard the *Arja D.* at the time. That made it easier to bail and recover. But the experience was unpleasant.

Since that episode, I had been reluctant to bring it along. Then, having convinced myself that a small boat would be useful either as lifeboat or ferry from an anchorage, I reneged, but not before I made a few changes: adding a wood frame high enough to support a taut canvas tarp covering the punt and shedding spray, rain, and waves. But now, as the little vessel wove like a cliff swallow through the chop, I grew uneasy about my decision to take it with me. Even though the canvas cover was well secured, water surged up the punt's sides and underneath the canvas with each slap of wave. It was taking water. The punt grew more and more lethargic. I just hoped it would float until we cleared the cape, and we could bring it alongside and bail. The end came quite suddenly, however. The punt slid into a trough, the water inside surged forward, the bow dipped, and a following wave held its nose under. It swamped.

We hauled on the tow-line. The boat was unresponsive and wallowed. Both Robert and I bent over the stern of the *Arja D.* attempting to draw the punt nearer. We struggled to keep a footing on our own rolling vessel, and our attention was so focused on the water-laden punt that the snarl of a big diesel engine nearby startled us.

The hull of a Cape Island fishing boat loomed alongside. John Ferguson swung the wheel over, his head sticking through the starboard hole of the wheelhouse, his wife standing on the working deck aft. They had just hauled the last of their three hundred lobster traps when they sighted our predicament.

"Need a hand?" he hollered. I freed one hand from the tow-line and waved an acknowledgement.

"Toss the line. We can lift 'er with the hauler."

John fed the line we'd tossed up through his lobster-trap hauler wheel and pulled a lever. The rope bit into the V-shaped slot on the wheel's edge and pulled steadily until the bow of the punt was drawn alongside. Then, with a groaning from the rope, the punt's bow lifted and rose into the air. Water coursed from beneath the tarp and out the stern. The little craft dangled mid-air for a moment or two, and then it rolled. The weight of water and the punt's cargo tore the canvas cover. Some of the contents tumbled out and went to the bottom, but the punt, drained of water, floated once again. A following sea and wind made the return to the Beach Point waterfront easy, if not quick, and we tied up an hour and a half later.

Dealing with the punt had been a fiasco, and a reversal so early in the trip had made me wonder whether my plan for this voyage was well-founded. Perhaps the sinking was a sign. Maybe it signalled the beginning of a string of calamities. If I had made a poor judgment in this, what failings hung upon future decisions? That morning I had left the dock energetic and excited. That same morning I returned, frustrated and troubled. In less than half an hour, though, I had arranged for someone to haul the punt home, and we were underway, this time unburdened.

The tidal chop had eased, but the sun had lost strength. Cool descended into cold; faint blue faded to grey; and light rains followed us. Our course led into Northumberland Strait, following a southerly arc around the coast of Prince Edward Island.

PEI, the smallest province in Canada, lies in the lower Gulf of St. Lawrence, bounded by Nova Scotia on the south, New Brunswick to the west, and Quebec in the north. But, unlike those regions, it has a different geological origin. It arose from debris deposited by melting glaciers just after the last ice age. Then, thousands of years of gulf currents lapped its shores and carved the Island into a crescent shape. Tidal rivers carved out lowlands into lengthy arteries, and the shoreline along which we sailed shifted from steep headlands, exposing the Island's deep-red soil, to bright sandy beaches and low grassy dunes.

In early afternoon, we passed the port of Wood Islands marking the southeast corner of PEI. A blue-grey line on the horizon, twenty miles across the Northumberland Strait, suggested the rocky, forested mountains of Nova Scotia. After we rounded Wood Islands headland, we rode more comfortably. The east-southeast wind fell on our port quarter. The air was cold, just fifty-four degrees Fahrenheit, and rain fell until we reached the broad mouth of Hillsborough Bay. That channel led to Charlottetown, the capital of PEI, and the birthplace of the Canadian Confederation, a city as significant to Canadians as Philadelphia is to Americans.

No doubt, Charlottetown would have been an agreeable place to stop for the night. It would have been fun. Still I had no desire to do so. Seemingly, neither did Robert. His reason remained his. My reason had roots in the leaden feeling that my trip could not begin until the shores of Prince Edward Island were behind me. Until then, all this was make-believe, like a child puttering in his sandbox. So, we sailed past.

At 2300, the night was black and moonless with only a dim hint of stars. I stared forward into that emptiness across a bow silhouetted by the muted incandescence of our running lights. Sometimes I thought I could make out something in the distance: a shifting of shape, a shadow against shadows, an apparition lingering in a dark cloud, ill-focused remnants of colour.

Before midnight, though, my vision had clarified what my mind had laboured to define. The vague light and amorphous shapes I had seen emanated from the Confederation Bridge, which spanned the Northumberland Strait between New Brunswick and Prince Edward Island, a distance of eight miles. Its navigation lights showed the safe shipping passage under the span. A glow shone from lamp stands over the bridge's highway bed. Headlights from midnight cars flickered from the elevated roadway.

The Confederation Bridge was the first permanent connection between PEI and the Canadian mainland in seventy-five thousand years. After the glacial meltdown, Northumberland Strait appeared but, in the dead of winter, the salt water of the strait froze solid. The first settlers, the Mi'kmaq, added runners to their birchbark canoes, like those on sleds, to cross both snow-covered, icy expanses and open patches where ice floes separated. European settlers used 17-foot vessels fitted with runners just as the Mi'kmaq had done to carry passengers and mail and supplies to the mainland, and by the early twentieth-century ice-breaking ferries carried engines powerful enough to batter through jammed ice. Still, well into modern decades winter crossings were unpredictable. Travellers could expect very long waits to beat through pack ice. The completion of the Confederation Bridge in 1997 eliminated that inconvenience.

BORDEN, PEI

On this moonless night only a trickle of lights moved noiselessly across the bridge. To starboard, however, a mass of yellowish-orange light glowed from the port of Borden. The lights were bright and distracting, and sighting the small buoys that led us toward the breakwater was difficult. A few minutes later we entered the harbour. The pool within was well-lit. We tied up behind several fishing boats on the centre wharf, fifty yards from the shore. The depth sounder registered four feet of water beneath us. I checked my watch. It was 0030. We had made seventy-five miles. That was a very good run, but it had been a long, long first day.

Robert was still asleep below when I woke at 0700 and started breakfast. The *Arja D.* has no proper galley. So I improvised a kitchen in the cockpit. I retrieved a camp stove and propane canister stowed under a rear hatch below the tiller. Everything else was below deck. An icebox stood beside the companionway ladder to starboard, and a small sink and freshwater tap had been set up on the port side. Below the sink were two shelves stocked with food and utensils. I lit the stove. It burned away the morning dampness. Soon, the smell of ham and eggs and coffee roused Robert.

We shoved off at 1100 on a course parallel to the Confederation Bridge. The bridge was quite long. In fact, at eight miles it became the longest bridge over ice-covered salt water in the world. It also seemed enormously high. Its pillars towered several hundred feet. Halfway across the strait, the bridge span rises in a great hump to allow heavy ship traffic to pass. We altered course, passed under the hump, and struck out for Shediac, about thirty-eight miles ahead, on the New Brunswick side of Northumberland Strait. The sun glared. The air was damp. The temperature, which had been comfortable on land, dropped to a cold fifty-seven degrees—yet, in spite of all this, both of us would have sunburned faces by the end of the day.

It should have been....That phrase creeps into my vocabulary often when sailing. It flags the unpredictability of sailing, its challenge and, at times, its danger, but it's also part of the uncertainty that draws sailors to the sea. Before we left Borden, I had punched the coordinates for Shediac Island buoy into my GPS, and by late afternoon the buoy *should have been* visible. The GPS indicated that it was within a mile. However, there was no sign of it. Ahead, the mainland and Shediac Island merged into one long shadow. No landform stood out. I turned back toward a point at the head of the bay, where I believed I had seen the breakwater to a small harbour. We headed toward it.

Robert stood watch on the bow for rocks or other hazards. The water grew uncomfortably shoal. We moved cautiously and slowly through channel markers that took us on a tortuous path toward a wharf. As we drew close to the breakwater, a confusing string of red buoys stretched in front of the narrow opening. To avoid crossing the line, which they created, I hauled quickly to port and ran softly aground in muddy bottom. The red "buoys" now were only a few feet to starboard and, below them through the clear water, I saw an underwater pipeline. I had misgivings about seeing no cars or people hanging about the small harbour. A decrepit factory rose above the wharf on the far side of the waterfront. I didn't like the look of the place. So I gunned the engine in quick bursts ahead and astern to make as short a turnaround as possible.

What happened next, as we made our slow retreat, was more than strange. It was bizarre. Approaching us from seaward was a Cape Island boat, the type of fishing boat most commonly used in this part of the world. Something about it struck me as odd and, as it grew closer, I became aware that it had been scaled down to about one-third the dimensions of most fishing vessels to something above toy size. Even more peculiar was its colour: orchid. The boat grew nearer. Gradually the orchid hue resolved itself in my eyes, and I saw that it was actually a hand-painted mural, which extended from the stem of the little vessel to its stern.

At the wheel was a tall man. At least he seemed tall. His head stuck up well above the foreshortened cabin top. He reminded me of a little boy straddling his ride-on dump truck. He wore a captain's hat, which seemed too small under a full head of black hair. The rest of his attire looked as if it had been snatched from a wardrobe room on the set of *Saturday Night Fever*. A floral shirt, big collar, loose fit, fluttering in the light breeze, buttoned halfway up his chest. Dress pants, polyester, tight, flaring out at the bottom. Short black boots, leather, elevated heels. We stopped and hailed his vessel as it passed.

"Where's Shediac?" I hollered.

"Next entrance," he replied, finger pointing north.

The working deck of a Cape Island boat is open, but his was not empty. The aft section was furnished like a patio. It held a cocktail table surrounded by several chairs, each one plastic and a crisp white. Several potted tropical palm trees had been braced against the washboards near the stern. Their long delicate green fronds drooped over and shaded his furniture and the occupant of one of the chairs, the only passenger aboard. She was short, female, and buxom. She had dark hair and curvy proportions. Her demeanour was indifferent, however, and she stared rigidly at the horizon. Ordinarily, I might have interpreted her detached manner as anti-social and boorish but, in this instance, I gave it no thought whatsoever. In fact, I attributed her manner to her nature and, in this instance, her nature was plastic. She was made of polystyrene. Inflated. Twelve pounds/square inch. Tethered into her chair lest she lift off in the light airs and drift away like an escaped beach ball.

I tried desperately not to gawk like a yokel at the governor's tea. So I simply waved thanks at the disco captain. I nodded politely to his lady friend. Then I shifted the *Arja D.* into gear, nudged the throttle, and tried not to appear astonished. Robert maintained a polite civility until we had passed the little boat and, unable to contain himself any longer, he fell forward, convulsing in noiseless hilarity.

We made Shediac, New Brunswick, a couple of hours later, and Saint-Édouard-de-Kent late the next afternoon, after a three-hour pounding from a squall. The day after, winds were light, the sky was clear, and the air was crisp, and, as it had been each morning of our trip, the temperature grew quite cold offshore. So we bundled into our survival suits. They were bulky and awkward to move in, but warm. Maintaining body temperature was a priority.

Another priority was the education of Robert in things nautical. It also kept our minds off the chill. He had gathered a basic understanding of safety and seamanship, having grown up in a fishing community like Beach Point, but he lacked the depth of knowledge, which would make him a solid member of a crew. Before coming aboard he had borrowed a book on sailing and had familiarized himself with the parts of a sailboat and principles of sailing. That morning he furthered his nautical education by learning the special uses of knots. We discussed emergency duties: use of VHF radio to call coast guard, fire control, abandoning ship. We talked navigation: rules of the road, chart reading, use of GPS and depth sounder.

By late morning the survival suits had come off. Long stretches of beautiful New Brunswick dunes slipped by our port side, and the abundance of wildlife along these shores grew fascinating. Flocks of black-and-white ducks leapt from one fishing spot to the next. Yellow-crested gannets circled nobly above and suddenly plummeted into the water as cleanly as bullets. It was a dazzling display. And the time passed quickly.

TRACADIE-SHEILA, NB

By noon we had passed the light buoy marking Sapin Ledge, a reef two miles east of the mainland. Beyond that, the surface was dotted with lobster-trap buoys as far as the eye could see. Boats were busy hauling the trap lines and harvesting their catches. We threaded our way through a maze of buoys, carefully avoiding the rope lines attached to them, some of which floated with considerable slack near the surface. We passed the Point Escuminac light, crossed the fourteen-mile mouth of Miramichi Bay, and ran northwest up the coast to Tracadie-Sheila, New Brunswick, our goal for that day's run.

To reach the town of Tracadie we had to pass through Tracadie Gully and into Baie de Tracadie. The bay is separated from the sea by a long, beautiful sandy dune. The gully is a narrow, stone-and-steel-reinforced slot cut through that dune. We entered the gully at slow throttle and, as we reached its other end, the bay opened before us. It was a beautiful vista, but there was no time to enjoy it.

Out of the corner of my eye I spotted the first buoy. It was a green port-hand buoy, and it appeared hard on our starboard side, not ahead. My first thought was *That's impossible. It must have broken loose or shifted*, for it lay less than twenty feet between itself and a sinister, grey wall of rock, which buttressed the edge of the gully! The *Arja D.* carried too much way to stop and ponder a decision. So I trusted the buoy, uttered a few oaths, dragged the tiller hard to port in order to swing the bow neatly to starboard. The boat slipped between the buoy and the rock wall. The distance between our starboard planking and the menacing grey rock shrank to ten feet. I hugged the buoy side of the channel. The depth-sounder numbers sank to single digits. Then a starboard-hand red buoy thirty yards ahead guided us four points to port. We cleared the rocks, and I felt dubiously hopeful that the worst, which might happen now, would be grounding in sand.

The sounder, mounted just inside the cabin top, was clearly visible from anywhere in the cockpit. It blinked out 5...7...6 feet of water below us...and the tide was still falling. We were on a northerly course again. The great dune stood on our starboard beam, parallel to us, two hundred yards distant. The vista had opened up, and it was quite beautiful. Beyond our narrow channel to both east and west were broad saltwater marshes, and wading birds of many species fed and nested among its acres of reeds.

In startling contrast to the breadth of the bay was its shallowness. Small groups of men, women, and children stood, ankle deep in water, digging clams less than a stone's throw on either side of our passing boat. Their small motorboats or punts bobbed gently nearby, grazing the mud bottom.

Channel markers became sparse as the channel bent northeast

Robert Martin sailing near Tracadie, NB.

and narrowed. Stunted spruce trees crowded the shore. We had covered about three miles, and ahead the channel seemed to vanish into a dead end. I still saw no wharf. Then another bit of water opened up. The channel grew narrower, one in which two vessels could pass with difficulty. The shoreline became heavily wooded. The slope of the riverbank sharpened. Another mile passed. Then the vista opened wide and displayed a pretty, but shallow bay, at the far side of which stood the town of Tracadie-Sheila, silhouetted against a lowering sun.

The Tracadie harbour facility was a mile and a half across the bay, at the foot of a low bridge. The bay was shallow and the channel meandered. Consequently, we criss-crossed the bay three times before reaching the marina near the bridge.

We steamed past the marina in order to take note of its layout. Then we rounded up and made for a clear opening at the dock. The tide was still falling, and our downstream drift proved too swift. I put the engine into reverse, but it wasn't enough. The stem struck a glancing blow against the wharf. A bit of smudged paint, coupled with a thimbleful of embarrassment, was the total consequence of the hit. But bad news followed.

Robert had decided to end his voyage and return home. He had been troubled with pain, unable to dull it with patent medicines, and he'd suffered in silence for the past four days. He admitted that he had postponed dental surgery because it would have prevented him from sailing. Now, however, reality was setting in. It had become impossible to continue.

Sunday was a day of rest and a day of sunshine punctuated with showers...and magnificent rainbows. One of them appeared to circumscribe the southern sky, and it rested one resplendent arc on the bow of *Arja D.* I took it as a blessing.

My now-blessed boat lay between two steep slopes formed by the Tracadie River. A bridge lay fifty yards north. Across from us was a large hotel and an immense, neatly cut lawn, which stretched to the shore and to a small dock at which was moored the *Cajun II*, a replica of a sternwheel river boat. It ferried tourists downstream on sightseeing tours. On the west side were two wharves, one belonging to the marina, the other a public wharf. Between the two was a boat-launching ramp.

The public wharf was used by fishing vessels. It was short, but rose high in the air. Widely spaced tarred tree trunks supported its deck. It had a gothic appearance similar to a wharf in the film *Popeye*. A short distance above the wharves was Chemin Principale, the street that ran parallel to the river.

For most of the afternoon, I idled about the little marina. Robert had wandered off to look the town over and make homebound travel arrangements. Later, in our kitchen-in-the-cockpit we heated beans and wieners for supper. We had thunder, lightning, and hail for dessert in the cabin. It was a short, sharp storm. After it cleared, Robert and I headed into town.

The town of Tracadie-Sheila had a well-to-do air about it. Along Chemin Principale, buildings were newly constructed or nicely maintained. Several malls had located downtown, rather than in some remote suburb. Sunday evening sidewalks were busy; the streets were busier. High-performance autos, sports coupes, street rods, choppers, and trucks too pretty for farm or fishery paraded back and forth along this main drag, and back and forth again, in a never-ending procession just as the cruisers did along Hollywood Boulevard in *American Graffiti*. Restaurants were plentiful; sidewalk cafes seemed inviting. The sounds of music spilled out of the windows and open doors of nightclubs and mingled with the aroma of sausages rising from the grills of street vendors. We passed country taverns, rock clubs, and the bump-and-grind shuffle of a strip joint and ended our last evening in Dooly's, a quieter spot where we could shoot pool and throw back a few cold beers.

The next morning's northwest wind was cold, even with the sun. Robert and I walked to the gas station next to the bridge. It doubled as the local bus depot. It was around noon when we got there. Robert was uncomfortable about the bus ride. Recurring

An auger of fair weather in Tracadie, NB.

headaches and nausea left him with little appetite. Only three other young passengers and Robert boarded. He left quietly and in pain. He was disappointed at not being able to at least round the Gaspé Peninsula. I was disappointed as well.

The marina was quiet that evening. Most of the weekend boaters had returned to their jobs. I had a final chat with Jacques LeBreton, the marina manager. He was energetic, cheerful, and helpful. He suggested that I chart my course through Shippegan Gully to Baie des Chaleurs instead of a straight course around Miscou Island. Doing so, I could enter Baie des Chaleurs twenty miles before the mouth of the bay, where the confluence of tides can kick up an uncomfortable sea. I took his advice and, if I timed it right, I could take advantage of a tide falling out of the bay to speed me to Grande-Rivière, Quebec.

A long, hot, steamy shower ended my last day in Tracadie. Tomorrow I would sail alone.

Chapter 3

CAMEO

I let go my lines at 0530, just before the heat of the sun dissipated the haze of night, and when the tangible is as indistinct as shadow. I crossed the shallow bay and threaded a path down the Tracadie River. Thick stands of spruce looked down, cloaking me even deeper in darkness. The throaty rumble of the diesel and the burble of saltwater exhaust were the only sensations stirring in my head, soothing as a heartbeat yet discordant against the backdrop of this beautiful, silent, rural space in Canada's Maritime provinces. A few yards ahead at water's edge, a startled doe raised her head from the river, stared for a moment, and bolted to the top of the bank, close to the safety of forest, and from there she watched man and boat slip past. Perhaps curiosity kept her there—for very few, if any, sailboats would have navigated these waters.

The sky brightened as I passed between the dunes and marshes of the lower bay. Tracadie Gully neared. I edged between the final port-hand buoy and the grey rock of the breakwater and blasted one long air-horn warning as I approached the blind turn into the gully. Then I swung the tiller, and the *Arja D.* slid into the watery slot, slipped between the lofty walls which parted the dune, and, freed of those confines, steamed into the Gulf of St. Lawrence.

The sky was sunless, still half asleep, a lifeless blue over the waters of the gulf. The New Brunswick coast stood out against it like a long black brushstroke and, within that darkness, hid more dunes and beaches and coastal plains. Ahead was Shippagan Island. Miscou Island. Then Baie des Chaleurs. Once across that great bay, I would be in the eastern waters of Quebec. To reach that benchmark, however, my course took me through Shippegan Gully fourteen miles north of Tracadie. The Shippegan Gully breakwater separates mainland New Brunswick from Shippagan and Miscou Islands and, just beyond it, a circuitous route winds several miles through sandy shoals to the causeway which links the islands. A lift bridge allows vessels to pass under the causeway. I swung back until the operator halted road traffic and raised the bridge. Then machinery rattled, cables shifted, pulleys revolved, and the centre span of the black steel bridge lifted horizontally.

As it did, I motored forward, looking from the deck upwards at the structure suspended above. Estimating distance at such a steep angle baffled my sense of depth. Feet seemed like inches. I felt a chill of doubt. Did I have room enough? Was thirty-five feet the height of my mast over the deck or above the waterline? Had I interpreted the chart thoroughly? What about the *Sailing Directions*? Was the data in feet or metres? And so on. But the forty-three-foot lift to the bridge was plenty of height for my mast, even taking the tide change into the formula, and I passed beneath the span quite easily.

The town and harbour of Shippagan lay to port, just past the bridge. Dozens of mid-water vessels had been laid up on stanchions and remained in various stages of refit at the shipyard there. I continued north past Shippagan and toward Baie des Chaleurs.

The trip across Chaleurs was long, thirty-five to forty miles, and it was dirty weather on both sides. Winds gusted and a confluence of tides kicked up a chop on the south side of the bay. As I approached the north shore, black clouds, filled with thunder and lightning, scudded along the coast. I struggled to keep on course and wriggle into my rain gear at the same time. The rainfall was short but heavy, and by 1900 I fetched Grande-Rivière, my first landing in the province of Quebec, and squeezed into a berth too small for the fishing boats in this very crowded port.

GRAND-RIVIÈRE, PQ

Signs on the tiny canteen a hundred yards down the wharf advertised fish and chips, burgers, and poutine. It was near closing time when I arrived. My feet thumped across quivering floorboards and the screen door slapped shut behind me like a mousetrap. Two ladies operated the canteen. One by one they came out from the kitchen.

"Hi, I wonder if you could help me. I just brought a boat in and I'm looking for fuel. Is there a service station nearby?"

"*Blah-bleh-vous quesqu'bablah-blah*?" the one asked the other.

"*Jai bleh-blah blah*," said the other. I sensed from their puzzled expressions that they had no idea what I was asking. They stared at me blankly as if waiting for the channel on a TV to change.

"I'm looking for fuel. For my boat. *Bateau,*" I said more slowly.

"*Bateau*?" The one's face brightened. "Ah!"

"Yes," I said, "yes. *Bateau*." I pointed toward the wharf. "And I need fuel. Fuel."

"Foo Ell," she mimicked, and her face lost brightness like an autumn cloud crossing the sun.

"Fuel."

"Foo Ell," the other repeated like a dutiful student in a Berlitz class.

Each of us shared an awkward moment of silence. Each of us stared helplessly. Then, the one rushed to the door and yelled, "Allo! Allo!" and waved to a fisherman in a passing truck. He braked. A cloud of road dust kicked up in his wake, overtook his pickup, and swept past it. He popped out of the cab and strode toward the little shop in which the ladies and I had pretended to converse.

"*Cette blah ble-bleh bateau*," said the one, "*mais il a blah-blah de-la blaté pour quelque blah d'autre blah-blah-da-da pas.*" She shrugged her shoulders.

"*Il parle pas be-blah de Francais*," said the other. "*Blah-de-blah-vous blah' déquesce que'il blah?*" Her finger darted in my direction.

The fisherman looked at me. The one lady looked at me. So did the other. If they had been doctors and nurses, I would have been the patient they had read about in clinical textbooks who had a malady too exotic to have been treated by the most learned members of their staff.

Still, the fisherman gamely took up the challenge. He asked me if I spoke French. I said no. Then, to keep the pump primed, I uttered a few more phrases and words: "Boat...*bateau* from Prince Edward Island...need fuel...diesel fuel..."

"Diesel?" he said.

"Yes, diesel."

"Ah! Diesel!" said the one.

"Diesel," smiled the other.

So, after I had retrieved a jerry can from the boat, the fisherman whisked me off to a service station in the village, interpreted with the station clerk, and cheerfully returned me to the wharf.

At 0330 a flood of country music from an English station throbbed out of a truck radio on the wharf above me and echoed through the pen of vessels. It woke me, and I wished the driver had chosen coffee to wake himself instead of the grating bellow of country angst. At any rate, I was now firmly awake. So was the wharf. More cars. More trucks. Fishermen's boots flopping down the gangway to the floating docks. Sparse fragments of mellifluous French hanging in the cool air. I rolled out of my bunk, slid the hatch open, dressed, and broke out the propane stove for coffee. More fishermen down the gangway, my boat in a small berth alongside it.

The fishermen here were friendly. They hailed me with a word in French and a wave. I replied, the only way I can, with a wave, a word, and a smile in English. But the foreign words bounced off each of our ears and fell away. Eyes dropped with discomfort and smiles turned shy, and the only communication that remained was that of one fellow seaman for another.

At 0500 I radioed the coast guard and filed a sailing plan, my first. Today I would round the Gaspé or a good portion of it. The coast was rugged, the water open, and ports scarce. They gave me a weather update. It was favourable. They also suggested several wharves were I might safely get into, if conditions changed, and several that might prove troublesome. My goal for the day was to fetch Pointe-au-Renard, which lay about forty-eight miles north.

PERCÉ, PQ

At 0530 I cleared Grande-Rivière. Fishing vessels from that port were hauling lobster traps upshore. In less than two hours I passed Cap d'Espoir at the northern approach to the mouth of Baie des Chaleurs. The lighthouse on the cape rose beautifully above sheer fifty-foot sandstone cliffs. Two or three buildings and old homes stood around it. From here the course bent northeasterly, and I began my ascent around the great Gaspé Peninsula. Île Bonaventure, an island wildlife sanctuary, appeared in the distance. The famous landmark of Percé Rock would be near Île Bonaventure. I strained to catch my first glimpse of it, but saw only what appeared to be an outcropping of rock west of Île Bonaventure. If that was Percé Rock, I thought to myself, then I'm not impressed.

The air had a chill to it, but the sun was brightening. The winds were light southeast, and the sea was flat. I grabbed my Thermos from the starboard cockpit stowage compartment where I kept whatever I needed near at hand: my GPS, camera, emergency flares, binoculars, safety harness, a spare chart or *Sailing Directions*, an apple or sandwich, and always a full container of coffee prepared at breakfast before departure. I opened the Thermos and poured a mug full. A veil of steam lifted off the rim until I capped it with a thermal lid.

Around me the sea world had come alive. It was feeding time in Atlantic Quebec. All manner of waterfowl were fishing here in the waters of Anse à Beaufils, the bay which opened just after the cape. The birds rose in large flocks of kind. They circled; they overtook me. They landed far ahead; they dove for prey. When I overtook them, they rose again. There was a continuous rush of movement in the sky above and on the water below. To my left and to my right. Both ahead and behind me. It was almost dizzying, and I felt a thrill at being in the midst of a grand natural aviary, and to be virtually ignored by them.

Then I saw Percé Rock. The real Percé Rock. Until now it had been obscured by Cap Blanc and what I previously had mistaken it for were tables of rock near Île Bonaventure. Even at a distance of two or three miles, though, the monolithic structure that Percé Rock presented was impressive.

Two great rocks make up the formation. Plateaus form the peaks of both, cliffs all around, the sheer faces of which drop either into water or onto a narrow band of rocky beach at their feet. The first rock, the smaller of the two, rises about 200 feet on a base of the same dimensions. To the west of it, a second great limestone mass reaches heights of 290 feet and stretches a third of a mile toward the shore. Midway, the forces of water and tide have bored a gigantic cavern, which penetrates the structure fully from one side to the other, leaving it to stand on two elephant-like stone pillars.

In this morning's light Percé Rock struck a defiant black profile against the paleness of the sky. But, as I drew nearer, the sun strengthened, the sky regained colour for the moment, and Percé Rock revealed its magnificent weathered texture in colours of greyish-greens, tawny yellows, pockets of black shadow, all laced together with marblings of white and, nearby, at the foot of a great ridge on the mainland, the village of Percé glittered like a smile.

Percé Rock slipped astern, and the mainland quickly fell away as I crossed La Malbaie. Ahead Pointe Saint-Pierre formed a low profile against the sky, now darkening, at the northerly end of the bay. Just outside of it stood Île Plate, an ugly, barren, low-slung little sandstone island which I cleared to the east and traversed the eight-mile mouth of Baie de Gaspé. Here the wind began to baffle and warm. Then it alternated between balmy and humid to heavy and cool. Suddenly the breeze turned northwest out of the head of Baie de Gaspé and grew very cold. Even in my survival suit it seemed cold. My bare hands stiffened. They were growing weak from lack of circulation. So I broke out a towel and wrapped it around both my hand and the tiller to keep my grip from failing. My free hand dug deeply into the pocket of my survival suit, and I hunkered down as best I could in the open cockpit.

An hour later, I cleared Baie de Gaspé and passed Cap Gaspé lighthouse, nestled prettily on the edge of a limestone precipice on the northeast peninsula. It stood against a backdrop of thick spruce forest rising almost seven hundred feet above the water's edge. By then, the cold had begun to abate, and by midday it turned quite warm.

A majestic coastline flowed by. Wonderful limestone cliffs rose sharply from the sea four hundred, five hundred, six hundred feet into forested mountains. No harbours, no buildings, no roads existed here. And above the rolling landscape of the Gaspé Peninsula was a parade of clouds. Broad swaths of stratocumulus painted the heights. Below them rode cumulus clouds sometimes small and puffy and almost comical, other times large, dark, sinister. The sky brightened; the sky darkened, but the sea conditions and wind below the cliffs remained stable, calm, and light.

The magnificent cliffs along which I sailed formed part of Forillon National Park. These cliffs decreased in height the more northerly I sailed and, by the time I reached Cap des Rosiers, they had fallen to an insignificant twenty feet. The lighthouse there, the tallest in Canada, rose ninety feet above them.

After rounding the cape, I adjusted course again. Ever since the beginning of my journey along the coast of New Brunswick and Quebec, I had followed a northeasterly course. As I eased the tiller to starboard, the compass needle swung to magnetic north for the first time and settled in at two points northwest. We were technically now in the Honguedo Strait, sometimes called the Gaspé Passage. Anticosti Island lay fifty miles east and below the horizon. Rivière-au-Renard lay twelve miles farther along this gradually westward-curving coastline. That town was my destination, and I made it at 1330.

RIVIÈRE-AU-RENARD, PQ

Rivière-Au-Renard is a rather spacious port with good water for small craft and mid-water vessels. Inside, two long wharves form a small basin. I eased into the basin, past a busy fish plant and a wharf filled with large fishing vessels. At the far end, the marina and its floating docks sat nearly empty this early in the sailing season. Nearby was a Canadian Coast Guard vessel.

I tied up in one of the marina's berths and radioed the coast guard of my arrival and closed out my sailing plan. Club Nautique Marina's office was a long, low, motel-like wooden structure. The clerk informed me of the rates, which were twenty-seven dollars per night. Now, being Scottish by marriage, underfunded as a pensioned-off teacher, and penurious by nature, I found this a bit steep and put in a counteroffer of ten dollars. Apparently this confounded the clerk who telephoned a friend to translate what I was asking. They conferred briefly in French and agreed that they would have to call the owner. While waiting for the owner's reply, I busied myself with the boat. I needed more ice and a few food items. These were available a few backyards away on main street at a grocery store. By that time, I had gotten word back from Club Nautique that I could stay for twenty dollars. I declined.

Instead, I sailed out of the basin into the more spacious expanse of the harbour. The winds were light, and the sky was clear. A hundred yards off the western shore I dropped anchor, went below, and let the gentle movement of the boat and the warm late afternoon sun rock me into an easy sleep.

Late afternoon and early evening were pleasant. I boiled up potatoes and carrots and fried several hot dogs. I watched couples walking the sandy shore and a solitary old man casting a hopeful fishing line into the water. To the east of me was another small breakwater, and inside of it was a fishermen's jetty.

I had become quite pleased with my anchorage and more than pleased with the vista that revealed itself to me. The town is nestled at the foot of forested mountains, and its homes and halls and general stores and shops rim the bay. Beyond the marina, fish factory, and the main street is a brick church and, like all Roman Catholic churches in Quebec, the steeple soars far above the skyline. At sea these steeples are better than a lighthouse in daylight hours as a landmark. But two other objects caught the eye too. The first was the town's reservoir several hundred feet up the hillside, a grey squat cylinder amongst the spruce. And hundreds of feet higher a tiny, white, wooden chapel and a massive wooden cross rising out of the steeply wooded mountainside.

My eyes were often drawn back to that chapel. It was solitary. And against the mass of darkening greenery it shone like a pearl on the black velvet of a jeweller's showcase. It was ruggedly simple. It was seemingly inaccessible, much like a hermitage. Yet it was inviting, much more so than the great fine church in the town below. And at 1900, chimes of vesper bells flowed like blessings down from the chapel on the hill, over the town and over the ships, among the couples on the shore, and around the houses of the bay. And it was comforting.

RIVIÈRE-LA-MADELEINE, PQ

The sun was clawing its way above the horizon as I hauled the anchor chain hand-over-hand to the deck at 0530. Thick, clay-like, black mud clung to the flukes. As the boat drifted listlessly in the light airs, I pried and scraped off the sods, flushed the anchor and the deck with water, and made fast the anchor in its chocks.

The *Arja D.* reached Rivière-la-Madeleine mid-afternoon. It was Canada Day, a holiday at least for non-fishermen, and many residents and tourists from a nearby campground gathered at picnic tables near the shore, sipped beer, and munched hot sandwiches or poutine from the take-out restaurant on the far side of the parking lot by the docks. I paid twenty-five dollars for a night's berth. I was too tired to haggle, and the friendly atmosphere made it easier to part with the money. I restocked my cooler with newly acquired perishables and melting ice. Then I took a walk.

Behind the campground and wharf was a sharply inclined, grassy embankment, which formed the barrier between the marina and the sea. It rose to a height of perhaps fifty feet and dropped in a sheer craggy cliff into the sea below. On the exposed cliff face, a raggedy strata of rock pointed skyward, the remnant of an ancient geological upheaval. At one time this bluff had been the side of a mountain like the many great mountains behind it. Little was left of it now. The Atlantic's waters had eaten most of it away. I looked down into that sea as the late afternoon threw long shadows onto it. The tide was low. Harmless waves spent themselves on the shore, and row on row of partly submerged, jagged rock broke the surface like shark's teeth.

Friday morning felt like a good morning. Unlike all of my previous days, this one began with a real sensation of warmth, suggesting perhaps summer would arrive soon. With the penetrating first rays of sun also came the drone of the first mosquitoes of the trip. They were sluggish and lacked direction and thirst for blood. And I left them to gather their desires on the shores of Rivière-la-Madeleine around 0830.

The sun lasted for another hour. The sky greyed. Peculiar alternating drafts of first cold and then balmy puffs of wind flowed over the vessel. Then showers wetted much of the day.

The landscape along this stretch of coast rose on the backs of heavily wooded mountains. They looked like enormous loaves of bread huddled against the ocean. Where two loaves met was often a village named Rivière This or Rivière-de St.-That. Each had a prominent spire locating the church, and each had a large cross on some nearby prominence pointing seaward. A highway ran between mountain and sea. Cars and campers moved briskly, together with an army of logging trucks. From my vantage point I could make out neither shoreline nor highway and, because of that, the vehicles seemed to flow almost magically on the rim of the sea itself.

SAINTE-ANNE-DES-MONTS, PQ

I rounded the mountainous Cap Sainte-Anne and the village of Tourelle, which lay in a pretty niche carved into its side. The sun glistened on the village and, as I cleared the cape, it glistened on the stately skyline of Sainte-Anne-des-Monts. The marina at Sainte-Anne-des-Monts lay between several wharves and breakwaters deep within a wide cove.

Silvain was in charge of the marina. He sported a tan too dark for the time of year, bleached hair, and several gold earrings in one ear. We were well matched linguistically—my four French words to his five English terms. He chain-smoked throughout our attempt at conversation. He offered to drive me in his quarter-ton truck to get diesel. It was a much-appreciated gesture, and off we went at a frenetic pace through the village.

Energetic, effusive, agitated. Silvain slipped through moods the way a clock slips through minutes. His one constant was an impression of dissoluteness and perhaps sadness, like a Keith Richards back from a Stones' tour.

CAP-CHAT, PQ

I decided not to stay in Sainte-Anne-des-Monts after refuelling. The weather was good, and the sun was high enough to make the next port before sundown. That port was Rivière Cap-Chat and, because Rivière Cap-Chat was a fishing port, I expected to get a berth there for five or ten dollars a night, much as I was used to on Prince Edward Island and other fishing ports along the Northumberland Strait. So I set off.

That decision proved ill-advised. Soon afterward, the sky grew pale. Easterly swells began to build. Halfway to Cap-Chat I saw a ripple on the water. It reached several hundred metres offshore. It was a breakwater, now mostly submerged in the high tide. I steered east of it. Gradually the sky had been filling with deep grey cloud. Rain followed—a heavy, steady, pounding torrent, driven by gusting winds. I could see Cap-Chat to port and cautiously eased toward it. Now the swells were on my beam, creating an uncomfortable roll on my final run to the harbour. Two doglegs past the outer breakwater brought me into a small basin with a few fishing boats tied to a U of floating docks. Another floating dock, extending along the west breakwater, was empty. I tied up there and went below and listened to the rain drumming on the deck.

Minutes passed and I heard a weak hail through the confusion of grey rain. I hauled back the cabin slide and poked my head out the companionway. A man stood there, dressed in greens and greys, holding a grey umbrella, which kept only his grey ball cap dry. Rain poured off the old man, perhaps sixty-five or seventy. His English was scant, but clear. He was the wharfinger, and he was to collect the wharfage. It was twenty-five dollars.

"Twenty-five dollars," I protested.

"Twenty-five dollars," he said.

"But that's too much."

"That is what it is," he said.

He was neither embarrassed nor hurried, neither conciliatory nor irritated, neither friendly nor defensive. He could just as easily have been giving directions to a simpleton on buttoning his shirt, or he could have been reading aloud to himself the breakfast menu at a diner. He stood patiently. Streams of water shot over the cataract of his umbrella and foamed into a white torrent on the dock. His sneakers were sodden; his trousers and jacket glistened in fading gloom of evening.

"At Sainte-Anne-des-Monts they charge the same, but that's a full-service marina. They've got showers, security, power supply, and other extras. What do I get for twenty-five dollars here?"

"There is the dock...There is a water tap."

"I don't need water." *Coals to Newcastle*, I thought, as I wiped the rain from my eyes and pushed a wet mass of hair off my forehead.

"And there is electricity," he said, paused briefly, and added "but that is extra." He waited patiently. "Do you wish to stay?"

I was tired. I was wet. It was nearly night. The weather was poor. I had been beaten. I had no choice. Reluctantly, I extracted two twenty-dollar bills from my wallet and handed them over.

"I have no change," he said.

I had no change, I said.

"I will be back with change." He turned and walked along the L-shaped floating dock, which lay along the breakwater, about a hundred yards long. He strode slowly, erect, with short deliberate steps and bobbing motion. It seemed he would never reach the stairs, which led up the bank along the shore. I watched him through a porthole. The rain poured; a mist grew; he disappeared.

A half hour later, once again his slow gait and bob caught my eye. I waited below deck a long time before he reached the boat. He handed me two wet bills, wrote a receipt, and handed it to me. In seconds the ink smeared and ran; the paper became sodden and matted itself into the contours of my hand. He turned and walked away, tossing a polite salutation behind him. Then man and umbrella faded into the wet mist.

How I wish I had stayed in Sainte-Anne-des-Monts!

Chapter 4

GREMLINS IN RIVER CITY

Saturday 0700. Day ten of my voyage. The morning was dull with fog, damp with mist, and a cool draft slipped through the tiny port in which I had spent a rain-filled night. It had been unpleasant.

Unpleasantness doesn't discourage me, though. At the heart of my endeavour is an optimistic spirit, and I remained optimistic enough to look forward to an idyllic voyage, a kind of poor-man's odyssey, fraught with challenge and achievement, disappointment and elation, hardship and good fortune. It's all part of the package. At least that's what I keep telling myself.

At this point, though, I was tied to a rain-drenched wharf at Cap-Chat, Quebec. Beyond the village spread an ocean-like expanse of water, the mouth of the St. Lawrence River—seven hundred miles northeast of New York, five hundred miles east of Montreal—where the jaws of the river gape sixty miles across, like a great cat's mouth and, when foul weather catches the mouse asleep, it bares its fangs. At that moment I felt like that mouse, especially now, shrunk by great landscapes on the brink of a great ocean. On a river wider than most of the Great Lakes. Lying against the remote, rugged, mountainous coast of the Gaspé Peninsula.

By 0830 the fog began to thin, and the weather report remained favourable. So I motored out of the harbour, steering a course directly offshore until I cleared the coastal shoals, rocks, onshore currents, and the sunken barge just west of the Cap-Chat harbour but, within half an hour, I encountered my first frustration of the day.

The fog returned and swallowed me. Visibility was zero. There was no going back. I couldn't risk going aground on a return to port and, because the weather reports still suggested clearing, I pressed on, but with the added precaution of putting additional miles between my boat and the shore. I went below and double-checked my charts. My next port would be Matane. I entered its coordinates into my GPS, adjusted course, and hoped for the weather to improve.

It didn't. It would get worse. And before the end of day I would question why in hell I was doing this.

The fog didn't clear that morning. Nor did it burn off in the afternoon. At times I could see perhaps a hundred yards ahead at nothing except the great curtain of grey, which encircled me. One had the illusion of moving yet not moving at all. Time passed, water passed, and it all became a bizarre world unto itself and, after a lapse of several hours, my new grey world seemed the only world, and my boat, the sea, the grey curtain, the leaden sky, and I seemed its only inhabitants. Once or twice a gull glided into view, and its sudden appearance became propitious and uncanny and strangely significant amidst the emptiness. And my eyes would fix on it curiously until it faded from sight.

Near midday a white hull emerged from behind the grey wall. Although I had been alone for hours—days even—it was not until I saw another boat in the midst of all this nothingness that I felt that empty touch of loneliness. His boat and mine were on parallel but opposite courses, separated by about seventy yards. It was a deep-water sailboat. Its dark red main was set, but it was under power. A canvas windbreak screened the cockpit. I saw no crew. There was no hail or wave, and the boat slipped quickly out of sight.

Several more hours of solitude passed. The sphere in which I moved pulsed like a slow lung, expanding to two hundred yards and contracting to almost nothing. Then, far off, I heard a sound. I couldn't identify it over the thump of my diesel. So I shut down the engine, listened carefully, and waited. I heard it again, some distance away. A foghorn. One long blast, repeating itself at one-minute intervals, a ship giving notice of its approach. I fixed its course by the increase in volume and shift in direction of the sound. It was heading my way, and I hoped it was a domestic ship rather than a foreign one. If so, it was more likely a duty officer monitored the radar and a seaman stood starboard watch. I restarted my engine in case a collision seemed imminent, and for each horn blast I heard, I returned the signal with my own air horn.

After four or five minutes, a ship materialized out of the grey curtain and cut a diagonal course across my port bow. It crossed perhaps a hundred yards ahead, safely ahead. Through my binoculars I watched the black hull of the car ferry *Vancier,* which had sailed out of Rimouski, Quebec, on its crossing of the St. Lawrence River to the community of Sept-Îles. In spite of the chill and dampness, clusters of people gathered on the passenger deck. Their fingers pointed at my boat and attended to my slow progress. Then boat and passengers disappeared altogether in a fraction of a minute.

I had experienced a thrill when *Vancier* crossed. A fragment of "the adventure of a lifetime" which friends and strangers called my voyage. I know they are right in calling it that—but *why* that is so I can't really say. In the past, whenever I returned home dishevelled and worn out after some short, solo sailing venture, I might expect my wife, a non-sailor, to laugh and ask, "Are you having a good time yet?" to which I would reply, "Yes," and really mean it, though I could not convincingly explain *why* to her or anyone else. The answer was elusive and quietly slipped away as the fog closed in again and left me with only my thoughts for good company.

An hour later a second ship hove into view and crossed my bow. This vessel displayed a smaller profile than *Vancier.* It was a cargo ship with a very low open deck forward, the wheelhouse aft. An enormous arm-like crane curled upon the open deck, like a quiescent serpent. It probably would have spent that morning grasping cords of pulpwood stacked a forest deep on its own deck, and spitting them onto some local wharf.

The afternoon passed slowly. My grey room changed little. The engine droned. Water streamed by the boards. Wavelets formed and faded. A seagull bobbed on the restless river. The mast creaked in its bed with each roll. Suddenly an unpleasant sound broke the routine. An unpleasant glow followed. Both emanated from the temperature-warning gauge on my control panel. A sharp buzz and a red glow meant increasing engine temperature. Quickly I pulled the fuel shut-off lever to kill the engine and sat there for a moment, stunned. This was not good.

I lifted the thwart seat just aft the companionway and peered down into the rear of the engine compartment. No hoses had given way. No seaweed had fouled the water intake. The oil level was full. Then I waited half an hour for the engine to cool and started it again. I leaned over the starboard side of the cockpit along the hull at the wet exhaust port. Exhaust smoke pumped through, but no water flowed. I shut the engine down again. The answer now became clear. The water pump had broken.

I had no choice but to dismantle the water pump and size up the problem. That inspection revealed that the screw holding the cam had broken, disintegrated, disappeared, something. There was nothing I could do. I replaced the faceplate, refitted the engine shield, shipped the ladder, and crawled back on deck, disgusted. The boat drifted downstream. *So much for an idyllic voyage*, I thought.

The tide had shifted, and the wind had piped up a notch. A light breeze brushed my face, enough wind to gain a bit of ground with the sails. So up they went. I poured a coffee and made myself comfortable at the tiller. The GPS showed that we had put thirty miles behind us. Under sail over the next two hours we might gain another five. As time passed, though, several problems arose: first, a calm was settling in, and we were no longer gaining ground; second, the day was becoming short, and attempting to find Matane in the fog at night would be risky. Anchoring in the two hundred feet of water was impossible and drifting was unpredictable.

I went below deck again with toolbox in hand, desperation in the wings, and new resolve in mind. I unshipped the ladder, removed the engine shield, disassembled the pump, and stared at the broken parts until something happened. Had I asked myself, "Can I fix it?," the answer would have been, "No." However, asking, "How will I fix it?" bought hope.

And I hoped to find something useful in a little ditty bag I had brought along. It contained a random assortment of wooden plugs, spare wire, fuses, screws, clamps, nails, in fact anything that might be useful to assist a jury-rig. Among the screws I discovered one which fit into the cam hole, but it was a wood screw, not a machine screw. It caught enough thread to hold, but it was too long and would shred the rubber impeller. None of the other screws fit. So I found myself staring at that screw until some other option broke the surface. It did. I took the screw, held it firmly in vice grips, and whaled on it with a hammer to blunt the protruding point. I fitted it in place. The threads held, and the pump pumped, albeit with a tolerable drip. Minutes later the engine was throbbing, and the *Arja D.* thrust its nose into the weakening foggy daylight toward Matane.

As we neared that port city, visibility diminished—twenty-five to fifty yards at most. So close to shore I reduced speed, and suddenly I heard another blast of an air horn. It was very loud and startlingly close off my starboard bow. I heard the deep throb of banks of pistons in a ship's engines pounding away. I returned a long blast from my horn. Then a massive black shadow rolled out of the grey curtain. It loomed closer than I had expected. A boat length away. I recoiled as if to escape it. I felt as helpless as one of those time-frozen warriors in a Roman tableau, struck once already and steadying for the final sword blow. I gasped, deeply so, and held it. A wall of dark steel crossed my bow. And then in seconds it vanished. Probably a ferry, I thought. I breathed again. And then again, a bit less fearfully.

I checked my GPS again. I was point-zero-one miles from the Matane breakwater light. Fifty-two feet! Yet I saw nothing. The ship that had nearly struck me was arriving or departing Matane. Yet I couldn't tell which. My engine was idling. I had taken the transmission out of gear. It would be reckless to move in any direction.

Needing some time to clear my head, I went forward, removed the jib from the forestay, packed it in its sail bag, and stowed it in the sail locker below. Then I turned to fixing the sail cover onto the furled mainsail. When I looked up again, the breakwater light had drifted into view, a few yards off the bow. The time was 2030...but the ordeals of this day were not over yet!

Chapter 5

IN YOUR FACE

MATANE, PQ

With a slow throttle I eased through the breakwater and entered the port of Matane. It was the biggest harbour I had yet visited. On my port side along the east breakwater was a ferry terminal, its docking facilities, and a railway spur for freight cars bound for the north shore. A long public wharf followed the shoreline on the south end. Several wharves jutted from the western breakwater. A large tugboat and a dredge appeared at the edge of the fog. Wharf lights burned diffused yellow-orange holes in the gloom.

My engine idled in the middle of the harbour as I searched for a place to tie up. Most of the wharves rose twelve to fourteen feet above my deck, making it difficult to either mount them or make fast a line. A small squadron of fishing vessels midway down the west wharf had floating docks, and that seemed the only place suitable for the boat. Space was open nearest the wood ramp to the wharf's roadway. So I pulled in and tied up until I could get my bearings. It had been a rough day and a long one.

Not five minutes had passed before a voice in shadows addressed me in French. I had not seen his approach, and already he was at the foot of the ramp. A small, balding, middle-aged man spoke officiously but was not dressed as an official.

"You can't stay here," he said in French. He didn't approach further than the ramp. He shifted to English when I didn't respond. "You can't stay here," he repeated. "This is a fishermen's wharf."

"I understand, but where can I go?"

"You can go to the marina."

"Sounds good. Where's that?"

"Five kilometres up the coast."

"Up the coast! That's not possible."

"You can't stay here."

"I have no radar. We can't even see across the harbour in this fog."

"You have to go."

"I don't care. I'm not leaving," I said firmly.

His suggestion...no, his demand...was nautical lunacy. We had reached an impasse. Short of being driven bodily from the harbour, I intended on going nowhere. Apprehension grew as our words shrank into a vacuous silence. I grew tense. Edgy. I worried how this situation might play out. By then a small group had gathered. A collection of fishermen who had been aboard their vessels came

Unending fog in Matane, Quebec.

on deck and intently followed the conversation. Another fisherman came down the ramp and positioned himself near the little man. He was more than curious, if body language can tell a tale. Both feet firmly planted, arms crossed, scowling stonily, he waited for an outcome. The little man pointed toward the lofty south wharf.

"You can tie up there. It's a public wharf."

"I can't get a line up that high. And there's no ladder."

"Alongside that boat then," he said, pointing to a rusting hulk warped to the quay.

"There's some kind of steel framework welded to her hull. I couldn't lie against it safely."

"You can't stay here."

"And I can't leave."

The scowling fisherman jabbed his finger in the air to punctuate virulent French comments. The little man spoke back quietly, plainly. Then he spoke to the other gathered fishermen. Then he turned to me.

"You can lay alongside the boat behind you. But you have to be gone as soon as the fog lifts...and you can't leave your boat untended overnight. Some may leave at four o'clock."

That suited me. I shifted the boat. The little man disappeared. The crowd vanished. A fishing vessel named *Munroe* slithered with a near-silent motor into the vacant spot I had just left. It was captained by the angry fisherman who had stood at the ramp next to the little man.

I slept lightly...uneasily.

At four, I was awake, waiting for the fishing boats to depart, but I remained below and in my bunk. From there I could peer out my portholes at the fog. It was still thick. I heard no rumble of engines warming up. In fact, the only sounds in my ears were the gnawing rub of boat fenders, the rhythmic lap of waves against hulls, and the soft clatter of chain link that bound together the floating docks. At five, nothing. At six, nothing. Then I drifted into a light sleep.

The fog would persist heavily until eleven. I was up and about at eight. The fishing boats were still tied up. There was little activity on them. Even the few who lived aboard were scarcely visible, nothing more than an occasional glimpse of a form moving behind the glass on the bridge of their vessel. In my idleness that morning I churned over the events of the night before. My recollections left me one minute dumfounded and in the next minute angry. If these twenty-ton vessels with all their radar, sonar, manpower, and digital chart plotter capabilities would not venture forth into this dismal weather, how in hell did they expect me to do so alone, on a small vessel, with no high-tech gadgets?

I passed the time with odds and ends after a damp breakfast on deck. I reset my watch from Atlantic to Eastern Daylight Savings Time, added a few rounds of tape over the jury-rigged water pump cam screw to keep vibration from displacing it, and then I wandered the wharf.

Around ten o'clock I met the harbour manager, Roger Arsenault. Again. He was the little man I had argued with the night before. He was working on the north end of the west breakwater. At the water's edge, warped against the concrete wharf, lay a large seagoing tug. It was disabled and under repair. Roger had run a heavy fire hose from a freshwater pumping station on the wharf to the tug. It had had its fill of water, and Roger was about to pack away the heavy hose, when I struck up a conversation. We chatted comfortably about the tug, about the weather, about the freighter that had crossed my bow yesterday, but spoke nothing about the night before. He struck me as pleasant, hard-working, and convivial when not caught between the fog, an itinerant sailor, and an obstinate fisher. I helped him drain the fifty yards of hose and coil it around the spindle of a large reel. Then I returned to the *Arja D.*

I made lunch, ate in the cockpit, and watched the ceiling of fog gradually lift with a strengthening morning sun. I could see clearly across the harbour now. Being Sunday, there was little activity. The one exception, though, was on the *Munroe*, just off my bow. A noisy gush of water drew my attention to it. I peered over my cabin top at the red-and-white vessel ahead of me, where a crewman manned a high-pressure hose, which swept across its decks and washboards in a methodical effort to strip away hardened dirt, scales, and seaweed. Behind the deckhand with the hose stood the angry fisherman of the night before. He appeared just as resentful, just as glowering, just as vengeful as he had on Saturday evening. He saw me and stared with a long, unbroken, threatening gaze.

I stared in return, quite sure that, when given the opportunity, he would find some means by which to punish me for a perceived transgression. So when the fog cleared the harbour about an hour later, I started my engine and headed for the entrance. But just as I cleared the ferry wharf, the fog again flooded in, engulfing me completely. I lost sight of everything. Then a blast of an air-horn shattered the stillness. A ferry was entering the harbour. It would run me down if I didn't act quickly. I recalled that there had been no obstructions to port. So I blindly put her helm hard over. In seconds, I rolled out of the fog bank, which hung about the entrance to the port. The harbour reappeared, and moments later, the bow of the ferry burst through the grey mist.

I could not leave port, but I preferred not to return to the fishermen's jetty if I could avoid it. So I motored a bit further south past the fishermen's wharf and past a dredge. The dredge was moored end-on to the west breakwater, more or less permanently, and made its own wharf-like structure. It carried a No Trespassing sign. Just past the dredge I dropped anchor in the southwest corner of the harbour. The anchor held well, the sun felt warm even through the high fog, and I dozed for two hours in my bunk.

By the time I awoke the fog had thinned. Even though it was late afternoon, I hoped to spend the night at the Old Port of Matane, a few miles east, where I would find the marina. So I hauled the anchor, scraped off the mud, washed it down, and stowed it in its chocks. I put the engine in gear and pointed the nose across the harbour. I gave it a bit of throttle. The boat moved sluggishly. I gunned the engine to 2,500 rpm. But there was no advance in speed. In fact, I was making no headway at all...and beginning to drift. I put the engine in neutral, ran forward, and dropped anchor. I fed out enough anchor line to seat the anchor soundly on the bottom. And when I looked up I found myself about thirty yards from shore, equidistant between the dredge and the fishing wharf.

Something had gone wrong. My first thought was that the propeller blade had fouled with seaweed or a plastic bag but, as I peered over the stern, I could see that it was clear of any debris. I put the engine in gear and examined the prop again. It was barely moving. My worst fear was transmission failure. I didn't want to think about that, and what it might mean. Not now. Not here, in a port where I was unwanted.

Besides that concern, I was at the end of my anchor line. I was stuck; I couldn't leave the harbour, and I couldn't step ashore. Meanwhile, a light northeasterly breeze had sprung up, and my boat began to swing restlessly at anchor—first wearing to starboard until pressure on the anchor line pulled the bow around, and then swinging to port. It followed a wide, continuous pendulum motion, which carried me from within ten yards of the fishing vessels on one side to within fifteen yards of the dredge on the other side. The rocks of a breakwater lay on my stern.

I needed some help to move my disabled vessel. I patiently waited on a passer-by to give me a hand, but the boats were unoccupied, and the wharf road was empty. No vehicles. No pedestrians. After a few hours, I liked my situation less and less. Soon it would grow dark. The fishing boats likely would move in the morning before dawn, and the awkward position in which my boat lay may impede their navigation. Rather than risk an accident, I called for assistance on my marine radio. The Canadian Coast Guard picked up my signal and my request to establish phone contact with the port manager. I explained my concern, and they relayed it to Roger Arsenault.

Roger arrived an hour later after he had finished supper. He boarded the dredge and made his way forward. I tossed him a heaving line. It arced toward the dredge's deck and into Roger's hands. I freed the anchor and, a few minutes later, made mooring lines fast around the deck cleats of the same fishing boat I had been alongside that morning.

I phoned Brenda from a pay phone by the harbourmaster's office and updated her on my difficulties and the probability of ending the voyage here. Then I wandered up the wharf toward the highway out of Matane, where I found a motel with a bar, and numbly watched a French situation comedy on TV as I sipped a shot of whiskey with my beer. A second whiskey and beer immeasurably warmed the long path back to my boat.

My second unsettled night in Matane. A light sleep, if any. The boats were to depart for fishing grounds. I had to be ready to shift my lines promptly. Someone letting my lines quietly go during the night and setting me adrift was not unimaginable. But as five o'clock and six o'clock passed, it became apparent that the fog had persisted, and today would be as yesterday. The vessels would remain tied up.

At 0830 I walked to a boat repair shop. The mechanic arrived, and in short work he found the problem: a damaged Woodruff key, a piece which locks the driveshaft into the transmission coupling. He returned to the machine shop and milled a new key and repaired the water pump. With everything in place, I started the engine, revved her in forward and reverse. Everything held and sounded good. My spirit buoyed again.

RIMOUSKI, PQ

During the sail to Rimouski, my next port of call, the landscape transformed itself. The steep-forested, mountainous shoreline shrank into short bluffs and gentle rises. Homes and cottages appeared more frequently at the river's edge and clustered around narrow sandy beaches.

The seascape had changed as well. Days before I had noted debris in the stream—twigs, small branches, lumps of weed, sods, small tree trunks, leaves, vegetation of varying kinds flowing from upriver. I had kept a sharp eye for logs. They could do damage. Today, I also had to watch for floating islands of vegetation—thousands of bits of vegetable matter which had rafted together and bound themselves into thin, brown mats, fifteen or twenty yards across. They could foul or damage a propeller. More importantly, they might also conceal a log, which could crack a boat's plank. So I carefully steered around these odd islands.

Further offshore, mid-channel, a few large freighters steamed toward Quebec and Montreal. These container ships looked like enormous railway freight cars when only their cargo decks were visible above the horizon. Several islands or reefs, three miles ahead, also caught my attention because they weren't charted on this stretch of the river. As I drew closer, however, they melded into the mainland. My concern had been a mirage of some sort.

The mirages slipped away as did the villages and towns dotting the southern shore: Sainte-Flavie, Mont-Joli, Sainte-Luce. A few miles off Sainte-Luce lay the sunken remains of the passenger vessel *Empress of Ireland*. It had sunk after a collision with the Norwegian freighter *Storstad*. Its number of dead—1,012 including 314 children—was exceeded only by the *Titanic*, a few years before. Despite the fact that this marine disaster was the most tragic in Canadian history, few people have heard of the *Empress of Ireland.* Its name is scarcely remembered because the start of the First World War overshadowed news of its sinking.

Two miles off Rimouski is the long wooded island of Île Saint-Barnabé. East of it is the channel into Rimouski. West of it are mud flats, thinly covered with water and peppered with immense boulders.

The harbour is divided into two separate sets of facilities and entrances: the western access, best suited for freighters and tankers, and the eastern access, narrow and opening into a snug, well-protected basin. A few large fishing vessels, a coast guard vessel, and a ferry lay against the commercial wharf. The ferry, which runs to Sept-Îles on the north shore of the Gulf of St. Lawrence, was filling with passengers as I entered. The marina contains over a hundred berths alongside floating docks, and it seemed nearly filled to capacity. I tied up and registered at the office. I had put sixty-five nautical miles behind me today. I was tired. Very, very tired.

Next morning began with a long shower. The shower in each stall was coin-operated. One dollar for an eight-minute supply of water. The water was hot; the room was steamy; and my sense of time washed away. Consequently, I found myself two bits short of a ten-minute shower when the faucet ran dry. *Who times their showers, anyway?* I thought. I stared indignantly at the dripping shower head. I stood, covered in suds, muttering through the foam, fumbling through my clothes, and desperately searching my pockets for enough change to start the shower again. Unfortunately, I had no dollar coins and was driven to collar the next person who entered the washroom to fetch me some change. Having just paid twenty-eight dollars for a berth, I had expected a free shower. At least.

Later, at the main desk, I enquired about local sailors who might have experience with conditions upstream. The desk clerk suggested Louis Arsenault on the *Louise III,* a spacious cruiser built by the owner himself. I hallooed from the dock, and Louis invited me aboard.

Louis was a cordial, mild-mannered, and highly knowledgeable man. He brewed a fresh pot of coffee, offered me a cup, and poured himself a refill as he finished his Corn Flakes breakfast.

The dining area of his boat had standing headroom and was nicely furnished with hardwood cabinets and trim. There was a full kitchen and a table large enough to lay out a nautical chart. Before the hour was done we had scrutinized two or three charts of the waters west of Rimouski. He was free with information, and forthcoming with cautions and advice. From him I learned that west of Rimouski the river begins to narrow considerably. As a result, the velocity of tides increases, and it becomes difficult to determine when the change of tides occurs. This becomes problematic if a boat steaming toward Montreal with a six-knot hull speed encounters an eight-knot falling tide. In those circumstances, one would best be in port or at anchor, but anchorages are few along the way, and the river may be several hundred feet deep. He stressed too that weather conditions and tidal conditions on the north shore differ from those on the south shore of the St. Lawrence. In addition, more islands lie in the passage ahead. They might pose a navigation problem in fog. Some are better navigated on one side or the other in order to avoid strong currents or heavy ship traffic.

I took notes.

Chapter 6

WHERE ARE THE STUNT MEN?

It was not yet 1030 when I steamed out of Rimouski and headed west toward Trois-Pistoles, Quebec. The winds were light, generally unfavourable in direction, and cool. The sky was clear. Once again it was a slow advance against an adverse tide, but I finally rounded Île Saint-Barnabé and watched its long silhouette slowly fall behind. Several smaller islands appeared, and I took the inside passage between them and the mainland.

More islands hove into view. Some wooded clumps. Others merely rocks. I took the outside passage for all of these. On my starboard side, the watery horizon lost its crispness against the sky. It became distorted. When it finally resolved itself, I could make out a faint leading edge of the St. Lawrence River's north shore, perhaps fifteen miles away and, rising above it, the radar tower which monitors incoming ships. It looked ghostlike, larger-than-life, and wavered like a desert mirage.

TROIS-PISTOLES, PQ

Near Trois-Pistoles, a few pilot whales surfaced. These whales, sometimes called blackfish, run fifteen or twenty feet long. Flanking one of them were smaller black-and-white creatures, which I took for whale pups. Beyond the blackfish and just past two rocky islets called Îles Razades, two milky white beluga whales played about.

It was just before 1830 when I motored into Trois-Pistoles. The waterfront and three wharves formed an irregular shape. The most formidable wharf served as a seasonal terminal for the ferry which ran to Les Escoumins on the north shore. The more remote arm of wharves enclosed a marina. As I entered the marina, the water level dropped enough to raise concern.

I met Michele Gagnon just after I had tied up. He was a short, kindly, soft-spoken, elderly man. His captain's hat and his jacket were navy blue. His beard was white. As I passed, he was carefully painting trim on his boat. He spoke English, and he told me that this harbour goes completely dry at low tide. The few small vessels which remain here nestle their keels into the mud bottom. Some prop against the wharf to keep upright; others careen or lay on their sides until the tide rises again. Clearly, this wasn't a good place to berth the *Arja D.*, but I had two hours to make other plans.

I enquired about charts of the area and local sea conditions, and Michele said he would fill me in. It was not long before Michele came back with several charts. I broke out a bottle of brandy, and we pored over the chart, which covered the Cap-à-l'Aigle and Kamouraska region. And then it was time to leave. The tide was dropping.

ÎLE AUX BASQUES, PQ

Île aux Basques lies off Trois-Pistoles. It's a small wooded island, a bird sanctuary, and a national historic site, named after Basques fishers who lived and laboured there when most of the continent was a mystery. I anchored off the east end of the island. Its navigation light was visible above the sand near the tree line. I stayed up long enough to ensure that the anchor had set and watched as more beluga whales gathered and danced with curiosity around the boat.

Thirty feet of water lay below me, and I payed out 125 feet of line. The boat rode well at anchor that night. Next morning I made a pot of coffee on deck, just before the rain began. Then I went below and studied the chart which Michele had given me. My next stop would be Îles du Pot à l'Eau-de-Vie (Brandy Pot Islands). This small island group, situated in the middle of the St. Lawrence, provides a good anchorage and is a convenient stepping stone to points upstream. From Brandy Pot I could reach Cap-à-l'Aigle on the north shore or Kamouraska on the south shore in the following day's run.

I had hoped to lift anchor around 1300 at the change of the tide but, as that hour drew closer, my plans disappeared in a thickening fog. The spectre of sailing into the middle of shipping lanes past numerous islands in rain and fog and in unfamiliar strong currents had no appeal. Add to that, cold. The temperature had been falling all day. By 1500 it had dropped to fifty-seven degrees. Two shirts, a sweater, and a quilted work shirt were not enough to stave off the chill. During the early afternoon, I lay in my bunk. I rested but could not sleep. The cold persisted and became almost a presence, like the glow of hungry eyes beyond the shadowy edge of a dying campfire.

All the while, conditions continued to deteriorate. A northeast breeze sprang up with the rising tide, and the *Arja D.* didn't take kindly to it. She pitched and rolled and yawed like an unbroken mare. I couldn't stand on deck; I couldn't move without a solid handhold below deck. In fact, the only spot offering comfort was my bunk, where I wedged myself neatly between the hull on one side and a canvas storm rail on the other.

During the late afternoon and early evening I experimented with several methods of steadying the boat at anchor. I payed out more anchor line, lowered the centreboard. I even streamed a sea anchor off the stern hoping that the rising tide would take it and add enough pressure to the stern to prevent the yawing. In spite of all this, there was no significant change in the boat's response.

Dinner was late. It consisted of canned fruit and a peanut butter sandwich. It was not safe to light a fire. The chill in the cabin was palpable. There was no cabin heater. It was too uncomfortable to read. Misting rain and showers continued intermittently. A curtain of fog cloaked everything in grey except a fragment of Île aux Basques, at the end of which I swung at anchor.

I poured myself a glass of brandy. A horn sounded. Through the grey veil emerged the Trois-Pistoles ferry on its return trip from Les Escoumins. The yellow lights burning on the passenger deck seemed gay and warm. The red and green navigation lights seemed sober and cold. The ferry crossed my bow perhaps forty yards away. Its wake touched the *Arja D.* and for a few moments altered the rhythm that the wind and sea had set against us. This was the third time that the ferry had passed me on my anchorage, and if repetition can spark sentiment, then circumstance can generate symbol. And so here, the ferry seemed more enriched than it deserved. The impact of it generated a puzzlingly meaningful moment for me in the same way as the light across a dark bay was to Gatsby in F. Scott Fitzgerald's novel or that the crossing of the sandbar was to Tennyson in his moving poem.

Then I wedged myself between hull and canvas bunk rail, let the brandy give up its warmth, and let the night pass. Once again there was rest, but no sleep. Wind drew out of the northeast, and the tide set southwest. The boat rolled and pitched. Oftentimes it lay crosswise to the sea. One hundred and fifty feet of anchor line was out. The ride was uncomfortable. Tedious. The mast creaked incessantly against the wooden deck partner through which it passed to its tabernacle on the keel. At some time during the night I raised the centreboard halfway. I had become concerned that the sudden snap of the boat during a roll might put too much pressure on it and damage either the centreboard or its housing.

The tide was still rising as I crawled out of my bunk next morning at 0800. I pushed back the cabin slide and climbed the short ladder to the cockpit. The rain had stopped. The fog persisted. The ferry once more emerged from its nest behind the fog in Trois-Pistoles, bent a path to clear Île aux Basques and my anchorage, and disappeared north into the fog.

Several ghostly white beluga whales played about the stern when I came on deck, but at my presence they turned shy and moved farther off. A large black seal broke the surface and stared at me like some dog wanting to fetch a stick.

The sea anchor, which I had set the previous night as a drogue off the stern, had fouled, probably at the change in tide. I hauled it alongside, up, over the washboard, and packed it away. The sea had settled somewhat from what it had been overnight, but it was still too dangerous to light a fire and cook a hot meal. For that reason, I had eaten little the day before, and it seemed that the same might prove so today. However, there was fruit and bread and cheese; I wouldn't go hungry.

A bit of warm weather would offset my having to eat cold meals. But that would not be the case today either. The early-morning temperature had dropped even farther to forty-two degrees. Also disappointing was the report on the marine weather station—two more days of fog, and small-craft warnings on the north shore.

At that news, I had to make a difficult decision. To go on would mean two more days and nights at anchor here, perhaps more. There would be a third anchorage off Brandy Pot Islands, forty miles or so west. Then another day to reach Cap-à-l'Aigle. Altogether, four or five more days to my next port and, during that time I would be unable to contact my son who expected to join me in Montreal.

To return to Rimouski would be less challenging. The weather downstream was reportedly more favourable; the passage was familiar; and I could contact my son about a change in plans before he boarded his plane.

My decision, therefore, was to return to Rimouski and wait until the weather settled. So at 1030 I raised the Danforth anchor and slipped away from Île aux Basques. The coast, which had appeared out of the fog for a short time before, disappeared again as I set a course offshore to avoid the islets just east of me. Then I punched in the GPS coordinates for the west light of Île du Bic and slipped into the last three hours of a falling tide.

Little did I suspect that the next twelve hours of my life would pass like a dream sequence. Not a nightmarish fantasy, but the kind of dream that wears one out...the kind of dream in which one feels hobbled, molasses-like in mind, in spirit, and in body, unable to perceive with acuity, unable to escape. It was the kind of dream in which a numbing sleep is punctuated with disturbing episodes and finally dissolves into a troubled sleep. It was the kind of dream that has no resolution, only the interchange of dread for apprehension and apprehension for discomfort in a wearying cycle

The wind blew nor'east up the river at 15 or 20 knots on my port bow. The temperature crept to forty-three degrees. Rain began to fall again. I shifted my sneakers for boots and donned the rain gear stowed under the starboard cockpit seat. My rain jacket had a hood, but I preferred a sou'wester for head cover. It shed water well; it didn't obstruct peripheral vision; and it didn't baffle the direction of sounds.

The ragged profile of several rocky islets passed to starboard, and an endless seascape of fog and water followed. Wave after indistinguishable wave slipped astern. No hint of coastline broke the grey veil for one or two hours. Then a prominent headland appeared ahead. I took it for an island, a substantial one, but the south end was obscured by fog, making identification impossible. As I neared it, a vessel appeared between me and the land. It was a tug. It towed a barge loaded with heavy construction equipment at the end of a long cable. The wind had stiffened to 20 knots with the change in tide. The tug and barge were approaching and running with the wind abeam. The wind had set the barge so far east of the tug that the barge, from my vantage point, appeared nearly parallel to the towing vessel. They were upwind, and I was unsure how much they were drifting toward me. So I gave them a great deal of seaway.

Once the tug had passed, I moved more northward and seaward around the island, curious that I had not spotted a lighthouse there. I followed a winding course around the west and north sides of the island, and then resumed my previous compass heading of ninety degrees magnetic. The land faded into the greyness.

Suddenly, a chill thrilled up my spine. My eye locked onto a small, black, rocky crag abaft my port beam. It emerged through an open spot in the fog. Then another split the surface, farther ahead, off the port bow. Small, black, tooth-like. My jaw clenched; my body shrank up; my eyes strained through the fog for other ghastly obstructions. But I could see nothing but fog and sea. I slowed the engine to a crawl; I checked the depth. There was ample water. If I headed away from the rocky outcroppings to the south, I would put myself in an inland channel. But I did not want to risk being that close to land in fog. Besides, the currents tend to set oddly and more strongly there. On the other hand, I did not know what might be lurking just below the watery surface if I moved north toward deeper water. I made a decision; I eased the bow north.

My plan, if one could call it that, was to thread the boat midway between the two rock outcroppings. There was plenty of apparent sea room. The rocks were about one hundred yards apart. What was below that football field of water, however, remained a perilous mystery. As I made my approach, I studied carefully the waves for any irregularity in their intensity or shape or colour; in short, any clue that might suggest a rock or shoal just below the surface. I throttled the boat to move only fast enough to make headway. Should I strike something, then perhaps I would not be holed. All the while, I continuously monitored the shifting numbers on the depth sounder.

I expected that the most hazardous point would be somewhere along a line between the two rocks. My unease mounted as that line drew nearer, in spite of the fact that the numbers on the depth sounder did not significantly change. The *Arja D.* slipped across the imaginary line. I grew more hopeful, and gradually the number of feet of water below the vessel increased. Soon I was in deep water. I breathed again.

Visibility improved in the deeper water. I could see for perhaps two miles. But all was grey: sea, sky, water, deck, and even time itself. Without the movement of the sun, or changes in blue, or shifts in cloud, or deepening and dimming of light, there was little sense of time. And whether I sailed for one hour or two or three, I could not judge but, during that interlude, the seascape I came upon was both remarkable and majestic. Lines of rollers marched up the river as far across as my eyes could see. Each roller was long, much longer than those in the Gulf of St. Lawrence or Northumberland Strait, where waves act like children streaming through a school hallway—jostling, rushing, stalling, merging—in an undisciplined but perceptible order. These waves, however, reached as far across the breadth of the river as the fog allowed me to see. Separately, each one was unbroken, orderly, and massive. Together, they possessed the discipline and precision of a cavalry regiment marching platoons and squadrons on line toward some decisive consequence. And like a mounted cavalry formation, they exuded a sense of power which could not be taken lightly. Although the strength of the wind had remained constant, the seas were building. What had been three-foot waves when the day began now had grown easily to nine footers. In spite of their size, however, their form was smooth, their approach was paced, their interval was comfortable, and the ride amongst them was exhilarating.

Eventually, those waves diminished in grandeur, and I settled into a monotony of dampness and fog and an odd vacantness of mind. I felt the cold in my idleness. The boat, its rigging, and my clothing dripped with wetness which set the cold in deeper. I reached for my Thermos. I poured out a mug of coffee. Three days old, it was tepid, but I drank it anyway. I grabbed a fistful of crackers and an apple below deck before the boat could veer far off course. I munched the snacks mechanically. They had little taste.

For some time, I had believed that I was well into open water. Then it became apparent that the currents were setting me onshore. Ahead, parting the fog, was a point of land. Island or mainland,

I could not tell. I approached it, keeping it on my starboard side about half a mile off. Its cliffs were high, sheer, and rocky. No shore was visible. Nor could I discern breakers near the base of its cliff.

There was no warning before the first of the waves hit. They looked twice the size of what I had encountered earlier. No. They were more than that. Much more. The suddenness of their appearance and the magnitude of their height stunned me. I had never encountered anything like them as a fisherman or as a sailor.

The first wall of water struck head-on. The bow dug into the trough at its foot and lifted neatly. The *Arja D.* lumbered up a mountain of water. I dreaded the crest. What lay beyond it I dared not imagine. *One fear at a time*, I thought. The bow mounted the top of the wave, pierced through it, hanging, it seemed, balanced in midair. There was a hesitation. For a fraction of a moment, I envisioned stalling, falling to one side, and broaching, but the momentum of the *Arja D.* pushed it through, and the boat sped down into the trough on the other side. At the bottom lay a great hollow between two waves. Another wave bore down. It was as towering, if not more so, than the first. The bow lifted smartly and we began the steep ascent. I started a slow count...one thousand, two thousand, three thousand, four thousand, five thousand, six thousand...until the boat reached the second crest. I quartered the crest more obliquely this time. Less of the bow overhung the reverse slope of the wave; more of the hull dug into the water; there was no pounding upon the downward drop.

I once read that aboard square-riggers a warning was given to helmsmen that, when running before the wind in a great following sea, never look behind. If a man at the wheel did, then it was believed that he could freeze in terror, and his inaction could put the vessel in jeopardy. Nevertheless, halfway up the slope of the third wave, I disregarded that advice, notwithstanding the fact that we were not in a following sea. I had to know where we stood in relation to land. Perhaps Lot's wife used similar reasoning before she stole a furtive glance at Sodom and was turned into a pillar of salt. Despite that, I spared one of my six seconds to look back and see what possibly may become my future. What I saw when I turned was not pretty.

Current and wave had driven me easterly. An unscalable cliff was astern. It was a lee shore and, against that rocky, sheer face of land, great waves hurled themselves to death like raging bulls against a matador's sword. Atop the cliff, thick woods capped the island and crowded around several buildings. One of them looked like a decommissioned lighthouse—round, tall, with a cone-like red roof. The others, block-shaped wooden structures, seemed abandoned. The whiteness of each stood out against damp green underbrush. Deserted, none showed signs of life.

The stark bluntness of it all staggered me, and I felt the shadow of fear hover nearby and stall somewhere between life and death. The onset of terror ought to have crippled me but, strangely, it didn't. Something else happened. Something odd. Some instinct kicked in, and somehow I knew that fear and terror were luxuries I couldn't afford, and somehow that stark reality enabled me to step through fear and, on another side, I found a place of cold clarity where I could draw on experience and knowledge, weigh options and make decisions, and be free from numbing emotions.

We dropped into another trough, and my concern shifted to whether we were clawing off this desperate shore or whether our movement was an illusion. I checked the instruments. Water depth registered fifty feet. The diesel was turning over at 2,800–3,000 rpm and my last estimate of speed, determined before this turn of events, had been 3 knots against the rising tide. By all of that, we should be making slow progress, but....

Another crest to tumble from. Another trough like an open grave to wallow in. The *Arja D.* handled all of them neatly. It had proven to be a good sea boat in the past. This test further added to my trust in my boat, and, as a result, I grew more confident. More hopeful. Less rigid. My death grip on the tiller less intense. Still, I thanked God that these weren't breaking waves.

As we were once again swept upward toward a crest, the boat climbed at thirty-odd degrees near the base and more steeply near the top. The full length of the 26-foot vessel clung to the slope and still I could see water well beyond the bow. Even then, the wave kept building and building and building. The leading slope had to have been forty feet long. Most likely more. The height of the wave, I could not guess. Something over twenty-five feet, I'm certain. We worked our way through six or eight of these waves. Then they moderated, almost as suddenly as they had begun, into nine-footers. Then six-footers. A final look backward confirmed that the cliff had dropped farther astern. That danger had been beaten back.

Yes, that peril slipped behind me like an awful dream, but a more subtle, systemic threat stepped forward and took its place. The temperature had warmed little. By late afternoon it may have reached fifty degrees, and rain had persisted off and on for much of the day. The clothing beneath my rain gear had grown quite damp. The rain had worked its way in during that long day. I was chilled. My hands and fingers were numb. It became troublesome to fasten the wrist buttons on my rain gear. It took slow and laboured effort to manipulate my handkerchief and to wipe my nose which was running continually from the dampness. I tried to keep one hand in my pocket for warmth and the other on the tiller but felt my grip on the tiller weakening. So I wrapped a towel around my hand and wished for gloves and imagined a warm meal. I had eaten little yesterday or today. It was difficult to leave the tiller to prepare food. So I munched on an apple or pear or a granola bar, whatever lay within easy reach. The last bit of coffee was cold, but the jolt of caffeine lent some comfort.

Fighting the rising tide was slow work too. It wouldn't turn until about 2000. Two more hours. The rain was slacking. That helped. Visibility still was poor, varying from half a mile to a mile, and that played havoc with navigation. I mistook Pointe à Santerre for Pointe au Père, and when I headed into the bay it enclosed, the water level began to drop, a signal that I was in the wrong spot. I headed offshore again, and at dusk I spotted the long dark silhouette of Île Saint-Barnabé. I knew then that this day's journey was nearly done. Rimouski lay just beyond its eastern end.

RIMOUSKI, PQ

Light of day faded quickly in the ever-present fog. Île Saint-Barnabé turned black against a charcoal sky. Past the end of that island I swung the bow southerly and began the approach to Rimouski. The water was deep on the entry, but I could see neither the town nor its lights. Just the veil of fog. Finally, about two hundred yards from port, two red, ill-defined glows emerged. The lights, which emanated from the breakwater lights, seemed like a bizarre double sunrise.

I slipped between the breakwaters into the harbour. At slow throttle the *Arja D.* barely cut a wake. The berths were filled with vessels of all descriptions, but not a soul was about. I idled midway down the rows of floating docks, and I tied fenders on the port side in preparation for docking. It was a slow process. My hands weren't working. Then, seeing no available berths, I rounded up to the fuelling station. I heaved the bow and stern lines onto the dock and jumped after them. However, my legs gave out, and I went sprawling across the wooden planks. I had not stood in more than two days.

I got to my feet, tied up, and slowly walked the ramp to the registration office. Its lights still glowed brightly at 2200 hours. An old man in yellow rain gear sat silently on a bench. Behind the counter a girl talked on the phone. When finished, she asked if I wanted to register. I nodded. She brought out an application card and asked me the name of my vessel. I said, "*Arja D.*," but all she heard was a feeble squawk. She looked up puzzled. I cleared my voice and croaked again, a little louder. She became more puzzled. I took the pen to write the required information on the card. My hands were splotches of blue and white. My fingers were numb. My hands trembled. An illegible scrawl dribbled off the edge of the card.

She looked quite concerned.

"Are you all right?" she asked. I nodded again, but I don't think she believed me. "I'll make you a fresh pot of coffee," she said and rushed off.

"*Très froid*," said the old man in the yellow rain gear. His only words. He never looked up.

Chapter 7

CALL FOR REWRITE

I slept like a dead man until eight. I did not dream. The dead never dream. When I awoke, I remained motionless and in a numbed stupor for another half hour or so. Gradually, I felt a lively warmth in the early-morning air and a strength to the sun which streamed through the portholes and illuminated my cabin. It suggested a playfulness from the world beyond my small cramped space, and this proved enough to rouse me from my bunk and to fortify me for what the day would bring. Still, something within me checked my buoying spirit from the elation toward which it aspired. Even though I couldn't identify it, even in my own mind, I sensed a growing weightiness—a burden that craved shifting.

My first shift, however, sent the cabin slide forward with a crisp thud. I stood up into a flood of sun and hazy blue. *A wonderful day*, I thought. I gathered my gear and made for the washroom. A long, hot eight-minutes-for-a-dollar shower. Then another dollar coin into the slot just for the sheer exhilaration of the steamy rush, the stinging warmth. The glow of that simple pleasure attended me throughout my breakfast in the restaurant on the second floor above the shower room and registration office.

I spoiled myself with a stack of waffles and syrup, a side order of fresh melons, slices of apple, kiwi fruit and orange, chunks of pineapple and, of course, black coffee. My table was in a cozy nook set against the back wall. The front wall was glass from floor to ceiling and wall to staircase, so guests could enjoy an unencumbered view of the harbour. I found a quiet joy in staring over the forest of gleaming aluminum masts of the marina. Among them, including my own, were two or three wooden ones, as well. Beyond that was a persistent haze of fog blanketing the St. Lawrence River. It hovered over the water like a seductive mystery and in great contrast to the cheery simplicity ashore.

The sunlight dimmed suddenly, as it does sometimes when a small cloud obscures it, but, in this instance, no such phenomenon had occurred. What had faded was not the light of day but my spirit, dampened perhaps by the sight of fog over the river and remembrance of recent days past. My change in mood was not profound, nor even significant, but it was perceptible, like one skip of the heart's beat or a variant puff of wind while at sea and, as I stirred my second cup of coffee, I became more contemplative.

I had been bothered lately regarding my ability to complete the first leg of my voyage, one that would take me to Chicago. First of all, the money to support my journey was running low. I had already spent half the money set aside on outfitting. Second, prevailing contrary winds had limited my ability to sail. I had to rely on the engine for power, and diesel fuel was expensive. Third, the price for berths was growing, the farther west I travelled. Safe anchorages were difficult to find. Finally, my timetable was falling apart. I should have been approaching Montreal now, but Montreal was five hundred miles upstream, a week or more of cruising under the best of conditions, and conditions this season had been unexpectedly cold and foggy. Finally, I would need many more charts to continue up the St. Lawrence, probably several hundred dollars worth. Obtaining them would add to the financial burden, and I didn't feel that I could afford much more.

Each of these considerations slogged through my mind as I stirred my second and third cup of coffee and weighed the practical against pride, and necessity against desire. In the end, the scales tipped toward an unfulfilled dream and, reluctantly, I resigned myself to the inevitability of that decision. I would be heading home.

My preparations to return began with a phone call to my wife, Brenda. I guessed that she would be delighted about my coming home but, being sensitive to my disappointment, she tried to mask her feelings. Then our conversation turned to my older son, Finley, and his plans to meet in Montreal. Later Brenda modified his travel arrangements. Instead, he would take a train and join me in Rimouski. I looked forward to having good company aboard again. In the meantime, the three-day lapse before his arrival would give me much-needed R & R.

After that, the day turned into one for small chores: refuelling, shifting to a permanent berth, replenishing ship stores, and banking. Today also became laundry day. So I bagged my soiled and wet gear, slung it over my shoulder, and trundled off to a room adjacent to the marina office. The room was small, busy, and hummed with the rhythmic slush-slush of washing machines and the muffled clink-clank of buckles and buttons tumbling in dryers. Two banks of machinery left little space for patrons to move. Even the five or six of us who were there made it crowded.

A group of four idled alongside their vibrating machines and waited contentedly for the end of a wash cycle. They caught my attention because they were not the usual marina hangabouts: middle-aged or greying businessmen, wives or girlfriends, or the odd family group with a day-sailer. They were young, sixteen or seventeen years old, three boys and a girl. They chatted with the excitement, bright eyes, and quick smiles of those who are close friends. The girl was strikingly pretty, blonde and fair complexioned, yet still retaining the last vestiges of innocent shyness. While she spoke, her eyes darted about as if drinking up the detail of some great wonder which she feared might soon vanish. The boys, each of them, were spirited and likeable and aglow with the thrill of adventure.

They spoke of boats and the water and, when I enquired if they were aboard a local boat, one of them replied that they were. I was not surprised at the answer. More so, I was caught by the ease with which he spoke to an older adult. I had half expected an awkward pause, a sense that I had intruded into a private world, or a shift in tone or demeanour. There was none of that.

I learned that they hailed from the Toronto area in Ontario. They were four of a group of seven, who crewed a 36-foot wooden ketch. Their boat was bound for Norway via Iceland, he said. Though I said nothing I was stunned at the enormity of that undertaking. Their adolescence, their naiveté, and their simple pleasantness jarred my sense of what physical strength, steely tenacity, and gritty seasoning I believed one should have to make such a voyage. On the other hand, perhaps their youthfulness prejudiced my opinion. Maybe I was becoming somewhat jaded with age, overly judgmental, unfair.

"Who is the captain?" I asked, hopefully covering up any trace of scepticism.

"We take turns," he replied. I interpreted his reply as meaning that they take turns on watch or that each takes a shift at the wheel. Still, I was taken aback, and I felt a misgiving arise in my mind and a concern in my heart at the inexperience, which bled from his choice of words.

My conversation with them suggested that they had had some sailing experience in Lake Ontario, but how much I never learned. They had gone aground once already in this vessel, upriver at Gananoque, Ontario, where they found themselves having to call the coast guard to pull their vessel free. But there was no damage that they knew of.

Two or three other older people were aboard, including the owner of the ketch. One of them arrived later, after I returned to put my clothes in the dryer. That young man was not much older in years than the others, but he was a head taller, more sober in mood, and more deliberate in speech, all of which suggested a gathering pool of strength and experience. That brief encounter was the last I had with them. I had hoped to visit the ketch the next day, but they had cleared the harbour sometime during the night.

Later that summer a radio news report told of a large wooden ketch from Ontario that had sprung a leak in stormy seas and sank off Newfoundland. There were two aboard that vessel. The owner died of hypothermia; his nephew survived. A group of young people which had been aboard this boat had disembarked before the vessel left mainland Canada. Another crewman left the boat while it had been dry-docked briefly in Newfoundland. When I heard the news, my thoughts turned to that pleasant knot of young people I had met in Rimouski...and I wondered....

During my second and third days in Rimouski, I puttered with small repair jobs and maintenance checks. Between chores, I often visited with Louis Arsenault. In summer he lived aboard the *Louise III*. He had an easy, quiet, dignified manner, which made me feel comfortable, and I could count on him for the loan of a tool or an offer of good advice. Beyond boating, we shared a common interest in music. He was a trumpet player with a fondness for swing, jazz, and South American rhythms. He also played classical guitar and kept a small guitar on board for fun.

As dusk drew near on my last day in Rimouski, Eddie Arsenault, Louis's brother, visited. We chatted about boats, hockey, and wandered about the marina grounds looking at several boats which had been hauled out for repair. One vessel in particular caught my notice. It had been designed by the same naval architect as my boat. The boat in Rimouski, however, was much larger than mine. It was close to 40 feet L.O.A. and looked to draw perhaps seven or eight feet of water on a full straight keel. It was clearly a blue-water boat. Its most fascinating characteristic, though, was that the entire hull, below the waterline, was sheathed in strips of naval copper. This had been a common method of protecting hulls of square-riggers and Clipper ships from wood-boring teredo worms, but it was something not seen in ship construction for probably seventy years or more.

As the evening sky grew dark, I returned to my little vessel for an early turn-in. There had been a warm feel to the air all day. Darkness fell, but the balmy warmth lingered, and I drifted into sleep. The alarm of my wristwatch woke me at 0200. The sky was black; the air was warm and damp; the marina was still. I leaned against the siding of the marina building waiting for Finley's taxi. He arrived from the train station around 0230. We went directly to the boat, and I got him settled in. He was wide awake and eager to leave and, after some orientation to the boat and after an early breakfast of scrambled eggs, we cast off lines and motored out of Rimouski just as the sky was lightening.

We had caught a falling tide. So we were able to make a comfortable 6 knots at 2,800 rpm. We steamed into a rising sun toward the old port of Matane where the marina was located. As I did with Robert on the first leg of the trip, so I did with Finley on this one—that is, I gave a crash course on knots and safety procedures. First on my list was that life jackets must be worn on deck and, if anyone is working forward, they must be tethered to a lifeline.

"Any exceptions?" he asked.

"No," I replied. He paused. I thought I perceived an expression which hinted at a momentary flashback to all the times I, as a father, had said that this or that must be or must not be—somewhat daunting now for a twenty-nine-year-old. Then he grunted in acknowledgement and nodded. His expression changed. The cloud which had momentarily crossed his face evaporated. It was clear that he had distinguished between me as father and as captain.

Overall, our first day out was comfortable and relaxing. We made the marina at Matane's old port in early afternoon. On our second day we spotted a plume of diesel exhaust from a distant fishing boat. Then another plume of smoke rose even further aft. But that sighting turned out to be not smoke at all. It was a whale blowing. In fact, it was one of a pod of whales spouting as they ran a course parallel to the fishing vessel and in the same line of sight.

En route we also encountered an unusual natural phenomenon. We were boarded by hundreds and hundreds of flying insects which, having left the safety of the shore, found sanctuary on our floating island. Among them were common houseflies, bees, hornets, dragonflies, moths, and several other species with which I was unfamiliar. Unlike the mosquitoes and blackflies and deer flies which come in search of a blood feast, these creatures seemed content simply to co-exist. Each found its niche on sail or line, on a sleeve or under a flap of a jacket, in the cabin or along a spar, and there each remained with little movement. At first, their sudden appearance caused dismay, but their non-threatening, timorous demeanour evoked in us a more tolerant, even charitable, response, so that we made few movements that might disturb or harm them. After an hour or two, the swarm fled as quickly as it had appeared.

SAINTE-ANNE-DES-MONTS, PQ

Finley's spirits became more and more buoyant as the day bent on. His stress as the principal graphic artist with a Washington, DC, advertising firm was melting away in the salt air and sun. By evening he was quicker to laugh and more relaxed. After supper in Sainte-Anne-des-Monts, he picked up my guitar and worked his way through a few strident blues tunes and attacked the strings with confidence and expression which made me quite envious.

Today was July 14. The French celebrate that date as Bastille Day, the anniversary of the people's storming of the Paris jail and the freeing of prisoners, and the onset of the French Revolution. I celebrate too. It's my wedding anniversary. This year's celebration, unfortunately, was via telephone in the marina's office in Sainte-Anne-des-Monts.

Finley and I cast off about 0530. The tide was rising. So we expected a slow run for quite a while. The twin spires of the church of Sainte-Anne-des-Monts rose above the town behind us as we sailed out the bay and headed east along steep, wooded cliffs. I turned on the GPS and checked our speed. It startled me. We were making 7.5 knots, and we averaged that remarkable speed for the next two and a half hours. Several times, we drove up to an incredible 10 knots. Against a rising tide!

A peculiarity of the tidal action in this region accounted for the phenomenon, but it was a temporary anomaly. After a few hours of exhilarating ride, we slowed to 5.5 knots. The tide had completed its change, and the weather changed as well. Clouds closed over us, and the wind piped up stiffly out of the northeast.

By the time we passed Mont-Louis, seas had begun to build. The waves were short and steep and irregular; the chop was unpleasant; and the boat pounded uncomfortably. We moved further offshore into deeper water and away from the undulating shoreline, which seemed to exacerbate conditions. We had begun the day's voyage under sail but, with the wind in our teeth, we had taken everything in and motored ahead. And now we had to reduce engine speed to ease the pounding.

Cap de la Madeleine, a rocky promontory jutting from the mountainous shore of the great Gaspé Peninsula, lay ahead. As we approached, the temperature plummeted, rain fell, and the wind stiffened to about 20 knots. The seas became more regular in frequency, but they also became steeper—about six feet.

It took two and a half hours to clear Cap de la Madeleine. We were barely crawling. On our starboard quarter a froth of waves beat across the rocky shoals, which extended a quarter mile off the cape. The land fell away southwest of that cape and the lighthouse, which hung on its edge. Mist and patches of fog were making up. But I could still see a few buildings ashore. Three hamlets formed the scattered municipality there. Beyond them, in a tiny cove beyond Rivière-la-Madeleine was a fishing harbour. The shoreline was an indistinct blue-grey smudge. I had some idea where the little port lay, but those same seas, which had been impeding our progress, had also buried many of the channel buoys which could lead us directly there.

The waves grew steeper, shorter in interval, somewhat irregular, and more dangerous. They were making from the southeast, but we had to work our way west to reach the harbour. All the while, the boat was tossing wildly and unpredictably. Sometimes we were hurled from our seats. Life jackets were on, of course. Now safety harnesses were donned, and we tethered ourselves to a U-bolt in the cockpit.

Timing was critical too. As each wave struck, we quartered the crest. As the boat fell into the trough, I hauled the tiller to port to make some westing. Then I swung the tiller back again to quarter the next wave. I repeated this series of manoeuvres over and over and over again in order to wrestle our way in. If I badly mistimed, we could roll onto our beam ends, or one of us might go over the side.

Occasionally, a couple of waves would come in quick succession, and they were a worry. At times, one would catch me unawares. Then the boat caught the crest more abeam than on its quarter. It lurched thirty degrees over. My feet braced crosswise in such a way that I would find myself standing on the side wall of the cockpit, one hand gripping the tiller, the other hand desperately clutching the washboard on the weather side.

It was slow work. It was exhausting work, both physically and mentally. It was a time of few words, and it was a time for complete dedication to one task—guiding the boat to which we clung through seas, which opposed us—and after another hour, we won some success. We had crawled further into the shallow bay. The contours of the mainland began to mollify the worst of the waves. The shore gained more definition behind the mistiness. I could see the distinctive rocky bluff which provided a natural shelter to the little port, but the channel buoys remained buried beneath the rough water. Carefully we edged in, further south and then west. I recalled the jagged teeth of rock that ranged in front of that bluff. I had viewed them from atop the ridge at low water on my outward-bound visit. Now they hid themselves below the water line, hungry for a ship's bottom.

We moved along slowly and parallel to the shore. Then we spotted the breakwater and the buoy marking the entrance. We slipped through and idled in the middle of the little cove. Finley readied the fenders and bowline. I prepared the stern line and manoeuvred in. A young man stood at the dock to catch our line. I swung in and reversed engine. The boat slowed. I heaved the stern line, left the tiller, and hurried forward to fend off the dock. Suddenly my feet went out from under me. I flew forward, headlong toward the cabin top. My full weight fell upon a corner, my rib cage catching the worst of it. I was stunned. My hand reached down to grasp the pain in my side. I felt my safety harness and realized that I was still tethered to the U-bolt, but had been too worn-out to be conscious of it.

I felt more at ease after I'd tied up at the wharf, taken off my foul-weather gear, and mounted the steps to the registration office. The office was warm and smelled of food. The office doubled as a canteen. Then I had a hot shower, changed clothes, and took a short nap in my bunk. Afterwards Finley brought a hot chicken and fries supper from the canteen. We hadn't eaten since morning.

The evening grew so cold that we hooked up a small electric heater in the cabin. We chatted until dark, and spliced the main brace with brandy to celebrate Finley's first taste of dirty weather. From the limited experience he had under his belt, my son learned that sailing was not the so-very-relaxing pastime that advertising agencies showcase in their television commercials. However, he said he had come to appreciate something today that he had not fully comprehended before. There are circumstances in which we are not at liberty to rest, reconsider, or stop. We have to press on.

When tired, one labours. When challenged, one perseveres. When confronted, one struggles. Those who live in a comfortable world may never fully comprehend that notion. Seamen, fishermen, sailors have always known it. Not that it is their choice. For the most part, it is a matter of no choice at all.

For Finley it seemed a kind of epiphany, a worthwhile one, I thought. And one that might be added to the handful of other counsels we gather about us in a lifetime, safely stored away like a rack of firearms, taken down from time to time, to be cleaned, oiled, inspected, and ready when circumstance calls for them.

We left the electric heater on all night. It took the edge off the damp cold, but it did little to dry our clothes, hung up on a line strung across the cabin. An overnight drizzle had stopped. The air was damp and cool when we motored out of Rivière-la-Madeleine to meet an unsettled mix of sun and cloud. We arrived in Rivière-au-Renard about 1700.

The following morning we sailed around the Gaspé Peninsula. Another day brought us to Grande-Rivière and Tracadie-Sheila's sandy estuary. With the revised weather update, we departed just short of noon. Again, fog settled in for most of the day.

At Richibucto Cape, the fog had thinned enough to see the slim, distant silhouette of Prince Edward Island against the darkening eastern sky. We pressed ahead and crossed Northumberland Strait on a twenty-five-mile night run to Prince Edward Island.

Shore light and navigation lights along PEI blinked. The running lights and masthead lights of a few vessels moved along

Finley, Jr. at the helm near Gaspé, QC.

the waterway. We took turns on the tiller in two-hour watches. Sometimes we slept; other times just chatted the watch away. Cape Egmont's lights grew large and bright after midnight. We considered a layover, but we were rested; the sea was good.

We followed a course up Northumberland Strait. The lights for the Confederation Bridge, spanning PEI and New Brunswick, glowed like a string of jewels. The scattered stars above had dissolved; the rich blackness of night had washed away. An ashen pallor hung about the face of the pre-dawn sky. By the time we passed under the towering centre span of the bridge a new day had emerged, clear, bright, and hopeful.

Finley piloted the *Arja D.* between the pillars supporting the bridge and continued along the coast. By the following afternoon we were travelling along a familiar shore. We could name the communities as we passed, even though most were little more than half a dozen houses at a crossroad. Often we knew the names of those who lived there. As we approached Cape Bear, the number of houses and cottages thinned. The landscape became thick with spruce. The Cape Bear lighthouse hove into view. Then the buoy at the edge of the Cape Reef.

We slipped into the small bay and slowly motored through the channel. To starboard, the long, sandy finger of Poverty Beach pointed for a mile across the bay and sheltered the inner harbours. To port, sandy beaches and small dunes of Beach Point sloped gently from short bluffs and scrubland. A small lighthouse blinked at Old Store Point. The narrow slot of water between the Point and Poverty Beach roiled with a rising tide. We felt a thrill as it gripped our vessel and heaved us through. Home lay just ahead.

Chapter 8

BUBBLES IN A THINK TANK

As the *Arja D.* slipped between shoals on the approach to its home port at Beach Point, the engine throbbed, the bow wave pulsed, and the wake hissed. Its motion was lively; its response to any shift of helm was quick; and the rising tide added the eagerness of a puppy rushing to its front door. I sensed the excitement, which sprang from the heart of this boat, much the same way as the energy of a spirited friend overspills itself and sweeps everyone else along on a stream of elation.

Yes, I sensed the excitement and, to some extent, shared in it. I looked forward to spending time with my wife, my children, and grandson. I looked forward to sharing the delights and difficulties of my trip with friends and neighbours. I looked forward to no schedules, no early departures, and no evening searches for fuel and supplies. I looked forward to a soft bed, a meal not fried or boiled, clouds requiring no suspicious look, and idle days in which a breeze could blow from any quarter and not provoke a frown.

It had been a good trip, to be sure. I had matured as a navigator and sailor. But it had been a long trip, a little over one thousand miles in twenty-eight days. And it had been a difficult trip—unseasonably cold, foggy weather, and several dirty days at sea. All this had taken a toll. I was weary, but most of all, I was disappointed.

Disappointment is a peculiar emotion. It often feels like a bare room in which one muddles about or does nothing at all. Yet it is neither like creeping through fog nor like standing slack-sailed in a calm. It takes the shape of an abyss between what one is and what one wishes. It can persist and fester or wither and heal, cripple the spirit or temper it. It smothered my spirit. And for many weeks after I made port, I could still feel the weight of it bearing down.

As fall drew near, I was not sure what fresh course I would set for myself. Some asked, "What are your plans for next year?" and suggested destinations such as the Magdalen Islands, Cape Breton, the South Shore of Nova Scotia. My wife bravely suggested a trip to New York. I replied rather vaguely to all.

Others asked, "Would you do it again?"

"Um...maybe," was the only response I could conjure.

As winter set in, however, I came to believe that even an abyss can be bridged and, while I did not speak openly about it, I began to see again the dream that had given birth to my voyage of the previous year. That vision of the future gained momentum—in my mind—and like all dreams, eventually struggled to transform itself into reality. Images conjured vision; vision kindled plan; and the plan fuelled action. In time, my evasive replies to friends gave way to intention.

"So, you're going again?" asked one bother-in-law, Ken Nicolle, a fisherman who had received the Star of Courage bravery award from the governor general for venturing out and saving the crew of a boat that had sunk during a gale.

"I believe I will."

"The same way?"

"Yes..."

I just don't like unfinished business, I rationalized to myself. More truthfully, I didn't like failure. I remained more guarded, though, about my long-term plan or even the object of the first leg of my voyage and, to queries about destination, I would admit only that my goal was to go as far up the St. Lawrence River as I could. That seemed to satisfy idle curiosity. It also spared me from declaring grandiose plans, which I knew could be crippled easily by any of a hundred hazards in the preparation or en route.

Once committed to the project, plans developed and preparations commenced. A few of these preparations included a better survival suit, a smaller sea anchor, a circuit breaker to replace my fused electric panel, a better chart light, and a second bilge pump.

Batteries which don't start provoke in sailors two responses, either a reddening face stoked by a mouthful of expletives, or a face whitening, drained of blood and numbed by the approach of disagreeable consequences. In anticipation of either of these worst possible worlds, I installed a second battery and, with it, a switch which could isolate one battery for starting only and the other for running auxiliary equipment.

I also bought two new safety harnesses. These would fasten to jack lines mounted on the cabin top. I bought a folding bike which could be stored under the chart table. The second piece of equipment, which Brenda found for me, was a collapsible luggage carrier to haul a five-gallon jerry can of diesel fuel. Many ports lack commercial fuel docks for small vessels and my ten-gallon fuel tank did not warrant the dispatch of a fuel truck for a fill-up. At the best of times, I have begged rides from strangers; during the worst of times, I have limped along from a fuel depot a half mile away with a forty-pound can in tow.

Gathering nautical charts was tedious as well. A long journey requires many charts, and they occupy considerable space. So, many boaters purchase electronic navigation plotters. They are convenient, accurate, and provide a vessel's position in real-time, but they have a downside.

First, navigator plotters cost thousands. Second, they're a significant drain on storage batteries. If battery power fails or the plotter malfunctions, the skipper will be left blind. Third, a more personal reason, I've always felt more comfortable being able to see "the big picture" on a chart and plotting my own course.

As a result, I decided to use paper charts. Close to forty charts came aboard, enough to navigate from Prince Edward Island to the beginning of the Trent-Severn Waterway in Ontario, where I planned to buy more.

Beyond the routine maintenance on my two-cylinder Yanmar diesel, there remained one other mechanical concern that deserved attention—the driveshaft. I had had trouble with it in Matane when the Woodruff key, which locks the shaft onto a faceplate, worked itself loose. Fortunately, this didn't occur at a critical moment, and a machinist repaired it the next day. Nevertheless, I still had concerns about why it happened. So, long before I had resolved to head upriver again, I removed the shaft and took it, propeller, faceplate, and all, to a machine shop and left instructions to make any needed repairs.

I reinstalled the shaft in May, but put off alignment for a few weeks. Engine alignment is the process of making the angle of the driveshaft perfectly match the angle of both the engine and transmission. When I finally tackled that job, I discovered that the engine would not line up, no matter how much shimming of engine mounts, shifting of gear, or shaving of bed logs I might do.

So I hauled the shaft out again and called on Kenny Emery, a man from the port of Wood Islands. Kenny is a large man with big hands and a benign smile that lingers almost unendingly. He moves slowly and talks slower, venturing observations on politics, history, the environment, and many other topics as he cuts, grinds, measures, clamps, oils, brazes, shaves, and eventually resurrects whatever tool, mechanism, or machine lies disabled on the bench before him. His opinions are thoughtful and well-phrased, and his statements often conclude with the feel of a question, as if he were saying, *What do you think?*

Kenny put my shaft on his lathe, lined it up, and started the machine. It rotated slowly, and just a few revolutions revealed everything he needed to know about it. He observed a wobble in the faceplate and a shimmy in the shaft. After turning off the lathe, he removed the faceplate from the shaft. He held it in his hand and examined it for what seemed a long time. Then he said, "There's too much play between the faceplate and the shaft. When the set screw is tightened, it throws the faceplate out of square." He paused, turned the grey shape of steel around in his hand. It seemed to draw as much wondrous curiosity for him as another might find in a meteorite or a fossilized footprint. He gathered his thoughts and continued, "If you used it the way it is now...then every time the shaft rotated...there'd be a small snap...eventually that snap would cause the Woodruff key to wear away...and fall out."

He looked up thoughtfully.

"I wouldn't want to see that happen to you on a lee shore," he added.

A few days later, Kenny had repaired the shaft, and a few days after that, I braced open the barn doors, coupled my 1990 Ford to the trailer hitch, and drew boat, trailer, and all into the early summer sun. A friend and former colleague, Thane Lelacheur, arrived on the appointed morning for the boat launching with his tractor. At the water's edge, he backed the trailer down the slip. The tractor gave a quick jerk forward. The boat jarred loose, eased back, floated freely in the water. That afternoon a boom truck lifted the thirty-three-foot mast and lowered it onto its seat against the keel. The boat was rigged before sundown. The next day, Saturday, more gear was put aboard. Then all was ready.

PART TWO

Chapter 9

THE REMAKE

What we were ready for was simple: to recapture the previous season's progress and add a great many more miles to the total. The goal, of course, was to complete the Great Loop, a circumnavigation of eastern North America. Two routes can be attempted, and there are variations within each. The US version logs about 6,000 nautical miles. My Canadian version, which includes the Maritime provinces, would rack up 7,500 nautical miles and is the more challenging route. I would start the first leg of that journey, though, with some good company. Peter Grant, an old friend, would sail for a week or so before he was obliged to return to his nine-to-five job as a systems analyst.

Our paths first crossed at the University of Ottawa in 1968, where we pursued graduate degrees in English literature. Later, in 1972, we set up writing and editing service for East Coast writers and gathered material for a collection of new Canadian writing from that region. Prince Edward Island was home base for the project, and by 1975 each of us had married and accumulated several children.

At some point, Pete and I had fully convinced each other that we could sail. We did not lie outright. Each had been aboard boats in some capacity, varying from ballast to cook's apprentice. Still, our exaggerations would have added a short cord of wood to the end of Pinocchio's nose. Eventually, we purchased a sailboat, a 26-foot whaleboat, a war surplus lifeboat from a Canadian destroyer. Fortunately, they are quite seaworthy ketch-rigged vessels and have been known to override the flawed commands of those as deluded as we were. Thackery once said that "a fool can no more see his own folly than he can see his ears." But in the next two years, by God's grace, we learned a thing or two about sailing. In fact, eventually both of us managed to get enough sea time and course work to complete certificates for Master of 40-Ton Vessels.

Thirty years passed. Then, June 25, 2005, less spry and less foolish, Peter and I reminisced about our youthful misadventures as we prepared to set sail. My wife, Brenda, Pete's wife, Kathleen, and her sister, Mary Lynn, waved from the jetty as we motored toward the steel and concrete breakwater. Optimism abounded.

We crept along against the now-rising tide, north through the Beach Point breakwater to the inner channel, then east. To starboard stood the Beach Point lighthouse. On our portside, a low sand dune named Poverty Beach ranged for two miles to the north.

We chatted as the coast bent gently to the west. During a lull in the conversation, I lifted the athwartship cockpit seat, just aft the bridge leading to the cabin. From there I could view the engine, transmission, and driveshaft. I checked them over. Everything sounded good, and everything looked fine. But then something caught my eye. A glint of light. I looked at the rear injector on top of the engine. Behind it a flicker of light again. I reached my hand out and touched the engine. My hand came up wet. It smelled of diesel fuel.

Unlike gasoline vapours, diesel fumes are not explosive. Nevertheless, I distrusted fuel seeping over a hot engine, and I imagined a spark from a generator or some other electrical connection igniting the fuel. So I shut down the engine, and we made sail.

Wood Islands lay fifteen miles south. The wind drifted out of the northeast at 10 knots, stiff enough to drive us to that port on Prince

Edward Island's southeast corner in a few hours. Once there, we could investigate the leak more closely or call a mechanic.

Three hours later, the Wood Islands light appeared ahead. Then it faded in a haze, and disappeared altogether in a gathering mist. A short while later, we sailed into the belly of that same grey, vaporous mass.

As the fog thickened, the wind fell flat and the sails baffled. Somewhere ahead, a sonorous rumble of diesel engines throbbed in the heart of a car ferry, idling at dock, loading vehicles, and preparing to leave port.

I pressed the starter, and the engine sprang to life. The noise was startling after the pious silence of sail and fog. The pulsing engine reverberated against the damp walls of fog and, in gear, the boat leapt ahead blindly. Our speed was dead slow because visibility was just a few yards. Still, it was a surprise when a green buoy suddenly

The author, left, and his old friend Peter Grant in 2005.

drifted by. I knew it must have been a channel buoy marking the entrance to the harbour, but the harbour had vanished into thick mist. I shifted the engine into neutral, but the buoy slipped out of our sight, and we drifted past it. Then another surprise followed in close succession—a great air horn blasted away all other of our sensibilities. As the sound faded, a white wall, the size of an airplane hangar, drew itself across the great cloak of fog. It was the hull of the ferry. Its engines, each the size of an elephant, quickened their thumping pace like the heart of some animal bolting after prey.

I noted the direction from which it had come, checked the bearing of my own vessel, and swung the tiller onto a new heading. Moments later, both the breakwater and the outline of the shore emerged from the mist.

Safely tied to the pier, I took a more leisurely look for the source of the seeping diesel fuel but, after half an hour, I was no better enlightened. Unable to investigate further, I called Lorin Panting, a mechanic not far from the Wood Islands wharf. Lorin said he would look at it first thing in the morning. That evening I brooded about the inauspicious second beginning of my trek, and that night I sailed through a confused sleep of shapeless, ill-lit dreams.

Lorin Panting's Garage in Wood Islands looked like an abandoned rural service station. The white paint on its wood-frame building is stained and peeling. A crumbling concrete pedestal marks the spot where the fuel pumps once stood and, on the broken asphalt pavement of a nearby lot, lie the remains of disfigured cars and rusting truck frames.

Inside, a small wood stove pumps heat fuelled by a few sticks of kindling. It takes the edge off a cool, early summer morning and the damp off the evening dew. Along the wall, a half-dozen grey and balding heads sit side by side on metal chairs, sip coffee or tea, and are silent only when someone new walks through the door, and then only for as long as it takes to size them up. All of them are friends of Lorin—retired mechanics, big-fisted fishermen, leathery farmers—and they form a scene found at almost every garage or general store in the county.

Lorin himself stood behind the counter. He was a short man, surprisingly witty and bright-eyed for eight o'clock in the morning, and he moved with a brisk gait which belied a workman in his eighties. No time wasted, either. In minutes we were driving to the wharf. In a few more minutes, he spotted the problem and the cause. An over-tightened clamp had cracked a clear plastic fuel return line. Lorin cut off the damaged edge, forced the hose over the metal tube, making a fit tight enough to seal without clamp. "That will be fifteen dollars, please."

We departed Wood Islands at 1030, passed the entrance to Charlottetown, and the picturesque Victoria Harbour. Nearby, the Tryon Shoals endanger a westward approach to that village port. Several years ago, an elderly solo sailor grounded his sailboat on those sands during a nighttime approach. He was unfamiliar with the area, and the sea was running high.

The incoming seas beat his hull and careened the vessel on its side. Succeeding waves swept over his deck. To survive, he lashed himself to the mast. After that, he could only pray he would not be swept into a black, roiling sea on that black, starless night. It must have seemed hopeless when no help came. No one ashore had witnessed the shipwreck, and he counted the hours of his solitary terror by the din of hundreds of waves and by the sweep of tons of water. At dawn he was sighted and rescued, but he never sailed again.

BORDEN, PEI

As we neared Confederation Bridge, the water turned choppy, but the port of Borden lay just ahead. It takes fewer than a half dozen boats to fill the public wharf in Borden. We found no vacant berths. So we tied up alongside another vessel. Because the hour was late, we rushed to find a restaurant.

Gateway Village was a few hundred yards away. It lies within the village of Borden, but it is not really a village at all. More, a fabrication. A prop. A tourist magnet. An elaborate construction of gift shops, restaurants, tourist information kiosks, interpretive centres, and craft stores. The PEI government constructed it after the bridge had been completed. It was a grid of broad avenues, along which developers erected dozens of spacious, cute wood-frame buildings. At nine o'clock, tourists having reached their cottage retreats, these stores turned out their lights and locked their doors. Gateway Village then takes on the appearance of a set on a no-longer-used movie lot.

Peter and I ordered the last platters of fish and chips at the last open restaurant in the village. We ate on the veranda, the restaurant itself now closed. The sky grew pale. The village grew indistinct in the fading of day. The walk back to the boat took us through part of the real village of Borden: small, modest, blue-collar houses nestled on tiny lots, each uncomfortably close to the next; narrow streets; yapping dogs; worn cars in driveways; broken pavement; children's toys dropped at the call to supper and forgotten; the violet flicker of televisions; the echo of a loud goodbye from half a street away; the galloping beat of a country-music tune; lawns manicured and lawns ragged. All of this made Gateway Village seem unnatural, false, and, on some level, as grotesque as a grinning mannequin.

It was dark by the time we returned to the boat. Lamps along the pier cast a bluish-white glare over the water. The *Arja D.* stood in the shadow of the *Crystal D.*, but something seemed out of order. The boat moved oddly. It seemed to hobble at its tether like a dog with a thorn in its paw. Then I noticed that the tide had bottomed out. The mud flats had crept to within six feet of the boat. The stern had grounded in the mud, while the bow floated freely in the first ripples of the rising tide.

The *Arja D.* was fully afloat when we awoke the next morning, but the marine weather station had issued a small-craft warning. The weather was still favourable: the wind steady 10–15 knots; fog patches were lifting; and the port of Summerside was only fourteen miles away. It was tempting.

We gave into the temptation and arrived around noon. As the report promised, foul weather struck. It blew hard for two more days. Then the forecast moderated. Light winds were promised, and it looked good for a morning crossing to New Brunswick.

We steamed out the channel at 0715 the next day. At the fairway buoy we shut the engine down and raised sail. The wind lasted another hour, but then the sails luffed and the boat began to drift. I cranked the starter, and the engine pumped away.

Our course took us across the Northumberland Strait toward New Brunswick's Richibucto Cape. Prince Edward Island slipped out of sight, and the sun slipped toward the horizon. A veil of soft pinks hovered over a bath of dusty orange in the northwest. Landforms grew dark, indistinct, dreary, and hardened into a black, amorphous profile. Above, the sky transformed itself into a clear, vibrant, liquid-blue.

The sliver of longitude upon which we floated became enveloped in the rush of night. A delicate necklace of warm, amber lights shone from homes beyond the invisible dunes and marshes which marked the low New Brunswick coast, and just above this gentle horizon blinked a vague, luminous speck—the planet Mercury. Further aloft, Venus glowed with ardent conceit. And atop the pinnacle of its arc, Jupiter reigned steadily and strong. The smallest, the nearest, and the largest of all our planets. Altogether they sparked the first light to confront a darkening, vacant sky. And in their wake flooded a heaven full of stars, summer constellations, and the incandescent glow of the Milky Way. Sporadic meteors streaked through the darkness and the anchor light on the masthead, scribbled playful arcs on the celestial blackness with every gentle pitch and roll of the boat. Around 2300 a radiant smudge appeared in the east and illuminated a huddle of low clouds. It kindled into a cool, orange ember, which grew into a fragment less than half a moon, weakly yellow at first, and dimly white and pale later as it climbed.

The night was beautiful, but I wished that the moon had grown brighter by this hour. It was now two in the morning. We had reached our waypoint off Tracadie-Sheila, New Brunswick, but we had not spotted the lights that would guide us through the break in the dunes. Nor had we passed another marker which we should have crossed along our approach a few miles further south. I went below and double-checked the latitude and longitude of Tracadie on the chart. It was correct. We should be less than a mile from the shore and the breakwater. The buoys should be lit and nearby, but we couldn't see any.

At least part of the problem was the nature of the coastline. The fifty miles of coast from Miramichi to Miscou Island is low-lying. Much of it is masked behind dozens of miles of sand beaches and dunes, many of which are detached from the mainland and form a protective outer barrier. Between dune and mainland are shallow lagoons and bays and the rivers and streams which feed them. Altogether they present a low silhouette in the daylight, while at night the silhouette mixes indistinguishably with the blackness of the sea. Lights from any towns behind it, however, are not obscured. So, a leading light or a flashing channel marker a quarter mile ahead might be confused with a blinking red light on a tower three miles inland. All depth of field was illusory. And the sprawling town of Tracadie-Sheila was busy with light—red, yellow, white, flashing, steady, and intermittent as we peered into the seamless black water and shore ahead. Those lights which were navigation aids and those which were deceits could not be separated. Not by me, at any rate. Nor by Peter.

So we cruised slowly north and south paralleling the coast, earnestly searching for something to confirm our GPS waypoint numbers and remaining alert for abrupt changes in the readout on the depth sounder. Getting ashore was by no means an urgent matter. Anchoring was an option. Wind and sea conditions were temperate. However, we had covered a respectable one hundred nautical miles that day, and we had been on deck for twenty hours. We were tired.

TRACADIE-SHEILA, NB

We were tired, but not exhausted. So we continued our slow patrol of the coast, gradually working our way inshore, and then we observed a red light shifting more markedly than the others as we made our passes. That meant it was closer. We motored cautiously toward it. Indeed, it was the very channel marker we had been looking for. Then a second marker appeared closer to shore, and beyond it was the narrow unlit cut through the dune into sheltered waters of a great, broad, shallow lagoon.

Peter posted himself forward with the spotlight to illuminate the steel-girded walls of the gully. As soon as the gap was cleared, I hauled the tiller hard to port. The bow swung to starboard, and we threaded through several miles of shoal water and narrow channel and past unlit markers. By the time we entered the Tracadie River, the gloom of pre-dawn gave a hint of shape to the objects before us. The river water shifted to grey and then to an ashen pale hue; the wooded terrain along the banks redefined itself in gloomy shadows and ragged textures. Then at the end of the canal-like river, the expansive inner bay emerged. And the skyline of Tracadie-Sheila. And the world gained colour—a soft rose, and pale silver, and a gentle blue.

Four hours' sleep was not nearly enough, but it was all that I could manage. So I rolled out of my bunk, clambered up the steps to the cockpit, hauled the propane Coleman stove from the rear hatch, and brewed some coffee in my open-air kitchen on deck. I was contemplating a second cup, listening to pancakes sizzle in the fry pan when Peter appeared from below. Over breakfast we discussed his plans to return to Charlottetown. His vacation time was over. Tracadie-Sheila was his last port on this journey, and he phoned to make the travel arrangements. The following day he returned to PEI.

I phoned home too. My daughter, Arja, answered, but it was difficult to hear her. The house rang with the laughter and jumble of chatter from relatives in the background. Brenda was hosting a potluck dinner party for my son Finley and his girlfriend, Leah. Finley took the phone. He was rather excited about joining me for a week of sailing. I suggested Rimouski, Quebec, as a good place to rendezvous.

As I hung up the phone, other familiar sounds faded from the ear piece: a boisterous voice of my brother-in-law, Ken, rising above the common din; a clatter of dishes; the metallic clank of tableware; and the girlish chime of Brenda. I felt both a twinge of isolation and a warm sadness.

Chapter 10

ANOTHER CAMEO

The pre-dawn sky was a flawless, vibrant aquamarine. The wind was hushed. A lustrous crescent moon hung high in the south like a splinter of opal. Even the dark side shone a radiant ebony, and together they dangled like a pendant about the neck of morning. Such a day heralded glory, invoked promise, and nurtured well-being, but in less than an hour the noble beginning would totter, then stumble and lurch headlong into the chagrin of a one-joke farce. And I would have the starring role.

It was not yet 0500. I stepped out of the shower room in the lighthouse-shaped marina building on the knoll above the wharf. The outer room, which served as an office and tourist information centre, had a washbasin where I shaved and brushed my teeth. Then I returned to the shower room to grab my knapsack of clothes. I felt a cold thrill of numbing alarm course up my spine as I turned the door's handle. Or should I say attempted to turn the handle? The shower-room door had closed and locked behind me. Inside were my clothes and kitbag. Inside were my keys to the boat.

I blundered out the door onto the porch with just a little more composure than a man who has suddenly come upon a corpse in his living room. My eyes scanned the marina, the boats below, the main street above, the bridge upriver. There were no cars running morning-damp roads, no people afoot, no quiet light burning in the cabin of fishing boat, cruiser, or yacht. The brilliant dawn sky, that half an hour before had grown pale with the quickening light, now had grown tawdry and false.

I had little choice then but to wait, wait until some boat owner with an early-morning concern for his boat would appear with a key to the shower room. An hour and a half passed before that someone arrived. I explained my circumstances, but learned that none of the club members had a shower-room key. A duplicate key could be got from Jacques LeBreton, the marina manager, but he was away for the holiday weekend. I should call him, one boater suggested. Jacques was an early riser, he said.

I waited until 0700 before I made that call. Jacques answered after five or six rings, sounding groggy, but obliging, and promised to be there in half an hour by boat. His cottage was downriver.

Jacques was prompt, dutiful. My gear and keys were retrieved and, before the wake of his cruiser faded into the face of the bay, I had let go my mooring lines and began to creep downstream, across the bay. Outside the barrier dunes, I headed north along the coast of New Brunswick for ten or fifteen miles. It was not an effortless run. The sea was lumpy, and I was glad when I was able to slip through Shippegan Gully into the protected waters. I navigated a meandering switchback of shoals and cleared the lift bridge at the town of Shippagan.

I put into the marina near there because my previous weather check indicated deteriorating conditions. A flight of wooden stairs led me to the marina complex above the wharves. Near the side entrance to the marina complex I passed an elderly man engaged in conversation with an animated young woman in her late twenties. Their topic was the weather too. I stopped and asked if she had heard a current forecast. She was lanky and sunburnt; her hair was short, bleached, and windblown. She had just arrived from Percé. She was travelling in a fleet of seven lean, powerful "cigarette boats." On their crossing of Baie des Chaleurs, however, they had been beaten about by six-foot waves. The woman had been shaken by the experience.

I bided my time at the marina for several hours. Then I learned that the front which had so distressed the cigarette boat crews had passed. To my surprise, the thirty-odd-mile crossing to Grand-Riviére turned into a pleasant sail. In fact, the entire day proved successful. I logged sixty-five nautical miles.

It took six days to sail from Tracadie-Sheila, New Brunswick, to Rimouski, Quebec, and, though I followed the same course as the previous year, it had a different feel to it. One circumstance strikingly different from the previous year's passage around the Gaspé Peninsula was in the number of waterfowl. Last year, birds were abundant, varied, and active. This year, even though time of day and date were nearly identical, rather few birds coursed through the air or bobbed on the surface. One condition strikingly similar to last year, however, was the weather. Winds remained light and variable, and a chill hung in the air with many mornings beginning at forty-five degrees (seven Celsius).

In the lower St. Lawrence River between Cap-Chat and Cap des Méchins, a brief flurry of wildlife stole my thoughts away from the frigid morning. Three large seals broke the calm of the water. Moments later I glimpsed a whale closer to shore. Its black hulk breached the surface twice more, quite close to my port bow. It made no noise and disturbed little water in its gentle but swift race upstream. It ran a course parallel to mine, but after its third appearance, it vanished. The sighting of the seals and the whale in quick time reminded me that several other conditions had changed on the river since last season. Fewer boats cruised; fewer freighters lumbered along. There was less debris on the seaway—no logs, masses of displaced grass from spring run-offs, and fewer seabirds plied the air or rode the waves.

RIMOUSKI, PQ

I had grown quite fond of Rimouski during my two brief stay-overs last year. Returning felt comfortable and even a relief, like sighting Carthage after a desert crossing. I was assigned a berth on the west side of the dock, near the marina ramp, close to where I had tied up before. Of the acquaintances I had made there, Andrew Laplante, a Rimouski high-school teacher, was first to say hello. He was aboard his boat, *Symbiose*, tracing the source of a battery failure.

It was not yet 0900 when my friend Louis Arsenault stopped on the way to his vessel, *Louise III*. Louis had helped me in the past, and we had corresponded during the winter. He invited me to breakfast. Over coffee and muffins in the galley of his cruiser, we discussed family, music, business and, of course, boats. As usual, whenever I visited Louis, we were interrupted by friends rapping on the hull or hallooing from the dock. They would chat briefly or, more often, come aboard, take a coffee, and share a story of their own.

After breakfast I returned to *Arja D*. The day was bright and warm. I had grocery shopping to do and took that as opportunity to try out my folding bike. It had been stored below deck, housed in a waterproof bag, wedged between the mast, centreboard housing, and a starboard locker. I hauled it up and through the hatch. It took a few minutes to assemble, and then I was on my way through the marina and along the access road toward the highway through Rimouski.

I must have looked odd on my machine. It resembled a type of stunt bike. The bicycle has only twenty-inch wheels, small enough to clear my hatchway. The handlebars and seat extend to adult height. The bike was comfortable, though wobbly. Gradually I began to attribute the instability of the bike not to any design flaw, but to my not having ridden a bike in fifty years. Still a trial run brought me safely to the mall two miles away.

Late in the afternoon, I visited Andrew. We uncapped a few beers and talked about ports upstream and river conditions, and whether to head along the south shore or cross to the north shore on the run to Quebec City.

The south shore, the coast along which I had travelled thus far, had the strongest falling tides and was thought of as better for a downriver passage. There were more villages at closer intervals, but waters in the approach to them are quite shallow for some distance offshore, and several of these ports go dry with a falling tide.

The advantage of a north shore passage was strong rising tides. Five- or 6-knot currents, added to the 6 knots of a driving engine, would propel a boat twelve nautical miles in an hour. If one could maintain that for two hours, then a boat would achieve what otherwise would have taken half a day's good sailing. On the other hand, the north shore is bordered by steep cliffs. There are few natural ports to put into, and the wind always seems stronger on that side of the river. Another disadvantage to the north shore is the great Saguenay River. The frigid Saguenay water pours into the warmer St. Lawrence creating thermal layers. The interaction of these thermal layers frequently results in dangerous riptides and turbulences. Wind and strong tides add to the problem. The result can be treacherous for small boats.

A basic rule for all sailboat traffic, however, is this: leave port with the tide in your favour; be in port when the tide turns. Otherwise, your boat will be treading water or, worse, losing ground during six hours of adverse current. The maximum hull speed of most small sailboats hovers around 6 knots.

By the end of the day I had decided on a sailing plan. Tomorrow, I would make the short run to Trois-Pistoles, and anchor off Île aux Basques for the night. Next day, I would continue on the south shore to Port de Gros-Cacouna. Day after, I would cross to Cap-à-l'Aigle on the north shore. Day four would take me to Île aux Coudres where very strong tides are common. Finally, Quebec City via the south passage of Île d'Orléans

During my last evening I was entertained by Louis Arsenault and his brother, Eddie, on the *Louise III.* Several people dropped in that night. One was a retired lawyer. He was in his eighties, but he looked much younger. In many ways he reminded me of a young Cary Grant—quick-witted, plucky, and self-assured, and wearing his hat cocked at a rakish angle. I learned that he was a widower. Tonight, his girlfriend accompanied him. She was a quiet, pleasant, attractive woman in her forties.

Finley would arrive by train shortly after midnight. So I killed some time in my boat, straightening gear and listening to the radio. It was nearly impossible this far north in Quebec to tune in to a clear English station. I grew bored. So at eleven o'clock I began an unlikely task—laundry. The washing and drying ended a little after twelve. I packed the clothes away in the boat. Then I waited for Finley's taxi from the railway station. The evening was damp, and the stars were obscured by the glow of Rimouski's streetlights and homes. One o'clock came and went. No sign of my son. I hadn't heard a train whistle. I waited until two o'clock. Still nothing. So I returned to my boat and fell asleep. At three, I was awakened by a racket on deck. A thump as the companion slide shoved ahead. The door rattled out of its slot. Finley stumbled down the ladder.

"Hi," he said cheerily. "There was a train derailment."

Chapter 11

TROUBLED WATERS

The tide fell most of the morning. So there was no necessity to turn out early. When we finally did, it was for a leisurely breakfast at the marina restaurant on the second floor, overlooking the boats and the harbour beyond the breakwater. We feasted on omelettes and French toast and plates of cut fruit. The coffee was good. So we had seconds.

Over the last cup of coffee Finley passed on all of the home news, as well as details of his delay the night before. His train had not derailed though. A freight train on the track ahead of him had. As a result, the passage was blocked. Bewildered railroad officials searched for alternate arrangements for stranded passengers, and eventually packed them into taxis and drove them to their destinations. It had been an uncomfortable journey but, after his arrival in Rimouski, Finley recaptured his excitement to sail again.

We sailed out of Rimouski at 1030. It had been sunny and warm at dock but, shortly after entering the river, the temperature chilled and drove us into layers of cold-weather gear or survival suits. The tide was still falling and wouldn't turn for another hour and a half. A 15-knot westerly wind bit into us, and the sea was snarly. It was tough progress driving upstream, but the four or five sailboats coming downriver enjoyed quick passage and good sailing conditions.

Later that morning, we neared the region where I had faced so much misery in '04—days of fog, bone-numbing cold, disheartening rain, and menacing seas. It occurred somewhere near the islands of Bic and Biquette.

Those islands came into view once again. Slate reefs fringed their shores northeast, northwest, and southeast, and their black, bony crags licked the surface at low tide. I trained my binoculars on them and searched for landmarks that might confirm that this was where I had been so endangered. However, nothing seemed to fit. There was a lighthouse on Bic, but the outbuildings seemed wrong, and their height above the sea was far less than I recalled during my ordeal. Was it possible that I had drifted inside the islands, nearer the shore? Cap a l'Original has two-hundred-foot cliffs and faces an open easterly sea. Could that have been my lee shore? Or Cap Enragé. I could see neither of those landforms so far offshore. Nevertheless, remembrance of it all provoked a shudder, and I wondered if other such hazards lurked ahead. I had no time for further exploration here and no more desire to worry about unforeseeable futures. So we kept moving west.

Wind stiffened, and rain sputtered and dribbled. A hint of fog grazed the horizon ahead, and a haze obscured shoreline to the south. The closer we neared to the deep, cold Saguenay River, the less predictable the weather became.

ÎLE AUX BASQUES, PQ

We reached Île aux Basques, the island fronting Trois-Pistoles, around quarter to eight. We stood off and anchored on the east end of Île aux Basques, just as I had the year before. The island sheltered us from much of the wind but, at anchor, the *Arja D.* still wanted to lie crosswise to the breeze. So I expected an uncomfortable night of rolling. Fortunately, the wind went slack as evening bore down; the sea grew light and calmed. In fact, conditions became so pleasant that I broke out the cook stove and heated soup and made coffee. The evening was agreeable enough that we could lie back, read a few pages of a novel, or catch up on our journals or letters.

I took a solitary turn on deck before bedding down. Bright points of light illuminated the village of Trois-Pistoles, a half mile away, on the southern shore. Three miles northeast a freighter glowed a brilliant amber, lit by a dozen deck lights. It was standing at anchor, perhaps waiting for a pilot to board or for an empty berth in the port to which it was bound. And less than a hundred yards to the west a solitary navigation light marked the east end of Île aux Basques. All of the lights surrounding us burned brightly, seemed to grow closer in the deepening darkness, and, like the embers in a dying campfire, they generated warmth and comfort enough to propel me into a light, sound, yet cautious sleep. I had experienced the worst here. I had learned that misfortune bides its time, and luck is untimely. So I slept with my clothes on and dreamt of pleasant things.

The wind and sea remained calm the entire night, and a gentle current rocked us to sleep. At dawn, the wind was idle and the sea placid. The sun rose with strength, but fog baffled its warmth. Banks of radiant fog swept by intermittently during the morning. And out of their grey recesses echoed the sounds of wilderness: squawks and chirps, growls and throaty warbles, wails and plaintive laments. Sometimes, a rhythmic flutter of wings beat the skin of the river. Then a drove of shags or bay ducks would emerge in low flight over the water and disappear into a cloud of mist. Sometimes a tumultuous shudder of water reached our ears as the heads of a dozen or more gulls plunged into a school of fry. Once or twice a whale, unseen and nearby, sounded with a deep, thunderous surge.

As morning grew full and the sun rose stronger, the fog began to break into pockets, and corridors and ghost-like wisps. Lines of ducks and packets of black-and-white dovekies dotted the silver surface of the river. Grasses, twigs, fronds, and clusters of seed pods floated past and, when the tide strengthened, they knitted together into long, sinewy mats of vegetation. The distant slam of a car door marked the wharf at Trois-Pistoles, and the thump of a diesel engine carried from the shipping channel far offshore. This morning and this place could only be described as idyllic and perhaps even magical. And it was almost impossible for me to believe that at one time, here and not so long ago, I had been desperately cold, hungry, and sleepless on this very anchorage...that I would face dangers and fears and hardships...and that I would teeter on the edge of failure to grasp a dream I had long sought after. Perhaps I'd paid my dues. Perhaps all that was far behind.

Most of the morning then became a time to kick back and enjoy the sights and sounds. I found nothing to repair, replace, or adjust aboard the boat. I was not pressed to drive on upstream like a salmon responding to a primal urge. All that remained was some book work on the tides and a wait for the best time to leave.

My concern about tidal irregularities had begun near Sainte-Anne-des-Monts. But, now, as the river narrowed to fifteen miles, the currents ran more swiftly, inconsistently, and unpredictably. If we had simply followed the standard tide tables, we would have lifted anchor at 0930, an hour after low tide at Rimouski, thirty-eight miles below us. In reality, however, slack water would not occur here for four more hours and, for several of those hours, the falling tide would create an immense whirlpool effect southeast of Île Verte and southeast of Île aux Livres. Île aux Basques, where we anchored, was at the edge of that vast eddy.

Two principles guided my decisions about how to navigate upstream. First, be in the next port before sundown. Second, arrive before the tide begins to fall. In order to achieve both goals, we would have to weigh anchor before the tide began to rise. If we waited until slack water at Île aux Basques, then we would not make Port de Gros-Cacouna until long after the strong falling tide had begun. So, it would better to struggle against a light current now than to be caught by a strong falling current later.

At 1230, we lifted anchor. A couple of miles offshore, the tide was rolling at a brisk 4 to 6 knots. Inshore, however, only a 2-knot current slowed us. We hugged the coast of Île aux Basques and stayed within rifle shot of Île aux Pommes, and our speed-made-good against the tide maxed at 3.5 knots for the next two hours.

We passed three low-lying islands during that time. Île aux Basques was a thickly wooded bird sanctuary and, when North America was a dark continent, it had been an outpost for fishermen out of the Basque region of Spain. Île aux Pommes was green, but largely bare, and with rocky shores. Both islands were slivers of land, honed into narrowness by the great tides. Île Verte appeared five miles upstream. A group of islets and reefs preceded our approach to Île Verte. We stood further offshore to clear them. Then Finley took the helm. I went below and slept for an hour. When I woke and returned to the cockpit, Île Verte was still slipping by our port side. The tide had turned, and by the time we reached the backside of Île Verte we were making better than 6 knots toward Port de Gros-Cacouna.

PORT DE GROS-CACOUNA, PQ

Along the five-mile dogleg into that harbour, the texture of the water alternated—patches of oily calm and troubled ripples. We had plenty of depth, but we were sailing between two areas on the chart where tides created dangerous water turbulence for small craft. What we witnessed merely hinted at their potential.

Port de Gros-Cacouna was constructed in the 1980s as a much-desired harbour for super tankers. Tens of millions were spent in construction, and several thousand jobs were generated by this megaproject. It was to be the jewel of the south shore, news reports of the time predicted. Nevertheless, sailing into Port de Gros-Cacouna this day was like sailing into a ghost town. There were no trucks or shipping crates, loading cranes, seamen, or longshoremen on the piers. There were no ships or floating docks. There were no fishing boats tied to the wharf, and there were no dry-docked vessels. No smoke lifted from chimneys, no doors were ajar, and no forklifts waited for loads. In the 1959 Cold War movie *On the Beach,* a US submarine surfaces in Sydney Harbour, Australia, searching for signs of life after radiation from a nuclear catastrophe destroyed human life everywhere else. The sub's captain, peering through his periscope, sees untended ships and the products of human enterprise in a gulf of loneliness. We saw even less in Port de Gros-Cacouna. Within our field of vision were no ships, no hints of human activity, just an eerie emptiness.

We dropped anchor near the northeast end of the harbour in the shadow of the mountain and close to the rocks of the breakwater. We stood in twenty feet of water and let out a hundred feet of scope, but the anchor dragged. We reset the anchor, fed out a hundred and fifty feet of line, and the anchor finally dug in. Several other boats arrived before evening, among them *Au Fil de l'Eau*, the yacht of Yvonne and Miriam, a Montreal couple that had followed us from Sainte-Anne-des-Monts and Rimouski. All anchored nearby.

The northeast wind calmed during the night, and that made a good sleep possible. The sea was glassy, and the water reflected blues and greys and violets in slow undulations. Far across the harbour tiny figures, probably villagers from Saint-Georges-de-Cacouna, tossed fishing lines off a wharf for an evening meal of flounder. The sun gained strength, and the wind piped up to 15 knots, a heavy fog rolled in, dissipated, and then rolled in again.

CAP-À-L'AIGLE, PQ

After lunch, we hoisted anchor to cross the St. Lawrence for Cap-à-l'Aigle on the north and drifted alongside Yvonne's boat to say goodbye.

Outside, wavelets and a light 10-knot northeast breeze greeted us. We pressed on, farther and farther into the river. A comfortable sea accompanied us there, and a lovely following wind boosted us toward Cap-à-l'Aigle.

Once again, the air this close to the Saguenay River was cold. So we donned survival suits. We cruised west for three miles to avoid several rocks. Then we settled into a northwesterly course across the St. Lawrence. A twenty-five-mile string of slender islands and sandbars runs midway along the ten-mile width of the St. Lawrence River and divides that waterway into North and South Channels. On our crossing a whale rose and plunged and dove in its brisk drive upstream, and a car ferry from Rivière-du-Loup crossed our bow and slipped between Île aux Livres and the reefs at Île aux Fraises on its passage to Stephenville. We followed the ferry through the pass but, once through, we continued NNW toward Cap-à-l'Aigle, twenty miles ahead. All along our North Shore passage a long range of granite mountains crowded the water's edge. They dwarfed the two cargo ships, which passed us. The freighters looked like children's toys.

Cap-à-l'Aigle opens into a marina and its network of floating docks. By the time we tied up, it was early evening. Services at the marina office were closing, and that prompted a flurry of activity to get keys, information, and diesel fuel.

My hope had been a pre-dawn getaway the next morning, but heavy fog discouraged it. Fog persisted much of the morning and didn't lift until late. The best time for a favourable tide appeared to be mid-afternoon. So, when that hour struck, we set off once more. By then I had worked out the course for Île aux Coudres, our next port. The tides along that island are swift. In summer, flood tides average 3.5 knots, while ebb tides commonly run 6 knots and can exceed 7.

ÎLE AUX COUDRES, PQ

Progress toward Île aux Coudres was sluggish for the first two hours. After that, however, our speed coursed up to 7 knots. A freighter passed us in the narrow strait between the island of Île aux Coudres and the North Shore. Ahead a passenger ferry pointed a way into the harbour. We followed it.

The small marina lay next to the ferry terminal. As we passed the docked ferry and turned into the marina, water depth fell to five feet. Then a small, rusting scow motored by. A tiny outboard motor laboured on its stern.

"How much water do you take?" he shouted and pointed toward the bottom of our boat.

"Two feet," I said. He nodded. Then he motioned for us to follow him and led us to an open berth among floating docks. The pilot of the scow was the marina's manager.

"How long do you stay? When do you leave? You leave soon?"

"Overnight. We leave in the morning."

"If you stay, you can't leave early. Seven o'clock."

"Why?"

The manager crouched in his little scow about ten yards off our stern. He extended his arm and circumscribed a great arc.

"The water all go," he said. "All mud."

"You mean the port goes dry?" I asked.

"Dry. Dry yes. All mud. No rock. Boat is okay. No rock," he added assuredly.

I believed him. Not that I had a choice. Evening was settling in.

Perhaps "settling in" was not the most apt phrase. Shortly after dark, a chain of thunderstorms dumped torrents of rain, and lightning shattered the black sky until about midnight. Between two of the downpours I ran from the boat to a telephone booth outside the marina's main building. I phoned my daughter, Arja, to tell her of the beluga whales I had seen. She had just finished training at the RCMP depot in Calgary where part of her police training as a National Park warden took place. As a biologist, she is especially interested in marine life and eager to hear about the sightings, even though second-hand.

Something felt odd at five when I woke. I rolled out of my bunk, slid the hatch open, and clambered up the ladder into the cockpit. There was a hint of fog. The morning was dim, but there was light enough to see that the water level in the marina was very low. I looked over the washboards. Four more inches of copper paint exposed itself above the waterline. We were aground.

I grabbed my gear and made for the showers. The ramp from the floating dock to the marina deck was much steeper than the night before. It was like climbing to an eagle's nest, and it was slippery from last night's rain. From the deck, I overlooked a mud flat, which hours before had been the harbour entrance. Nothing could get in or out.

When I returned to the boat an hour later, however, it was floating, and by seven, as the marina manager had predicted, there was enough water to clear the harbour. The water was calm, almost glassy in the stillness of morning. We cruised along the coast of Île aux Coudres at 6.5 knots. I called up the GPS waypoints which would guide us through the inbound shipping lanes of the North Channel to Île d'Orléans, take us across the tip of that large island, and lead us into the narrows of the South Channel, the gateway to Quebec City.

Between waypoint one and waypoint two, the rising tide boosted our cruising speed to 9 knots but it lasted less than an hour, dropped back to between 6 and 7 knots and, as we approached waypoint three, twenty-five miles out of Île aux Coudres, the wind built to 20 knots, and a considerable sea rose behind it. What I'd expected to be a quick, balmy run to the South Channel became tumultuous and uncomfortable. Six-foot breaking waves knocked us about. They struck mainly on our beam, and we rolled so precipitously that we buckled safety harnesses and tethered ourselves to a jack line.

We stood four miles off the land. Several freighters and a large passenger ferry plied the same waterway, a mile nearer the shore and then, strangely, the water beneath our keel dropped from sixty to just thirty feet. Finley took the tiller once again. I went below and took a fix on our position. We had been driven three-quarters of a mile off course and were on the edge of a shoal area. A quarter mile to port, two rocks pricked the surface and churned the breaking waves into foam. I altered course northwest and headed toward the shore. In doing so, we were running before the sea, a much more comfortable position, but care still had to be taken not to allow a wave to pitch us sideways.

The closer our approach to the shore, the more imposing the mountains appeared. They were a massive range, fully wooded and well-rounded. They hugged the water's edge and lifted two to three thousand feet into the sky. I had considered putting into some local harbour. But the dark hills fell steeply into the river. No beaches ringed the coast. No coves offered shelter. No ports appeared as refuge.

We returned to our original course after half an hour. We had cleared the offshore obstacles. Now we cruised through deep water, but the curvature of the coast stirred riptides and eddies. We struck some good luck, however, as we approached waypoint four. There, the strength of the waves dwindled, their force broken by a string of islands mid-channel, three or four miles to windward.

The waters in which we sailed now were at the head of the lower St. Lawrence River. Beyond here, the great river narrows dramatically like the neck of an enormous bottle and, like a cork in that bottle, is Île d'Orléans. That island has two navigable channels around it. Both lead to Quebec City. The first of these is Chenal de l'Île d'Orléans, the main channel for in-bound ships. The second is, Chenal des Grand Voisier, the outbound passage, and it runs along the south shore of Île d'Orléans.

Quebec City had been the goal of our day's work. However, as the tide teetered on the edge of falling, that became improbable. Our choices now were two: run downstream along the river's south bank to Montmagny, or push ahead up the Chenal des Grand Voisiers to Saint-Michel-de-Bellechasse and hope that no ebb tide overwhelmed us. Montmagny was farther. It also meant a two-mile run through the St. Thomas Banks, an extensive coastal marshland. So we struck out for Saint-Michel instead.

SAINT-MICHEL-DE-BELLECHASE, PQ

Around noon the mouth of Chenal des Grands Voisiers opened before us. The canal was a mile and a half broad at its mouth. We planned to strike the coast just below Saint-Michel, work our way up to the channel buoy, and survey the harbour entrance before heading in. It was six miles to Saint-Michel, and it would take an hour to reach it.

It took only half that time, however, for thick, grey clouds to billow above Île d'Orléans. By the time they rolled over us, we had reached the buoys leading into the port, and were about to swing toward it. We held off for a few minutes, waiting for a large sailboat coming downriver. It appeared that it would turn into Saint-Michel. Then it altered course again. Its crew scurried about, securing sails and deck gear.

It was evident that they had seen what we had seen. The once-grey clouds above Orléans had turned black. Lightning crackled all along their length. Then a squall hit us with a roar of wind and a dousing rain. The first blast struck with explosive force. The boat rocked, and the brim of my hat snapped against my face with a sharp, slapping report. By the time I peeled it away, everything had disappeared: Île d'Orléans, the sailboat twenty yards to starboard, a small sailboat ahead, the channel buoys, the entrance to Saint-Michel, the shore. Even the bow of our boat vanished from our sight. Had it not, we could have seen little anyway, because the wind-driven rain struck our faces so painfully that we could not look to windward, and it pricked our eyes so harshly that we could not open them.

The boat was still rumbling slowly toward shore, a shore that I could not see, and toward shoal water that I knew was there. I felt below me for the throttle handle and shifted the transmission into neutral. The engine ticked away at idle. The boat lost its way and bobbed quirkily in the confused water and wind. Rain drilled onto the deck like bullets. Drops burst on impact and spattered in myriad directions. We slung our heads and, unable to oppose the bite of the hard rain, we stole only furtive looks about and cringed like a pair of beaten dogs.

And then it was over.

As quickly as it began, it ended. The change was sudden, startling even, and like soldiers emerging from a foxhole after a bombardment, we poked our heads up and looked around. The rain had ceased, and the mountain of cloud rolled away. The sky was clearing, the sun was brightening, and the outline of Saint-Michel was crisp in the post-storm air.

We motored through the short chain of buoys and found a berth at the end of the first dock. Finley cast the bowline onto the dock, jumped after it, and hauled the bow gently in. While he snugged the bowline around a mooring post, I hurled a coil of stern line and followed after it. Moving was sluggish. The squall had struck so suddenly that we had had no time to don oil clothes. Our cool-weather clothing, denims, sweaters, and quilted shirts, were sodden. We felt fifteen pounds heavier. Our shoes squished, gurgled, and spurted water with each step we took. I felt like a circus clown.

Once the boat was secure, we took a change of clothes. We wrung out the wet gear, hung some of it over the boom, and spread the rest along the foredeck and cabin top. Only the cockpit was free of laundry. Then, feeling a bit more civilized in appearance, we made for the marina restaurant.

"Is it time for a beer?" I asked

Finley grinned.

Chapter 12

TOWARD BREAD AND CIRCUSES

By 0900 the tide had turned to flood, and we left the quaint, picturesque, and quiet Saint-Michel. The sun glowed brightly, and the sky was a rich deep blue. Ahead, a line of power cables spanned the mile-wide breadth of the river, and in the distance we saw our first hint of the port of Quebec City: the dry docks, wharves, and towering cranes of Davie Shipyard near Lévis. Here the two channels around the island of Orléans merged into one at Quebec City. At that juncture the water changed character, growing more turbulent from eddies and gnarly from a chopping sea.

Water traffic became heavy as well. A large schooner slid in front of the Quebec skyline. The passenger ferry, *Louis Jolliet*, its three decks filled with passengers, crossed from Quebec toward Lévis. Several small sailboats dotted the seascape, and powerboats buzzed near shore.

Most impressive of all, though, was the city itself. It was built on a headland between the St. Charles and the St. Lawrence Rivers. A steep, foliage-covered bank skirted the water's edge. The tips of half a dozen towering office buildings and hotels sprouted from the plain 250 feet above, but not even they could keep one's eye from being drawn to the massive edifice of the Château Frontenac. Its ruddy stone walls dominated the city; its numerous wings and towers spread across several city blocks; and its vintage green copper roof proclaimed an old-world charm for which the city is best known and, by comparison, the sprinkling of steel and glass and plastic and polymer constructions east of it, and which comprised the modern face of Quebec, seemed insignificant and transitory.

As we closed on the city and bent more southwest into the curve of the river, the stone walls of the old city revealed themselves. They enclosed much of the European flavour of Quebec, the roots of which reach back to a trading post established by the explorer Champlain in the early 1600s. Then the Citadel. This strategic fort guarded Upper Canada from the British until the French defeat upon the Plains of Abraham, just west of that garrison.

As Quebec fell behind us, dockyards, ship basins, ferry wharves, tanker terminals, yacht clubs, marinas, and coast guard wharves lined a busy shore on both sides of the seaway. Our speed increased, but a brisk headwind drove against us and kicked up quite a bit of spray. The chop did not let up. So it was not a carefree day, but we made Neuville by 1430 and were satisfied with the thirty-five miles we had covered.

NEUVILLE, PQ

While ashore at Neuville, my navigational concern focused on the Richelieu Rapids we would traverse tomorrow, and I wanted to gather as much information about that obstacle as I could. A grey-bearded sailor in a boat tied behind ours offered the first advice. He spoke of a peculiar tidal flow at the rapids. Normally a six-hour flood tide follows a six-hour ebb tide. The Richelieu Rapids, however, ebbs for ten hours, leaving only a two-hour window to move through it on a flood tide. And the passage was best made in daylight and with good visibility. We took leave of the Bearded One after a short chat. He returned to the repair of his limping engine.

The building used as the marina clubhouse could easily be mistaken for a private residence. It was a storey-and-a-half structure, somewhat Cape Cod-ish in design, architecturally plain, gabled windows, steep roof, but with a subtle Quebecois accent. The main floor held the office, toilets and showers, and a large common room with a telephone, computers, displays, and a small well-equipped kitchen and comfortable chairs. The upper level was more club-like—varnished woods, upholstered furnishings.

After dinner, I slipped back to the clubhouse with *The Saga of Cimba*, a fascinating account of a 1930s voyage from Nova Scotia to Tahiti in a 35-foot converted fishing schooner. I was alone in the common room most of the time, and this suited my reading, but occasionally, I would put the book down and listen to the muffled laughter and chatter of those outside on the deck. It was a jovial crowd, mostly small family groups. Wine flowed; children scurried about the deck furniture, climbed the stairs to the second-floor lounge, or struck out for teeter-totters and swings on the lawn next to the clubhouse. Every now and then, *madame* or *monsieur* would pass through the common room and greet me. A nod, a smile and a word, and then I would return to the adventure stirring from the pages of my book.

At one point, a girl, perhaps twelve or thirteen, stood in front of me. I put down my book. She said hello. She spoke to me in French. I explained that I had little French. She spoke again. I caught the word "*musique*." I apologized again. Both of us grew embarrassed at the impasse. She left; I returned to my book. But, a few minutes later, she returned with an older gentleman. A translator and perhaps her grandfather. He explained that she wished to know if the music she and her friends were playing in the upper room was disturbing my reading. I assured him and her that it did not. They looked pleased. Then they left.

She returned to her friends upstairs; the man returned to his party on the deck; I returned to my reading, albeit distractedly, because my surprise persisted. I could not remember the last time I encountered a young person so considerate of another's feelings, especially those of a stranger. In a time when many young people have schooled themselves in a stylized rudeness or indifference, and in a time when many youth believe entitlement is a birthright, gentleness of spirit and thoughtfulness become luminous virtues and, just as Portia says in *The Merchant of Venice*, "So shines a good deed in a naughty world!"

From a high point on the shore we had a clear view up and down the river. The tide was low and, for a hundred yards out from the high-water mark, we viewed hundreds of loose boulders strewn over that now-exposed shoal. Our charts clearly mark this shoal and others, which extend considerably out into the river. At higher tide, however, the untrained observer would only perceive a wide and presumably deep expanse. While our charts didn't clearly indicate the best course in or out of Neuville, our *Sailing Directions* did.

The Bearded One, however, suggested something else—a shortcut. By following the visual bearing of two landmarks on the south shore, we could strike a diagonal line upriver and cut several miles from our morning's trip. He had used it himself on a number of occasions, he said. Such was the advice he gave in the afternoon, but at dusk, a sailboat making an approach to Neuville along this "shortcut" hung up on a sandbar, a third of the distance across the river. Several boats went to its assistance, tried to haul it off, but with no success. She stuck fast as the tide fell. And there she remained all night, gradually laying further and further over as the tide dropped to its lowest ebb.

It was an embarrassment, which measured itself in hours of waiting, during which time the crew of that vessel probably suffered as much humiliation as a Puritan on a public pillory. Later, the Bearded One echoed a similar chagrin, as he recanted his flawed nautical advice in favour of more conventional wisdom:

"Perhaps you should consider just heading straight out to the marker," he said.

Neuville faded behind. Donnacona passed on our starboard. We steamed along at over 5 knots until we reached Portneuf. Its wharf and village were vaguely visible offshore. Here, where the river bent, was the staging area for traversing the Richelieu Rapids.

Already a loose gathering of vessels had formed. Four or five sailing vessels and half a dozen cruisers lay ahead, moving at slow throttle or drifting. A few more vessels emerged from the harbour of Portneuf and joined the pack, which now strung out for half a mile. At about 1430 the first of the boats started to move. The rest slowly gathered way and streamed after them. As we turned into the bend in the river we saw the approach of a Canadian Coast Guard vessel. It stopped; a deck crane hooked onto a port-hand buoy, hoisted it, and repositioned it near the approach to the rapids.

Several characteristics of the Richelieu Rapids raise caution in mariners. First, the falling tide can reach 8 knots. Second, it's only passable for a few hours each day and that causes a bulge in river traffic. Third, the passage is narrow. Although the river is a mile and a half wide, there are drying banks, shoals, and rocky islets, which reduce seaway to four hundred yards. The main shipping channel itself is scarcely three hundred yards wide. Add a freighter or two into a mix of sailboats and other pleasure craft and there is potential for problems. Of course, fog, thunderstorms, and strong winds complicate such a situation.

On this day, however, even though traffic was busy, weather conditions were good. Other than the coast guard ship, no other heavy commerce was moving through at the same time as we were. The tide was still falling somewhat and, as we entered the narrows, our speed dropped to 3.5 knots. We struggled a bit. Boats with heavier horsepower overtook and passed us. Ahead, and at the second bend in the dogleg which encompassed the rapids, stood Île Richelieu. Near it rose a squat, red tower which housed a navigation light and a Racon, a navigational device which broadcasts a Morse code beacon to guide large ships. Black rocks split the surface of the water on both sides of the passage.

It took nearly two hours to move at our snail's pace from Portneuf through the narrows at Richelieu. By then the heat of the day was beginning to take a toll. The cold and even cool weather, which had characterized our passage so far, had fled. The temperature now had climbed to near ninety degrees Fahrenheit (over thirty degrees Celsius). Gradually we stripped off sweaters, sweatshirts, and heavy denims and hurled them below onto the bunks. Finley was down to bathing trunks and sunglasses by mid-afternoon and had found it comfortable enough to stretch out his six-foot-five-inch length athwartship on the narrow bridge between cockpit and cabin.

The heat seemed to sap our strength and vigilance more eagerly than the cold. As a result, we changed watches on the tiller with greater frequency. During one of those shifts I had gone below. The shade of the cabin and the cooler air flowing back from a partly opened forward hatch offered relief from an oppressive sun.

I was lying on my bunk in semi-conscious state of sleep when I heard an alarmed shout from the cockpit.

"Dad!"

I staggered across the cabin floor and leapt onto the deck. I was still groggy, unsure of my surroundings, unable to perceive the distress, and hardly conscious enough to speak.

"The guy is crazy! He nearly hit us," he sputtered angrily and went on to explain.

A 36-foot cruising sailboat had approached quickly from astern and overtaken us. After passing, it unexpectedly veered sharply across our bow, startling my son. By then, my eyes had focused, and I looked ahead. The vessel was hard on our starboard bow, her stern separated from us only by yards. That vessel had reduced speed too. Now the distance between our two vessels was closing, but the elderly skipper and his family seemed so self-absorbed in conversation that their heads never turned to appraise their position in the seaway.

Here, between Pointe des Grondines and Deschaillons-sur-Saint-Laurent, the shipping channel narrowed to a few hundred yards. I took the tiller again. *International Rules of the Road* state that an overtaking vessel has the burden of responsibility to stay clear of the other vessel until it's well past that vessel. That hadn't been the case here. All I could do was to move clear and reduce the chance of collision. I edged further to port, further into the channel and reduced speed.

In just moments, however, a wild card came into play. That wild card was ahead at a bend in the river—a freighter heading downstream toward us. It looked large in profile and, as it swung its bow and bore down, its girth seemed to absorb most of the width of the channel. It seemed so. Of course I knew it was an illusion. There was plenty of sea room, and I knew that the freighter would lie close to the port-hand buoys. The freighter was two miles west when I first saw it. It would pass in a few minutes. The skipper of the other sailboat saw it too. As the freighter neared, he panicked, threw his wheel hard to port, and swung across my bow a second time. I blasted a warning signal with the air horn, but he continued his manoeuvre and, with the sudden swing of his wheel, he closed the distance from my boat. Still he took no notice at all of our presence just behind him, and he also showed little concern for the freighter. He continued to sweep across the channel and crossed the freighter's bow as well. The last I saw of that vessel and its reckless skipper, it was making for a small marina, all aboard still seemingly oblivious, and I wondered how that the vessel had never been wrecked before.

As we sailed deeper into the Canadian heartland and ever so gradually south, the landscape changed. The shore grew less steep and more peppered with homes and cottages. The sense of wilderness which might have been imagined before Quebec City slipped away just as decorative maple and poplar supplanted the pine and spruce. In the upper stretches of the St. Lawrence, the passage narrowed and traffic increased. No longer could a vessel pass half a horizon away with no more concern than that of an eagle circling or a gannet diving. Almost every hour a ship with rusting plates and foreign flag thumped by. Canadian freighters piled high with containers or pulpwood. American ships with ore out of Lake Superior.

All of them hundreds of feet long, dwarfing my 26 feet of wooden planking. Tankers from Montreal or Detroit. They would loom large, fifty or seventy-five yards off our beam, a bow wave foaming before them. We could see master or mate at the helm behind the glass of the bridge; we watched pairs of seamen leaning over rails or against steel hatches, puffing cigarettes. We could read clearly the painted name, the stencilled words on hatches, and the port of registry shadowed in the curvature of stern plates. One vessel which passed us near Trois-Rivières bore the name M.V. *Rt. Hon. Paul J. Martin*, a Canada Steamship vessel, 750 feet long, named for the prime minister and former owner of that company.

As it passed, I brought up the bow to meet the stern wave which spread out in a broad V-shape behind it. The waves they generated were for the most part gentle. Most annoying about passing vessels was the fury of water stirred up by smaller powerboats. A few were considerate enough to reduce speed when they passed a sailboat; most simply blasted by at 20 or 30 knots, and excited bow waves which were steep, fast-moving, and capable of vigorously snapping a sailboat's hull. If caught unaware, we could be tossed off our seats. Their disturbance of the water also caused us to lose headway and stall. More worrying, however, was the tremendous torque those waves created. Each violent jerk to the hull by such a bow wave transferred a wrenching motion which multiplied with each succeeding foot up to the masthead. And I could not help wincing every time that spar shuddered and snapped in response.

In mid-afternoon we entered Lac Saint-Pierre. This lake opened up from the narrow constraints of the St. Lawrence to an expanse five miles wide and roughly fifteen miles long. Except for the dredged shipping channel, the lake is shallow, averaging just nine feet, and along its perimeter lay thousands of acres of marshland, much of it a protected bird sanctuary.

While the lake was just fifteen miles end to end, the shipping channel followed a loose S-shaped path, making a four-hour passage out of a twenty-mile crossing. Frequently, we passed small, speedy outboards fishing along the edge of the channel. The water was glassy; the heat became a weight. The shoreline was a fuzzy blue line at the rim of our visibility.

We followed the buoyed channel. Halfway across, we stopped in the stillness of air and in the stillness of water and replenished our fuel tank from a jerry can stowed in reserve. It was a slow siphon from can to tank. All the while, the boat bobbed inconsequentially, the sun burned a slow fuse through the haze, and we stared blankly at distant artificial islands and cribs erected to control ice flow during the winter and spring break-up. After we gathered way again, thousands of gnats swarmed aboard. They clung to our skin and clothes; they blanketed the deck and spars and sail covers. Then they vanished just before we entered the archipelago of islands at the western reaches of Lac Saint-Pierre. Those islands had the look of a natural park. Most were wooded, and revealed no sign of habitation.

SOREL, PQ

It took another hour to slip through the islands, return to the limitations of the narrow St. Lawrence, and reach the town of Sorel. The sunlight already was dimming at 2000 hours when we tied up. An attendant hurriedly topped up the fuel tank and the spare jerry can. Meanwhile, Finley cooked a special supper: chicken breasts sautéed in chopped tomatoes, onions, and mushrooms. Darkness fell upon us quickly, so quickly that Finley could no longer see the simmering pans on the stove. So I held a lantern to illuminate his final labours. We ate at 2100 and shared a single lantern beam to find and fork the morsels onto our plates. This would be Finley's last supper aboard the *Arja D*. Tomorrow we would land in Montreal. From there he would head home to Washington, DC.

Next morning we left the marina and made for mid-channel. Two passenger ferries crossed us, one from Sorel, the other from Saint-Ignace. We moved through the industrial waterfronts of Sorel and neighbouring Tracy. Hard on our heels was a large bulk carrier. It came from behind minutes after the criss-cross of ferry traffic.

A mile on, the river bent south. As we swept around that elbow, another bulk carrier steamed down toward us.

A heartening brightness which had characterized the early morning soured and dulled into cloud. Rain sputtered intermittently between showers, splinters of sun, and veils of haze. Seven miles along, just past Lanoraie, the channel split into two waterways, a small-craft channel and the main shipping channel. Both run roughly parallel to each other, separated either by shoals or a series of low islands. We entered the small-craft channel. We expected this diversion to be less busy, even though a bit longer. Surprisingly, we also found it speedier and picked up half a knot.

Just before Montreal, near the island of Sainte-Thérèse, the main channel and the small-craft channel intersect and cross. We continued on the small craft. Five miles ahead was a fixed bridge, and beyond that was Montreal. I checked *Sailing Directions* for specifications on bridge clearance, but the margin of error didn't look good, so we backtracked until we found navigable water between two islands in the Boucherville chain. We took that shortcut and emerged in the main channel just below Montreal East.

It was here that our motor died.

When a motor stops, it feels like the stopping of your heart. You don't die, of course, but there is a shock, a concussion which stuns the senses, a momentary helplessness, an unformed question. I looked round. Our position was precarious. Two bulk carriers were anchored three hundred yards across from us. We were drifting into the main channel, but not yet into traffic lanes and, as yet, no vessels were moving up- or downriver.

I cranked the engine a number of times, but it showed no sign of sparking to life. Finley went forward, freed the anchor from its chocks, and dropped it over. The line payed out through his hands; the fluke bedded in the mud and the bow rounded up. More line out. Another twenty-five feet. Then Finley tied it off.

When a diesel dies, it's the result of a problem with fuel, compression, or air. I looked at fuel first. I lifted the front cockpit seat. Below it is the engine compartment. A clear plastic hose feeds diesel from the tank to the fuel pump. To my surprise, only traces of fuel lay in a low bend of that hose, suggesting that the engine stopped because it was starved of fuel. The fuel tank is a gravity feed, and it should provide reliable service if there is no break in the siphon, and there didn't appear to be. I checked the tank next. I plumbed it with a measuring stick. The fuel tank was empty.

Both the tank and the spare can had been filled at Sorel the night before and, by my reckoning, we should have had enough fuel to run the engine for another twenty hours.

Finley hauled the spare fuel can from its storage area, and we siphoned it into the main tank. I tried the engine again. It wouldn't catch. A few more times. Still nothing. I primed the fuel filter. Then I tried again. Nothing. My last effort was to bleed the injectors of air trapped in the fuel lines. I put the wrench to it. Finley cranked the engine a few times as I watched the lines alternately bubble and spew diesel fuel. When the bubbling ended, I tightened the nut, securing the fuel line.

Back on deck I tried the engine again. It turned over, but it coughed and stalled. After a few more tries, the engine caught, balked once or twice, and resumed a regular thumping beat.

Along the next four miles of river, the landscape flourished with concrete and steel in a seamless ribbon of commerce. Freighters and tankers, bulk carriers and tugboats, and even a few decommissioned, rust-bleeding hulks lay alongside the wharves of cargo terminals and grain elevators and pipelines. Gantry cranes and travelling cranes and ramps hovered over those ships' decks like prehistoric predators. Longshoremen, seamen, and labourers, if they were there at all, became dwarfed in the scale of their environment and rendered invisible.

MONTREAL, PQ

Toward the heart of Montreal, skyscrapers and church spires replaced railway yards and warehouses; parkways, malls, and apartment buildings displaced the tank farms and fenced-off container lots; the sweet smells of oil and petroleum and the faint, acrid odours of welding torches, chemical cargoes, and standing pools of waste slipped out of the grip of our senses. A new vista opened. Here, in the middle of the harbour, on the edge of night, the skyline deepened in shadow and stood out boldly against the sky, bright but blanched of colour. The city seemed ready to come alive, and the excitement of that inevitability sparked exhilaration in both Finley and me.

Even though the hour was getting late, our plan was to have a night on the town. This was Finley's last night aboard. He would catch his train to DC tomorrow morning, but tonight he wanted to buy me dinner, and perhaps we would have a drink or two at some Montreal club and listen to a good band. At one time I had thought about securing a berth at the marina in the Old Port of Montreal. It was downtown, centrally located with good access to transportation. However, river currents there were quite strong. So that spot was not well-suited for sailboats. Instead, we cruised slowly along the shore opposite Longueuil. We passed one or two marinas or yacht clubs.

A third one was ahead on Île Sainte-Hélène. Downtown Montreal lay on the opposite shore. A bridge and a subway link the two islands. Besides that, Île Sainte-Hélène is next to the canal I would enter when I departed Montreal. So it would do quite well, I thought.

Marina de la Ronde was located at Port Sainte-Hélène. It was built on Île Sainte-Hélène, a man-made island, created from debris excavated from construction of the Montreal subway system, and site of Montreal's world-famous Expo 67. The marina had seen better days. Little new money had gone into the place. It carried an air of seediness, like some motel next to a strip club. Everything was well-worn, patched, or dingy, except for the crisp, upscale cost to tie up my boat for the night. That was not enough to dampen our spirits, however. After all, we were in Montreal, or close to it. A magical city.

Marina de la Ronde, we discovered, also possessed yet another unique characteristic. It sits on the perimeter of a large amusement park, named La Ronde. The marina property itself crowds a narrow access road along the shore and consists of several small portable buildings which serve as office, laundry rooms, and storage cubicles. Behind these is a steep bank, rimmed by a steel fence. Encircling and overwhelming the entire marina is the amusement park complex. An enormous roller coaster eclipses the marina. Next to it looms an administration building and, here and there, poking above the trees, are the towers of magical places and the spinning arms of thrilling rides.

Our excitement for that excitement waned, however, when we learned that we had no marina access to local facilities. All restaurants were in the amusement park. Access to the Metro terminal was in the amusement park, as well, and La Ronde charged thirty-two dollars per person to enter the park, even from the marina. The one accommodation which park authorities made was this: if we paid the sixty-four-dollar entry fee, we could buy food at one of the restaurants. However, a twenty-minute time limit was enforced. If we did not exit within that period, then we would forfeit our entry fee. It was 2030; we were hungry. So we laid our money down, grabbed a submarine sandwich at one concession stand, and a beer at another to wash it down. We pocketed our deposit and squeezed out through the turnstiles.

A parking lot lay ahead; the lane to the marina led from it. We passed a young couple pushing a baby stroller. They had been turned away from La Ronde as well. The lady seemed bewildered.

"But where will we eat?" she asked her husband. Disappointment shrugs, but seldom replies.

Other circumstances dashed our hope for a great evening in Montreal. Access to the Metro followed a similar deposit- and time-limit policy. Added to this was the complication that the park would close before we returned from the city and gates would be locked. A taxi was an expensive alternative, but this option also became impossible after we learned that a team of pyrotechnic specialists would be setting up explosive charges for a fireworks display at La Ronde. They would be working all night. During that time, bridge access to the island was prohibited.

In other words, we were trapped.

Back at the boat, Finley packed some gear. Later we shared some brandy and toasted Montreal. Then we poured some more brandy, groused about the marina, and carped about La Ronde. The steep bank behind the marina was dark and backlit with carnival merriment. The skeletal steel fabrication of the gargantuan roller coaster was brightly lit. It hung above our heads. For hundreds of yards through the still air, the clack of ratchet and chain echoed as it hauled strings of passenger cars up its incline. A moment of silence. A shrill roar followed. Wheels screeched against rails. An ugly cacophony wracked the air. And all of it was outstripped by a choir of shrieks, as dozens of adolescent riders hurtled downward into a mimic of terror.

Chapter 13

DO NOT PASS GO

A sourness permeated the morning. Part of it drifted from the empty skeleton of a roller coaster hanging in the sky off our stern. Part of it pulsed from La Ronde's loudspeakers during an early-morning sound check. Part of it oozed from the tawdriness of the marina, like an old tenement peopled by worn-out lives. Finley returned from the shower, angry. A leaking hand-soap dispenser had soiled his change of clothes. He tossed them into a washer, but the machine wouldn't accept quarters. So the clothes, wet and sticky with liquid detergent, soaked in the tub until an attendant showed up an hour later. And part of the discontent came from thinking about Finley's imminent departure.

His taxi arrived at 0715. La Ronde still closed; access to the Metro still closed. And he departed for the train station in Montreal. Tears welled up as the cab sped away; a reflexive lump swelled my throat. A sense of loss slowed my steps, but the sadness of friends departing is really a feeling of sorrow for one's self. I knew that. Yet it didn't quell the feeling.

During the next hour or so, I scrubbed and hosed off the clay-like anchor mud which had dried on the foredeck, and at 0900 I slipped my lines and left Marina de la Ronde for anywhere else I could make it into.

I backtracked to one of the marinas I had seen on our arrival. The closest and the smallest was scarcely two hundred yards away. Club Nautique de Longueuil.

Club Nautique de Longueuil was a private yacht club, but it accommodated sailors like me from more far-flung quarters. The setting there was idyllic. Two parallel channels had been dredged straight into the shore for one hundred yards. Each channel was equipped with two banks of docks. Between the two channels was a grassy park area about forty yards wide. The park had several picnic areas, scattered benches, and a barbeque tent. Mature maple trees screened out much of the day's hot sun. A pathway led to a clubhouse on a grassy knoll behind the park and boating area. The brick clubhouse looked more like a home than anything else. Only a few soda vending machines and an ice freezer on the veranda gave away its more public nature.

A few club members chatted and smoked and sipped coffee at 0930.They were friendly and helpful, and boasted that their club was a wonderful place to spend some time and much more relaxing than "the circus up the road," a cutting, but not malicious, reference to a large commercial marina a mile away. But the point of the remark was well taken. In fact, one did feel better here, more relaxed, more at home. Trees gave the club grounds a rural flavour, and a ridge behind the clubhouse screened out noises from the nearby highway and businesses in the city of Longueuil. Thicker groves masked the perimeters from whatever lay beyond them. In fact, the only evidence of being in an urban area was a spectacular profile of Montreal's skyline across the seaway, and even that was half hidden by foliage.

I eagerly parted with the twenty-nine-dollar berthing fee. Later in the morning I unpacked my bike and drove to a shopping centre for groceries. In the early afternoon, I refuelled. This proved a minor inconvenience because the yacht club had no fuel dock. As a result, I had to take the boat to the "circus," the Plaisance Marina, a mile downstream. It was a large operation, well-maintained, crowded with boats and tourists, and definitely a commercial enterprise. However some of the personnel were summer help, careless or inexperienced, a bit slow to catch lines, and one girl was too quick on the trigger of a fuel nozzle and sprayed my deck with diesel. She became confused when her attempts to hose it off with water failed. In the end, I pressed the staff to give me a bottle of liquid cleanser, a solvent for oily substances, which I used myself to clean up the deck. Then I happily returned to the quiet of the yacht club.

Before Finley's departure that morning he had urged me to spend some time in Montreal. He knew that the experience at La Ronde had been both unpleasant and discouraging and that I had a half-formed intention simply to shake the dust off my sandals and head upstream straightaway. The cordial reception I received at the yacht club, however, had mellowed me considerably. So I took Finley's advice that I "have to see Montreal."

Getting to Montreal was relatively easy. I rode my bike from the yacht club to the "circus," next to which was also a terminal for the small high-speed passenger ferry to Montreal. I caught the 1530 ferry. It was a ten-minute ride from Longueuil to the old port of Montreal. The afternoon was breezy, warm, and sunny. The ferry pressed against the stiff currents near the old port and put into a quay next to the small-craft marina. Then I spent the afternoon exploring the old city.

Montreal is a city with an international flair, and the *old quarter* is as cosmopolitan as any New World city can be. I wandered its narrow streets for several hours. Shops and restaurants and art galleries rose from cobbled lanes. If the buildings were not brick, then they were massive stone structures like the Notre Dame Cathedral or the museums or the civic buildings. In the passing crowds I caught fragments of not only English and French, but also Spanish, Polish, and Filipino and German, the tonal melodies of Asian languages, and several unrecognizable African dialects. One could smell waves of curry and sausage, incense and roasting meats.

I had earlier passed by the Ghandi Restaurant and, though I had never before eaten Indian food, I felt a strong craving for a taste of it, much more so than for anything else. Many of the restaurants in the old quarter do not open until the supper hour. So I wandered through a few more shops until it opened at 1700. It was worth the wait. The restaurant was humble in appearance, long and narrow and rather small, less than a dozen tables, but very nicely furnished. On the waitress's recommendation I chose Poulet Tikki Alfresi. It was a very spicy dish of chicken with tomatoes, onions and peppers, and rice. The aperitif was a crisp, tortilla-like bread with three sauces—peach, mint, and another very hot one. And the wine was a robust Chilean Cabernet. It was one of the finest meals I've ever eaten, even after taking into account that my own dreary cooking during the last month may have tainted my culinary judgment.

My late sailing start the next morning began at 0900. After a few last-minute preparations, I slipped out of the yacht club. Four or five sailboats wallowed on outside anchorages. At the buoy I bent west, passed La Ronde, under a bridge, and into the concrete-banked canal which led to St. Lambert Lock. This lock was the first of several which bypassed the Rapides de Lachine above Montreal.

Down the slot of canal a mile ahead, two pleasure craft tied to a stand-by dock near the big water gates fronting the lock. A Canada Steamship Lines freighter filled the lock. Its superstructure towered above the lock's doors. As the water drained from the lock, its upper decks grew lower and lower until I could see only the top of its bridge. Finally, the big steel doors swung wide open, and the vessel emerged and throbbed slowly forward toward me. We cleared each other about half a mile before the lock. The two pleasure craft had left the tie-up area and moved into the lock. They manoeuvred against the portside wall. Instructions were hailed to them by lock personnel, and crewmen wound their lines around mooring bitts or rails mounted on their deck, so that the vessels would stay tightly in place when the lock was flooded again.

This would be the first lock I would pass through. I was unaware if there were any sign-up procedures, whether there was a fee to be paid, or how it would be paid. But the mouth of the great lock remained open. I was in mid-channel, approaching. No one was waving me off. A red light near the approach had changed to green. So I stood-on for the opening.

The lock itself was an enormous steel rectangle, large enough for any vessel on the Great Lakes. Its walls rose at least thirty feet. So I felt as if I had entered a ravine. Voices of lock personnel and boat crews, and the putter of engines, and the slush of water reverberated from wall to wall to wall. I moved dead slow once inside and eased toward the portside wall behind the two small cruisers. Then one of the line handlers hollered from above.

"How many are you?"

From such a sharp angle below all I could see was a tilted head, part of a chest, and a gesticulating forearm.

"Just one," I shouted.

"You need two to pass the lock," he said.

"But I don't have anybody else. What can I do? I came from Prince Edward Island."

"I don't know. Those are the regulations. Go back to the stand-by dock. There's a phone line on the dock. Call the office. Talk to them. But right now, I can't let you through."

It was difficult to turn about in the swirling waters of the lock, and I did not do it smartly, but I managed to exit the lock. The big doors closed with a resolute clang, and I pulled up to the empty stand-by dock. My phone conversation with the supervisor was disappointing. For safety reasons, every vessel must have at least two line handlers on deck. The only solution was to get another hand onboard or go back the way I came. Sometimes, he said, you can borrow an extra hand from another vessel in transit.

I waited two hours at the dock. A few vessels came; none had extra crew. Eventually, I grew discouraged and returned to the Longueuil marina. At the registration desk, Yvonne, the manager, said he might be able to find someone to help me clear the next two locks. There was a girl, he said, who liked boats and hung around the yacht club. She might, he suggested. He called. Nadia spoke English and said she would, but not until tomorrow morning at 0900. She must make some arrangements. In return I would pay her bus fare back to Longueuil.

In the meantime, I drove my bike across the city. Traffic was thick and, at one point, I took to the sidewalk. By the time I returned to the marina at 1730, I had covered close to ten miles, the longest distance I had biked since I was fifteen.

At the marina, however, bad news awaited. Nadia could not help me tomorrow. Then good news tripped on the heels of the bad. Yvonne, the manager, believed that a man named Real Doré could replace Nadia, but Real would not be available until noon tomorrow.

Real arrived around 1100 the next morning. He was an older fellow, a paramedic on extended sick leave. At 1130 we left the marina and set out for the St. Lambert Lock. It was busy today with small-boat traffic. But the wait was short. Lock staff called in the powerboats first. Once inside, they were rafted together, the heaviest boats in first. The linesmen dropped two ropes, one to hold the bow in place and the other to steady the stern, and the crew of that boat would draw their vessel against the wall of the lock. Then a smaller boat would come alongside the first. The second boat would catch deck lines thrown from the first boat to hold the second boat's bow and stern. A third and perhaps a fourth boat would follow suit. Then another large boat would be drawn up just astern of the first group or raft, and on and on until all boats were secure.

In this flooding of the lock, the *Arja D.* was among ten powerboats and three sailboats. All of the sailboats were rafted together. Against the wall was a large red vessel, *Linnea*. It had been turned back from the lock the previous day for having only one hand aboard, just as mine had been. Next to it was *Bosco*. And the *Arja D.*, being the smallest, lay on the outside.

Even as the last vessels were being rafted together, the steel doors of the lock swung shut and locked in place. Moments later, over half-a-million cubic feet of water spilled into the lock from underwater pipes. The water's surface came alive. Powerful eddies swirled about the boats, the turbulence from which was especially hard on the sailboats. Round hulls and deep keels catch a force of water like a sheet of plywood catches a stiff breeze. Our raft bent back like the arm on a clock. The red *Linnea* rotated. Her port quarter jammed against the greasy lock wall. One of her deck rails crushed under the pressure. Extra hands from *Bosco*, joined by Real from my boat, crossed over to help draw her bow in. I stayed aboard and put my engine in forward gear to take some of the pressure off. Both efforts helped straighten the raft.

The turbulence waned, the linesmen extended a pole onto which we attached our lock fees, the doors opened, and we moved out of the lock one by one and into the canal. In those three or four minutes we had risen almost twenty feet higher in the lock.

For the next seven or eight miles the canal parallels the St. Lawrence River and, by doing so, it bypasses the Lachine Rapids. During the quiet passage from the St. Lambert Lock to the lock at Sainte-Catherine, I found Real pleasant company. He spoke English well, talked freely, and was good-natured. He too had a boat. His was at the Longueuil yacht club, and soon he planned to retire.

We cleared the Côte-Sainte-Catherine Lock. That lock seemed easier, in spite of the fact that the lift was thirty-five feet, twice that of St. Lambert's. Perhaps we were better experienced, or perhaps the engineering that controlled the water flow was more efficient. At any rate, I dropped Real off at the end of a small wharf at the edge of a shallow pool above the lock. A car and some friends were waiting there to pick him up. The wharf was difficult to approach. So Real had to jump the last few feet to reach the wharf, and I had to awkwardly back out of the tiny channel. Goodbyes were peremptory.

The canal extended for another hour and a half of sailing before feeding into Lac Saint-Louis, a shallow expanse of water which reaches from the Lachine Rapids to the west mouth of the Ottawa River. Three quarters of the way across that lake I headed toward the south shore where the town of Melocheville marked the entrance to the Beauharnois Canal. At the entrance of this canal was the third lock I would have to enter, the Lower Beauharnois Lock. Of course, that also meant my finding a second deckhand to navigate it with me.

I approached the entrance to Melocheville cautiously. The water level was dropping. It was a natural harbour, but quite small, and the mouth of it was broad enough to swallow only one vessel at a time. I spied a camper trailer park near the western arm of the harbour's entry, and at the edge of that low, rocky spit was a man vigorously waving and pointing to a sign. A bit closer and I could read it: DANGER SHALLOW WATER 4 FEET!

I waved him off. Four feet was no problem for me. I made for the nearest open berth. I registered at the office and refuelled and, as I was supervising the refuelling, another boat was making for the entrance. That vessel was the red *Linnea*. By the time the captain was close enough to read the warning sign, his boat bumped to a halt midstream. Fortunately, he too had made a very slow approach and, with a few bursts in reverse, he successfully broke loose, backed out, and took his boat around the point to a concrete wall which fronted a public park. He tied up there in the company of one or two other large vessels.

My first concern in Melocheville was locating someone who would accompany me through the lock. Omer Arseneau, who operated the little marina, agreed to make some phone calls to that end. Meantime, I explored the area.

Melocheville marina is separated from the Beauharnois Lock by the lock's spillway and a wedge of fenced-off land. A public road dead-ends at the marina. I walked from there toward the town a half mile away. Ahead was a restaurant and nightclub, a park area, several residential blocks.

I had gotten no farther than the nightclub before my path crossed with Jukka. Jukka Vasko displayed a formidable presence. He stood about six foot eight and weighed perhaps 350 pounds and spoke English with a thick accent. He didn't walk; he lumbered.

"You have blue wood boat?" he asked as he approached me on the street.

"Yes," I said.

"I have red one. Over there," he said wielding a tree-trunk arm toward the concrete retaining wall beyond the nightclub. "My boat too deep. Get stuck."

I couldn't place his accent. At first I thought he spoke some remote French Canadian dialect. Later that seemed unlikely. We chatted there for a while. Gradually, my neck began to ache from looking up at him. He said that he too was on the hunt for a temporary deckhand, but he had had no more luck locating one than I had.

"We go for beer later, yes? One, two beer."

I walked over to his boat after supper. Then we headed to the nightclub near the marina. Chez-Something-or-other was bustling at 2100. It attracted an older clientele of campers, locals, and cottage dwellers, ranging mostly between the ages of fifty and seventy. We took a table near the bandstand. Every table was crowded, the atmosphere cheery, the patrons surprisingly active, and the dance floor filled. A small band backed by synthetic percussion effects pumped out songs from traditional French hits to classic rock tunes like "Mustang Sally," CCR's "Down on the Corner" and "Bad Moon Rising," as well as country music songs of Garth Brooks and Tim McGraw. Daniel, the owner of the club, kept the place lively. He sang with the band, and he coaxed the female customers up to dance, and his waitresses joined in with the line dancing between their tasks of shifting platters of food and drink.

All the while, Jukka lifted pints of beer with great delight and grew quietly jovial. He also grew talkative.

"...Baltic...the partners...to Montreal then...," he said. There was pride in his tone, but the rumblings of boisterous customers swept most of his words away.

I tried to appear attentive and nodded approvingly.

"...worse there...*nibblin' on sponge cake*...not the Germans... *wastin' away again*...solo from...*here I haven't a clue*...," said Jukka, leaning back in his chair, oblivious of the singer's lyrics shredding his sentences, oblivious of his deep soft voice being indistinguishable from the bass guitar's reverberations.

One time he became animated, and then an intelligibility broke through the merry confusion of the place. "That girl pretty!" he said. "You think pretty?" he asked, poking his finger toward an attractive blonde a few tables away.

"Absolutely!"

Such intelligibility was fleeting, though, and soon I was trying to piece together isolated words and torn phrases in the hope of uncovering a thought, but "...try to cheat...big sea...the coastal...fly home..." was all that I heard and, as time went by, his accent, tottering under the weight of lagers and ales, collapsed into a mutter out of which I could make no sense at all.

My mind gave up the struggle to salvage something; sleep was tugging at my consciousness. My thoughts drifted to the fact that I had no help yet for tomorrow. So, as Jukka ordered his fifth or sixth or seventh beer, I said goodbye and left that happy place for the boat.

The next morning, Omer, the marina manager, told me that his calls to get an extra hand for my lock passage had been unsuccessful. So, as a desperate measure, I began to make enquiries of everyone I met on the street. That led me to one or two leads, but they came to nothing. Late in the morning I learned that Jukka had been no more successful than I, but that was no consolation. It left only one option: to go to the lock's stand-by dock and wait for a vessel which was able and willing to share an extra crew member.

I arrived at the dock outside the Lower Beauharnois Lock around 1130. Jukka sailed in about half an hour later, and invited me aboard for coffee. His boat lacked the gleam of well-oiled wood and the showroom sparkle of most yachts I had seen on the river. Still his running gear was heavy-duty, the boat was well-equipped, and his hull was sound. So one could perhaps overlook some untidiness. I already knew that he was single-handing a voyage. It wasn't until we had a chance to talk at length, without the raucous murmur and amplified drive of nightclub music, that I learned he was a Finn, more specifically a Laplander. He co-owned the boat, and he had sailed with a few friends from Finland. They had flown home from the Azores. He had carried on alone to Brazil, through the Caribbean, along the Atlantic coast, and up the St. Lawrence River.

His destination was Toronto. He would store the boat there and return to Finland, the home he had left over a year before.

It was more than an hour before another boat arrived. And then a second. Both were cabin cruisers. One of them held a family beginning a vacation. Six were aboard: parents, two older teenagers, and several young people. Two of them agreed to help Jukka and me. An older son joined Jukka's boat; Stephanie, his girlfriend, came aboard the *Arja D*. Stephanie had a limited English vocabulary and was not familiar with boats, but I was able to make clear what she must do when we entered the lock, and she did a good job at handling the lines.

We cleared two locks that afternoon, the Lower and the Upper Beauharnois Locks, for a total lift of eight feet. Both locks lay within a mile of each other. After that, Stephanie and her boyfriend boarded their family cruiser. Jukka and I and a few other boats strung out in a long line heading upstream. The twelve miles of canal were a comfortable passage but offered no remarkable landmarks. A few bridges, the Port of Valleyfield. That's about it. I had hoped that the Port would be a suitable stopover, but the look of it suggested that it was strictly a commercial vessel terminal.

SALABERRY-DE-VALLEYFIELD, PQ

Lac Saint-François opened up several miles past the Port of Valleyfield. The lake is shallow, averaging twenty feet in the east and shoaling to ten feet in the west with a dredged channel zigzagging around low areas. Having given up on Port of Valleyfield, I sailed into the lake with the intention of cutting back toward the town of Salaberry-de-Valleyfield. The town can't be seen from a seaward approach. It's tucked into a bay on the eastern end of the lake. Several islands and points of land hide it. A safe approach to town, however, requires staying on the main channel for three or four miles, even though this diagonal leads away from the town. It was while I was on this diagonal course that Jukka appeared astern. I slowed until he was on my beam. He was heading for the town of

Valleyfield too, he said. There was no channel buoy marking the change in bearing for Valleyfield, however. He had run out of nautical charts for this region, but he argued that Valleyfield was west. His reasoning was based on some tourist map. I argued that it was northeast. I had charts, and I had waypoints to mark the bearing, and I told him. For some unknown reason, though, he continued west, and I shifted northeast. In half an hour I entered the waterway which wove its way through Baie Saint-Francois and into the town of Valleyfield.

Chapter 14

FRIEND OR FOE

The crossing of Lac Saint-François was a relaxed series of doglegs that took until noon to cross the lake. At the far end, I sailed through a cluster of thirty or so islands which led into a narrowing St. Lawrence River. A number of the islands revealed cottage retreats. Others were undeveloped and formed part of an Indigenous reserve belonging to the Akwesasne Mohawks.

Powerboat traffic increased in the area and, as it was lunchtime, I pulled off the main channel and drifted in the shallows near two small islands. Several modest cottages occupied each of them. I could hear the shouts and whines and laughs of children. Parents reclined on lawn chairs shaded by verandas, sipped icy drinks, and watched me glide across their panorama. The day had grown very warm, and I wished I had some cover, and I wished I had a cold, cold drink. I stole below deck and made a peanut butter and jam sandwich and poured a mug of coffee. I also took the opportunity to examine my chart for marinas in the region.

Today I was to meet my cousin, Bob Zack, in Massena, New York. He had taken a bus or train from his home near Chicago, and tonight he would join me for part of the journey. My cruising to Massena, though, was looking more and more difficult. Massena had navigable access to it a mile or two up via the Grassy River.

However, no public wharf or marinas appeared on my chart. A closer look at my charts also led to a second problem: the US and Canadian *Sailing Directions* had conflicting differences regarding clearances on the two bridges along the Grassy River. There was no simple way to resolve the discrepancy. So I put the charts and references aside and motored back into the main channel. Massena was out. The alternative had to be some Canadian port.

CORNWALL, ON

Cornwall Island splits the St. Lawrence into two channels. I headed toward the north shore and the city of Cornwall, Ontario. A bridge, a dam, and rough water lay further ahead, but before those obstacles was Marina 2000. It had water enough to navigate, and it was situated close to the centre of Cornwall.

The marina had a crisp, new look to it. Several boaters standing idle near one of the docks turned-to and caught my lines. I fuelled up. They caught my lines again when I moved to a permanent berth. Moving the *Arja D.* through a marina is always a concern. One drawback to the design is that the long straight keel prevents the boat from making tight turns. Second, my two-blade prop doesn't bite the water vigorously enough in reverse to slow it quickly. Third, The *Arja D.* backs to starboard weakly, and only under ideal conditions.

It was 1500 by the time I tied-up and registered at the office. My next goal was to contact Bob in Massena and let him know that he would have to meet me in Cornwall. The nearest pay phone was in the Civic Complex a few hundred yards away. Among other things, the Civic Complex is the city's hockey stadium and, as I trudged up the concrete stairway to this immense structure, I found myself alongside twelve-year-old hockey players carrying taped sticks and gleaming skates. Fathers toted gear bags as large as their sons. The temperature was mid-eighties. Each of them looked as if they had been wilted by the heat of day. Beads of perspiration dotted their foreheads. Shoulders drooped. Mouths gaped like stunned fish in the bottom of a dory. However, they found some relief inside.

The hallways of the Civic Complex were broad, spacious, cool, and nearly empty. I found one payphone; it wouldn't work. I tried another; I dialled 411; but I got nowhere. In order to reach the information operator I needed the area code for Massena, but that area code was not available through the Cornwall telephone directory, nor through the local Canadian operator. Nor was Massena, New York, known to US operators who searched their database for it. Massena simply was not listed. I didn't believe that I was asking for the impossible, like Five Mile House, PEI, or Slocum's Hollow, Pennsylvania. It's a real town; over thirteen thousand people live there. If I stood on the roof of this building, I could see it just six miles away.

I walked the halls of the Civic Complex, stopped passers-by, and asked if they knew the area code. No luck. Soon I began to feel like one of the dupes filmed on *Candid Camera* or that I was descending into an uncanny episode of *The Twilight Zone*.

At the end of a main corridor I found myself at the entrance to the Don Cherry bar and restaurant. The smiling hostess did not know the area code either, but she gathered a cluster of young waitresses. One of them had dumped a boyfriend from Massena, and she remembered the number. I was thankful and relieved, returned to the payphone, and dialled the information operator at that area code. A perky, recorded message told me that information operators cannot be accessed via a public pay phone. I was stymied again. I hung up.

Massena's promotional literature describes that town as "the Empire State's best kept secret." Yes, I thought to myself, and as enigmatic and tourist-free as *Brigadoon*. Or *Shangri-La*. At that point I trudged back to the marina, feeling like some humiliated mutt.

Better luck lived at the marina. The young man at the desk made a few inquiries on the house phone and came back with the hotel's number. After several calls to cousin Bob, we made arrangements to meet at the Customs House where he would enter Canada from the United States. I would be there by 1800, I said.

It was not a long walk to the border crossing, I was told. That was an understatement. I left the marina at 1700. A very brisk pace brought me to customs an hour later. I had seen the bridge from the marina. I expected to find the border crossing at the Canadian end of the bridge, but that was an error on my part. The border crossing was halfway over the St. Lawrence River, on Cornwall Island, and that added at least another mile to my trek.

Cornwall Island is to smugglers what Las Vegas is to gamblers, a good place to make big money. There are several good reasons for this. First, it's close to the US. Second, it's where many islands conceal cross-border movement. Third, waters on the southeast edge of Cornwall Island intersect many jurisdictions: the United States, Canada, New York State, Ontario, and Quebec. Finally, Cornwall Island itself and many other nearby islands belong to the Mohawk tribe, and Indigenous reserves legally are quasi-nations. So, smugglers have found that, as the various law-enforcement agencies butt heads over borders and procedures, they can slip like mice between the tangle of government feet.

Interestingly enough, at the border crossing on Cornwall Island, there are two separate lanes of incoming traffic. One is for the usual cross-border traveller; the other is for First Nations people. North American Indigenous people have special status in traversing borders and, for that reason Mohawk police guard that customs checkpoint.

The increased risk of smuggling undoubtedly encourages border police to look with a sharper eye. The post-9/11 atmosphere certainly intensified that response. But why my cousin Bob's entrance to Canada would send up a red flag, I cannot imagine. Nevertheless, it did.

He arrived by taxi from Massena. He waved from the back seat of the cab as he arrived at the customs booth. I was leaning against a rail just past the gate. However, after a few brief questions at the taxicab, guards escorted him into the customs building for an interrogation. He was detained there, alone at first. Then one or two officials peppered Bob with questions; they rifled through his baggage; they ran his identity through computer databases. A third customs officer arrived and asked the same questions as the first, only more aggressively.

I was still leaning against the rail just past the gate forty minutes later, and I was beginning to worry. To pass the time, I chatted with the cab driver who had come from Cornwall to drive us to the marina. He was Sri Lankan, talkative, good-natured, and patient under the circumstances. Eventually, Bob was released, duffel bags in hand, and the cab driver loaded his gear into the trunk of his vehicle.

Bob was puzzled by his detention. It stumped me too. He looks neither like a drugged-out hippie, nor like a wild-eyed fanatic. At sixty-seven, he probably posed little threat to public safety. As a retired gunnery sergeant who had spent twenty years in the US Marine Corps, he had developed a respect for authority and the habit of clear communication. He had plenty of identification: current passport, driver's licence, and US government identification papers. He had referred his interrogators to me, ten yards away, as a person who could verify his identity and his reason for entering the country, but the guards were not inclined to speak with me. Finally, he had plenty of money—cash, money orders, and credit cards—to prove that he wasn't some deadbeat looking for an easy bone to gnaw on in Canada.

What Canada Customs found that was seemingly too far-fetched to accept was that Bob chose to enter Canada by taxicab. They grilled him on this, Bob said, over and over again. Clearly, they must have thought, such unorthodox transportation smacked of criminal intent or sordid secret.

We continued by taxicab away from the customs station along the Cornwall Island highway which led across the bridge to the city. Our Sri Lankan driver slowed to stop at the toll booth for the bridge crossing, but the Indigenous attendant waved us through. The cabby hesitated for a moment, touched the gas, but kept looking in his rear-view mirror. He seemed confused.

"What's up?" I asked.

"I don't know," he said. "He didn't stop us to pay the toll."

"Why is that?"

"It has never happened before...I don't know. Ah! He must think you are Indians," he said. "That is it! They are exempt from tolls."

This was the second time I had been mistaken for an Indigenous person. The first was thirty-odd years before in Ottawa. At that time I was attending a party made up largely of Algonquin people. My university chum, Peter Grant, was across the room chatting with pretty Annie White Duck.

"What tribe do you think he's from?" Peter asked her, pointing to me.

She studied me for a minute and replied, "Iroquois."

"Iroquois," she repeated, this time more confidently.

Skin darkened from a month on the water, high cheekbones, Slavic eyes all contributed to the mistake in ethnic origin, and these were traits cousin Bob shared as well.

It was a lazy start the next day. Breakfast in a local diner, some housekeeping chores aboard the boat, familiarizing Bob with the rigging and safety procedures. All these consumed half of the morning. Then it was a two-hour sail to the first of two locks we would transit today. The wait at the Snell Lock was an hour. Five sailboats and half a dozen powerboats rafted up inside the lock. One of the first sailboats to enter was a beautiful forty-foot blue-hulled ketch, but its skipper had trouble manoeuvring it against the port wall. No lines could be made fast to it. Eventually he was asked to leave the lock and re-enter. He tried it again. He approached the wall at a shallow angle to a point just a few boat lengths behind our place in the lock. Again, he found trouble lining up. On his foredeck a well-tanned and well-shaped young woman tried unsuccessfully to snag one of the cables hanging on the lock wall. It was too great a reach for her boat hook. The boat purred forward and reverse, forward and reverse, several more times. The silver-haired skipper shouted directions to her in a timely fashion. Each time she reported with four-letter expletives in a seaman-like manner. Although the blue ketch caused a fifteen-minute delay, most of the boaters found it a cheap price to pay for the salty amusement.

The Wiley-Dondero Canal links the Snell Lock with the Eisenhower Lock, and for a three-and-a-half mile stretch we cut through a slice of the mainland of upper New York State before returning to the St. Lawrence River. The second lock went more smoothly. Bob had caught onto line handling in no time, and after we cleared the last lock, we were ninety feet higher on the waterway.

MORRISBURG, ON

Waiting to transit the locks slowed us considerably. We covered only nineteen miles that day, but it took us seven hours to do so. By Sunday evening we found an anchorage near Morrisburg, Ontario, just off Auld Island. From our anchorage we could see the edge of a memorial park which commemorated the 1813 Battle of Crysler's Farm, at which American soldiers moving on Montreal were defeated by a much smaller contingent of Canadian troops and a Mohawk band. That battle, in effect, stopped the American effort to take Canada during their War of 1812 with Britain.

That evening was clear and calm, but thick clouds filled in as night drew near. We cooked a thick steak, seasoned it with onions, matched it with canned corn, and washed it away with beer.

But sleep was uneasy. Heavy showers punctuated the night, and peculiar currents tugged at the boat. Peculiar currents had tugged at my mind, as well, over the last few days. They concerned my cousin and the fact that we scarcely knew each other.

Prior to two days ago I had not seen Bob for twenty-odd years. That occasion was a family reunion hosted by Bob's sister in Wheeling, West Virginia, for members of my grandparents' family. Before that meeting, we had not gotten together since 1959, the year his son, Michael, had been baptized and a few years after Bob had enlisted in the Marines. During these past forty-five years, there was an occasional exchange of Christmas cards and second-hand reports from relatives on what each of us was doing with our lives, but nothing more. I had settled in eastern Canada, and he was posted with the 1st Marine Division in San Diego.

By the time I had committed myself to a voyage up the St. Lawrence and through the Lakes, Bob had retired and he and his family had moved to Chicago. It was natural then that I should renew contact, let him know of my plans, and suggest that we get together some time. Our interchange resulted in his offer to join me for part of the trip.

"Has the thought occurred that you and Bob might kill each other before the trip is over?" my wife, Brenda, asked.

She was right. That possibility had not fully formed in the head. In fact, I probably had spent more time in the last four decades discouraging knock-on-the-front-door missionaries than I had communicating with my cousin Bob. I should have been quite apprehensive about spending a month in close quarters with a person who, in reality, was a stranger. I should have said, "Thanks, Bob, but there's no room," or "I booked that part of the trip to a friend." I'm a writer; I could compose a book of excuses for any occasion, if I wished. But I didn't. And I wouldn't...because for some enigmatic reason, he did not *seem* a stranger.

"Robert!...Robert!" I echoed, somewhat crossly. The words slurred like a drunkard's oath, and a trickle of foamy spittle dribbled from the corner of my mouth. These were my first words. I was not yet one-year-old. My mother laughed; my Aunt Margaret laughed too because she had just fired off the very same reprimand at her five-year-old son Robert, as he ran with noisy abandon into and through the house.

Both of our families lived in Syracuse, New York, at the beginning of the Second World War. The last time that Robert and I played together would have been 1947, when my father's work took us from Syracuse to other New York and Pennsylvania cities over the next ten years. By the mid-fifties, Robert had enlisted in the Marines and disappeared from this scene. Then a gulf of nearly fifty years slipped between our two lives. No wonder, then, that Brenda, my wife, would express reservation about the success of our reunion. As did Bob's wife, Barb.

Our first meeting in Cornwall, therefore, probably was no different than two old dogs that meet on a road and circle one another with slowly wagging tails. We measured temperaments and gauged responses, but the result of all that subtlety, manoeuvring, and caution was unforeseen, quite surprising, and perhaps even serendipitous. In less than a couple of days, it seemed that we once again had become just two little boys playing in the front yard of 249 Clover Ridge Drive in Syracuse during the spring of 1947, and I looked at Bob as I had seen him then, as a "big brother" and, more than that, I now saw him as a best friend.

Such a seamless resolution seemed unlikely. That it happened so simply was puzzling, and for a moment my thoughts returned to my childhood sailing dream, the boats that peppered my life since, and the voyage I pressed ahead on despite the obstacles that discouraged it. Since then I sometimes question whether change is really inevitable over time. Perhaps change is an illusion. Perhaps what we become is no more than what we have always been.

We hauled anchor at 0715. The decks were wet with rain. Eventually the day cleared. The sun grew strong, and the temperature soared to ninety-five. Morrisburg, Ontario; Mariatown, and the Iroquois Lock slipped by. Stubborn adverse currents struck us near Cardinal, and we crawled forward at between 2 and 2.5 knots. After the Ogdensburg-Prescott Bridge, the current mellowed. We put into Prescott for refuelling. Then we had a hot, but quiet run to Brockville.

BROCKVILLE, ON

The Three Sisters Islands lay midstream just before the city of Brockville. We ranged inshore to get the lay of the land along the city's waterfront. Broad windows of expensive homes blinked through the foliage, which crowded the bank east of the downtown area. Shade trees flattened into a parched grassy commons. A long concrete wall fronted the park. Picnic tables, a small boat ramp, strolling couples, and playing children appeared and faded.

Beyond the park was a municipal marina. One or two powerboats stood off the entrance until several others exited. It was busy with traffic. I saw no masts indicating sailboats. I saw no empty berths, only a glare of white plastic hulls and the glint of chrome. We slowly motored on.

A small grove of masts sprang from behind the next breakwater though. So we poked our bow through the entrance and held our position until I noticed a small open space at a floating dock fixed to the inside wall. At least, I thought, we could tie there temporarily.

Minutes later, a red-haired man approached. He had two moon-faced children in tow. He introduced himself as duty officer for that day here at the Brockville Yacht Club. He was friendly and courteous, but his news dimmed our hopes of staying. He said that ordinarily the yacht club is not open to the public. It does, however, have a reciprocal agreement with other yacht clubs to make accommodations for each other's members and boats, but we didn't fit that criterion. Not only did we not belong to a regional yacht club, but we did not belong to a yacht club anywhere.

I was not put off by their policy. Nevertheless, I did ask if he knew where we might find a berth in the area or even a suitable anchorage. He would ask around, he said. One of the few people at the yacht club during this supper hour was Garth, and it was Garth that the duty officer collared for advice.

Garth was a middle-aged, loquacious contractor who had moved from Saint John, New Brunswick, to Brockville thirty years before. He was a long-time member of the Brockville Yacht Club; the red-haired duty officer was new to the club. Garth was amazed to learn that we had sailed from Prince Edward Island in such a small boat, and he was eager to hear details. In the end, he assured us that we were welcome to stay overnight. Coming from such a distance, he insisted, was just as significant as belonging to any yacht club.

So we filled out the registry in the shade of a picnic table at one side of the drive-in basement to the clubhouse, and I pulled out my wallet.

"Oh no," Garth said, "there's no charge! It's the same as if you were a visitor from another club."

Then Garth gathered up several nautical charts and spread them out on the picnic table. For the next hour he pored over our route upstream. Brockville was the easternmost edge of the Thousand Islands, and there was much to learn about that region.

Not only was Garth an avid sailor, but he also had a keen sense of civic pride, and he insisted that he take us on a quick car tour of Brockville. The quick tour took an hour, or so it seemed, for we were famished. Nevertheless Garth's excursion through the city was interesting, and we were treated to glimpses of many stately homes, scenic drives and lanes, and even a real castle. We learned that Brockville was the oldest incorporated town in Canada, and the country's first railway tunnel was built there. In fact, it ran underneath city hall. Garth pointed to a tall brick chimney near city hall. It rose straight from the underground tunnel. It had been built to clear the underpass of the thick, poisonous fumes generated by coal-fired steam engines.

Garth also pointed out practical buildings: grocery store, liquor store, and several restaurants. Later, after he drove us back us to the waterfront, Bob and I took one of Garth's recommended dining suggestions—Bud's Steak and Seafood Restaurant—for Cajun-style salmon and Bavarian beer from Brazil.

We did not meet Eric until the next morning. Eric had a W. C. Fields nose and a military bearing. He had sailed in waters around Malta and Greece, and he, like many others, was attracted to the novelty of a classic wooden boat's mast in the midst of a stand of aluminum spars. He offered us advice about threading through the Thousand Islands, and then he helped swing our boat around on our departure.

The lighthouse on Skeleton Island marked the entrance to the Brockville Narrows, a confined and busy deep-water channel between dozens of islets and rocks and shoals, strewn across the St. Lawrence River for three or four miles upstream. The islands are rocky and wooded. They rise sheer from the water, but submerged rocks lie near many of them. Most of the islands are privately owned cottage retreats; some are maintained by the Brockville

Parks Commission, others by Parks Canada. The dredged channel between the islands is surprisingly direct, and a stone hurled from the deck of any vessel would fall on some island.

After the Narrows, we struck out on a small-craft channel. It wound closer to the Canadian side of the river, avoided steamships, and precluded having to clear customs in an American port. Grenadier Island, one of the largest islands in the chain, divided the seaway into a shipping channel and a small-craft channel. The small-craft channel led northwest and tightened. A corridor named the Raft Narrows led us toward the Thousand Islands Bridge, which spans the St. Lawrence and connects New York's route 81 to Ontario's highway 401. Near that bridge we entered a beautiful archipelago.

Sometimes it was a challenge to fix on the correct passage through the archipelago but, in our effort to do so, we passed through a scene full of wonder and beauty. Willows, maples, poplars, and cedars forested the islands and shores. Mansions replaced cottages; estates supplanted lots. Stone and brick masonry shaped walls and towers into magnificent structures which stood like fortresses. Chateaus were commonplace. Private avenues and cobbled walkways ambled toward gated entries. Immense stone walls barred curious eyes of passing motorists and reserved the colourful flourish of gardens and verdant lawns to privileged gazes. It was here that much of the opulence of Ontario secreted itself within the privacy of islands.

By late afternoon, we had cleared the Gananoque Narrows and entered a relatively open patch of water. Three miles ahead lay the town of Gananoque, Ontario. The sky was dark and thick with low clouds. We spotted a marina and steered through its breakwater. It looked busy. No berths were apparent. We saw an empty hole on a wharf near the pump-out station. So we pulled alongside and tied up. Large cruisers and houseboats loomed on the opposite side of this wharf. Moments later one of the marina attendants arrived.

"Do you have reservations?" he asked.

"No, we don't," I replied, "but we're looking for a berth tonight."

"We're filled," he said. "There's twenty boats on a waiting list."

"Okay if we stay here for half an hour? I want to make some phone calls." A roll of thunder rattled across the darkening sky.

"You'll have to leave now."

"Can I take a few minutes, then, to use your washroom?"

"No."

"Not even the washroom?"

"No," he replied curtly.

"May I have time to comb my hair?" I asked, taking a comb from my pocket.

He sneered and turned.

He hadn't gotten to the end of the wharf before the clouds loosed a torrent. It was a sudden, heavy downpour, too heavy to even to see the marina entrance. So we sought refuge below until the rain subsided.

BATEAU CHANNEL

We managed to get our half hour ashore, albeit sequestered below deck, and as soon as the rain subsided we quietly slipped away. A coast guard cutter stood near the channel to port. To starboard lay a dredge, permanently anchored. Upstream the seaway narrowed. Groups of small islands gathered ahead of us. Sailboats and cruisers, themselves unable to find a marina, had anchored close in, but even near the shallow coves of these islands, little room remained for another boat to swing at anchor. So we pressed on. We entered the Bateau Channel, a quarter-mile wide slot between Howe Island and the mainland, a corridor leading to Kingston.

An hour later with evening fast approaching, we eagerly sought some place to tie up or anchor safely. The terrain along the shore was wooded. Few docks or houses penetrated the mask of foliage, and the thick green shoreline offered the illusion of remoteness. Then we saw what appeared to be a small marina. In fact it was the Trident Yacht Club, a private facility. We cruised by slowly and tried to judge whether or not we would be rebuffed here as well. The light was dim; we saw no activity. We swung round for a second go-by, and I began to feel like a schoolboy yearning for sweets as he shuffles past an ice cream parlour.

Then we saw it—what the schoolboy never sees—a hand waving us in. The hand motioned us toward a short dock, which fronted the waterway and led to the clubhouse. I can't recall who the hand belonged to, whether it was Jim Fletcher or Lee McCabe, both of whom were at the dock when we came alongside. Jim's granddaughter, a twelve- or thirteen-year-old, took the lines so smartly that I took her for a young employee at the club. Jim and Lee found an unoccupied berth next to Jim's vessel, and we shifted our boat into the more protected confines of the marina, where they caught our mooring lines again. Jim's wife joined the small group, as did their ten-year-old grandson. Both children were bright and inquisitive, wanting to know all the technical details about the *Arja D.* Finally, I let them have the run of the boat. They delightedly scampered below like cats after mice, while Bob and I chatted with the others.

Later, Bob and I barbequed a steak on a propane grill near our dock. I managed to get enough elevation on the yacht club's deck to call home on Bob's cellphone. There was no manager around that evening to register. So we would have to arrange that tomorrow. During the night the wind wailed through the rigging of neighbouring vessels, and I was happy to be snug at dockside rather than swinging at anchor.

Instead of setting up our propane camp stove on deck or firing up the barbeque near the wharf, we cooked up pancakes and eggs in the yacht club kitchen. Jim, his wife, and Lee arrived as we were preparing breakfast. Jim's wife was a teacher and, having retired from twenty-five years at that job myself, we had some perspectives to share on the state of that profession.

At 0900 Bob and I were ready to leave. The registrar for the yacht club had not arrived and, according to Jim, would be delayed for some time. Not to worry, Jim assured us. Just leave when you're ready. Lee agreed, and added that there would be no charge for our stay-over. It would be a courtesy for such long-distance sailors as we.

Both Bob and I were touched by the hospitality shown us at this and the last yacht club we had visited. It was a warmth which lingered as we pulled out of the marina's enclosure into the Bateau Channel. As we looked back, though, we saw another hand waving from a man rushing down to the short dock. He hollered and wove again. As we drifted alongside the dock, Lee passed us the morning newspapers.

"Something to read on your way," he said.

KINGSTON, ON

It was only ten miles from the Trident Yacht Club to Kingston, but it took us until 1400 to reach it. After we left the confines of the Bateau Channel and entered the expanse of Kingston Bay, the breeze was fair enough to raise a sail, and that gentle draft carried us toward Kingston. It was soothing to hear only the slap of canvas and the rub of rigging, and to feel the heave of the vessel as if it were simply one more part of all other natural things. Sounds and feelings that could lull one into a soft dream.

Cedar Island appeared to starboard. We turned toward it. Then, the ramparts of Fort Henry came into view. Then the grounds of the Royal Military College. Beyond it all, lay the city of Kingston and Confederation Basin, a large marina, where we were able to get one of the few remaining berths.

The location of this marina was perfect. It bordered the heart of downtown Kingston, and we spent the afternoon roaming its busy streets with three practical goals in mind: to find a repair shop for Bob's camera, to purchase charts for the Trent-Severn Waterway, and to refill our icebox with fresh food. Midway across one intersection we ran into Jukka Vasko, the Laplander from the red *Linnea* who had disappeared from sight somewhere near Valleyfield, Quebec, a week ago. Jukka was walking his bicycle at the time and bound for a late lunch at a Greek restaurant. We agreed to meet him there after we had retrieved Bob's camera from the repair shop but, when we returned to the restaurant half an hour later,

Jukka had disappeared once again. So we continued on, located a marine supply store, and bought most of the charts we needed for the Trent-Severn system. We headed down steep, sloping streets toward the waterfront and cut through a municipal park at the foot of that incline. There, occupying most of one park bench, sat Jukka, a pleasantly inebriated giant, his big fists manoeuvring an immense Greek sandwich cautiously toward his gaping mouth. At the sight of us, he smiled and roared and saluted us with his sandwich. Jukka promised that he would visit our boat after supper.

"I will bring beer," he said, "and we will talk."

He arrived around seven that evening, a case of bottles under one arm, and over the next several hours, we pieced together Jukka's story from tangled fragments of his half-drunken Finnish accent. Jukka was at the end of a two-year voyage. He had left his job as an environmental engineer and embarked on a sailing adventure with friends, each of whom eventually returned home. His voyage began in Finland and took him to Cape Verde Islands, Brazil, Cuba, French Guiana, and up the east coast of North America. By the time he hit Brazil he was sailing alone.

He spent a month in one Brazilian port, and that is where trouble raised its head. According to Jukka, a port official tried to extort money from him. When the official demanded payment, Jukka refused. That evening, he was visited by thugs in a rubber raft who threatened to kill him if he didn't pay. He confided this threat to another Brazilian who offered his services to murder the port official for fifteen dollars. Jukka declined the bargain-basement offer. The next day he left Brazil, slipping out of port just before nightfall.

Twilight lingers for only moments in the tropics. Darkness comes swiftly. He motored ahead, cleared the bay, and was making for deep water when he heard a fast-approaching motorboat somewhere off his stern. He cut his engine, quenched his running lights, and raised sail. Then he bore off on an altered course. He knew he was being hunted when the rumble of the motorboat engine began to cut a pattern across the black night. At some point, he heard random gunshots. He altered course again; the sound of their motor faded; and he escaped through the silence of his sail.

Jukka's plans were to return to Finland after laying up the red *Linnea* in Toronto. He was running out of money and had to get back to work. The co-owner of his boat would arrive to sail it further into the Great Lakes.

It was dark when we finished the last of the beer. Jukka returned to his boat to prepare for an early departure tomorrow. Bob and I gathered up the emptied bottles. Then we wandered the main street and ended up at Brandee's bar. The lounge was crowded Wednesday night. A four-piece band pulsed out a jazzy rhythm; a Black female vocalist shaped a blues interpretation of some old standards; and beer was four-something a bottle.

We departed Kingston after a stop at a bank uptown and a nearby post office the following morning. In the past month I had gone through a vast number of charts, perhaps forty. I had no room for them in my cabin, yet I did not want to destroy them. So I bound them up in an enormous roll and mailed them home. That made room for the fifteen or so I had purchased the day before, as well as a few others I would take out of storage.

BELLEVILLE, ON

After Kingston, we entered Lake Ontario. That sense of open water, however, lasted no more than two miles. Then we entered another sheltered water route behind Amherst Island. It led to the Bay of Quinte, along a Z-shaped river-like passage to Deseronto, and finally to Belleville, Ontario. Winds grew light, and temperatures climbed into the nineties, and there was nowhere to escape the heat.

We arrived at Belleville in late afternoon and refuelled at the marina. My most pressing business in Belleville would be arranging for un-stepping my mast. Tomorrow or the next day we would enter 250 miles of the Trent-Severn Waterway, which links Lake Ontario with Georgian Bay on Lake Huron. That waterway has many fixed bridges with low clearances. So the mast had to come down. There were two places in Belleville where we could get the mast un-stepped, one of them was Morch Marine.

Peter Morch, the service manager, said they could take the mast down, but I'd have to bring the boat in right away. So Bob and I motored over, tied up, and stripped off the sails and rigging ourselves. An hour later, we'd finished. Then Matthew, the yard manager, drove a motorized crane to the wharf's edge and lifted the mast clear of the deck. After that, Bob and I built a cradle to carry the mast above the deck so that it would neither obstruct our mobility nor interfere with the tiller. By 1330 we'd finished the cradle, and secured the mast and boom on top of it.

When we returned from lunch, we settled our account. Peter Morch considered the sweat equity we brought to the job and, what might have been a two-hundred-dollar invoice, was only forty.

"I just wouldn't feel right charging you guys full price," he said.

Chapter 15

LOCK AND LOAD

For the last four days the temperature had broached ninety-five, and it looked like it would reach that level again. Eleven miles separate Belleville from Trenton, Ontario. By mid-morning Trenton airfield, the military base which dispatches search and rescue flights for the Great Lakes, passed to starboard. The city of Trenton lies beyond the air base, nearer the head of the Bay of Quinte on the Trent River. A bridge, which spans the river, carries a banner-like sign that reads, "Welcome to the Trent-Severn Waterway."

The Trent-Severn Waterway is a snaking 240-mile path from Lake Ontario to Georgian Bay on Lake Huron. It was created by a series of man-made canals, rivers, and lakes of central and southern Ontario. Construction began in the 1830s but was not completed until 1920. It was adequate for barges, but too shallow for heavy shipping. Nevertheless, it shortened commerce routes, promoted settlement, and served logging interests. Eventually, however, railway and truck transport diminished its practical value for all but sailors and pleasure boaters. For them it became a wonderfully scenic route to the upper lakes and a shortcut which bypasses all of Lakes Ontario and Erie and part of Lake Huron.

A mile and a half up the river, we pulled into the slot of water leading to the first lock, tied up along the concrete retaining wall, and purchased a transit pass from the park warden on duty. Over the next week, we would clear forty-two conventional locks, twenty swing bridges, two lift locks, and a railway shuttle before dipping our bow into Georgian Bay at Port Severn.

We cleared three locks in our first four miles up the waterway. Altogether they lifted us sixty-eight feet above the level of Lake Ontario. The walls of each lock were made of reinforced concrete and were slimy with blackened marine growth. Once boats had entered a lock, one or two of the lock's crew walked a large wheel round and round until the mechanism of gears connected with it opened or closed the floodgate. Though these lifts were not as turbulent as the massive locks on the St. Lawrence, we struggled to keep the boat parallel to the wall, especially now while we had the mast and boom cradled and extending precariously beyond our bow and stern.

Between locks, the channel was usually less than a hundred yards wide. It's treed to the waterline, and the bank drops sharply.

Mast cradled before entering Trent-Severn Waterway.

Each lock had a rest area. We tied up along the concrete wall after lock number three, the Glen Miller Lock. Two or three picnic tables spread across a neatly kept grassy spot, and we ate lunch there and stretched our legs for half an hour.

The route beyond was often narrow, usually winding, and always surprising. Weeping willows dripped garlands of foliage into shadowy likenesses of themselves in the river. Elms spread their trunks in graceful skyward arcs. Beneath them, sturdy maples, delicate lindens, and poplars filled the low horizon with fresh hues of green and yellow; groves of rough and fine texture, diverse in shape and proportion, pleased the eye. Solitary fishers cast lures from boats screened by overhanging limbs. Others angled in small groups on ledges beneath bridges and trestles. The channel meandered through narrow corridors, between fields of verdant marshland, and past assemblies of cottages. Sometimes, the waterway grew busy with boat traffic; other times, the river spread out in a great watery solitude.

CAMPBELLFORD, ON

By 1900 the heat began to abate, the sun lost its harshness, and the colours of the river began to soften. After lock twelve, we entered Campbellford. The river narrowed, and suddenly I found myself in the midst of a pretty, suburban, residential area. It was an odd and unexpected juxtaposition, so much so that my awareness of being aboard a boat was swept away. At least for a few moments I had the sensation of leisurely driving my car down a canopied boulevard on a lazy Sunday afternoon. Tidy bungalows and split-level homes lined the way handily on each side of us. Quiet avenues followed the riverbank. The vehicles that travelled them moved unhurriedly and not much faster than we sailed. Lawns were mowed to the water's edge, children played, couples strolled the walkways; dogs barked and engines hummed.

Old Mill Park is in the centre of the city. We docked there, tying up along the wall. A small cement building in the park housed the tourist information centre, and the attendant informed us that docking was free. However, there was a thirteen-dollar charge for the washrooms and showers. The surrounding park was grassy and partially treed. A string of temporary bleachers had been erected along the edge of the riverbank for those joining the civic holiday festivities being celebrated that weekend. By the time we arrived, the day's activities had concluded. However, a number of empty tents were scattered across the park for the next day's activities and games. The Poor Edward band would play music; local groups would compete in cardboard boat races; and pick-up teams would struggle in tugs-of-war. In the middle of the park stood an enormous reproduction of the Canadian two-dollar coin, the "toonie." The twelve-foot diameter, silver-and-brass-coloured coin was elevated from the ground on a concrete pillar, and resembled an enormous metallic lollipop.

At the west end of the park, near the bridge which unites both sides of the city, appeared another unusual sight. A sign painted on the side of a parked refrigerator truck read: "Have you been to church lately?" It was not a religious reference, as one might think. It was the slogan for Church Key Brewery, a local company. Bubba, the truck's driver, walked by the boat as we were making supper and struck up a conversation. He talked boats, and he talked beer.

"Would you like to try one?" he asked.

"We would."

Bubba returned with three dark bottles, labelled Decadent Chocolate Porter. It was wonderful, a unique, rich, pleasant taste, and we downed them eagerly. At the same time, Bubba was quite interested in learning about our trip. So we gave him details of where we had been, and we discussed where we were going.

"Would you like to try another beer...a different one?" he asked

"We would."

Bubba returned with three more dark bottles, labelled Cranberry Maple Wheat. This second beer was better than the first, a lighter, springier flavour, and it led us without effort into a place of mellowness.

It was about that time that Nancy arrived. She stopped to offer a flattering comment on the *Arja D.* and stayed to converse. Nancy was, I would guess, in her late seventies, silver-haired and trim, polite and filled with curiosity about all things and people around her. She spoke in a clear, crisp British accent.

"Yes, I should like one," she replied to Bubba's offer and he hurried to fetch a dark bottle for Nancy.

We learned that Nancy had been a sergeant with the British Army stationed in Israel. In her monologue she spoke with admiration for John F. Kennedy, Winston Churchill, and Golda Meir. Her tone was quiet, unassuming, and wistful. Her husband had died two years ago. Now she was "putting in time until the pearly gates opened...," she said. Some of that time she put in involved ferrying seniors less mobile than she in her Volkswagen van. She also biked about town, was an enthusiastic bird watcher and, before she departed, she kindly offered to drive us for groceries or anything else we might need in town.

Bubba remained after the sun burnt out its last ember of daylight. Then he recalled, "I have one more beer you haven't tried."

He returned from the truck with several dark bottles, darker now in the shadows of evening, darkened still more by the black label, which read in thin gold letters, Holy Smoke.

Holy Smoke was a different beer, heavy and bitter, with an aftertaste I did not enjoy. Perhaps it was brewed for a British palate. At any rate, after Bubba left for the evening, I poured the dregs of Holy Smoke beer into the Trent River. That act of rejection, I realized later, would force me to toss away a stock response that I had used for years: "I never met a beer I didn't like." That paraphrase of a Will Rogers's one-liner had served me faithfully on many occasions. I would miss it.

The rivers and canals led generally north and west but sometimes dipped south for significant stretches. The sun was hot, the sky a hazy light blue. We encountered several more locks, most of which lifted us six or seven feet. At Healey Falls, however, a pair of locks flooded us twenty feet up. These locks, called "flight locks," were unusual in that they were a two-stage lock system.

The Healey Falls Locks lifted us high enough to match the level of Seymour Lake. Nappan, Slaughter, and Hardy Islands took us on an ess-shaped route across the lake, but it was important to keep within the narrow buoyed channel because broad shoals and marshy areas cover most of that lake. Then, once more we entered a river and its narrow confines.

Rice Lake lay ahead. It's shallow and marshy, about sixteen miles long and several miles wide. Then we entered the Otonabee River, where the channel narrowed and the banks of the river disappeared in extensive marshland, a seeming wilderness.

BENSFORT BRIDGE, ON

Campbellton passed. Bensfort Bridge as well. The chart identified a marina there, but we didn't see one. The chart marked a public wharf just beyond the bridge. We looked for it and saw a tiny dock, probably a private one, next to a cottage. Just beyond it, a long jetty protruded into the river. We headed for that, but pulled up short. No other boats were alongside, and it was in disrepair, flimsy, and probably safe neither to lie against nor walk upon. Nothing lay ahead but Peterborough, and we would not be able to reach that city until after sundown. So we turned round, backtracked a few hundred yards, looked at the stubby dock, and then drove forward again toward the dilapidated structure. Perhaps we could anchor somewhere, I thought.

Several cottages looked out from the shore. Wisps of smoke rose from a barbeque by one house close to the rundown jetty. A man in front of it gave several broad signals with his arm. Then he left the barbeque and walked briskly along the edge of the water. He motioned us both in and toward the stubby landing, which we had passed by.

The barbeque man was Grif, a former school bus driver. The dock to which he led us was indeed the public wharf, big enough for our vessel and not much else. As Bob and I tied up, two more men appeared, fascinated by the arrival of a wooden sailboat and filled with questions we tried to answer.

"You should talk to Johnny Walker," one of them said.

"He builds boats too," added the other.

Then Willy arrived. She was an elderly Dutch woman drawn to the dock by the unusually large gathering there.

"Johnny would like to see your wooden boat," she echoed. "I'll fetch him." She disappeared up a steep lane which crossed a shady road to the village.

Johnny Walker and his wife, Willy, returned a few minutes later. They were a short sturdy couple, both well into retirement years, both energetic. Johnny walked with crisp, resolute steps and a bit of swagger; Willy descended the incline of the lane with a firm deliberate pace. When they reached the boat, Johnny asked only a few questions, but studied the *Arja D.* as intently as a guard at a border crossing might examine a hippie's van. Then, he invited Bob and me to his home after we had finished settling in.

Johnny was indeed a boat builder. In a small outbuilding was his latest creation, a Friese Schouw—a vessel which might have graced the seventeenth-century canvases of van de Velde. It was a small working vessel, which he described as the pickup truck of Dutch merchants. It was from a Renaissance design and built in a small shed next to his house.

It was not more than 20 feet long, carvel construction, painted black below the waterline, and all bright work above. A leeboard kept the shoal-draft boat from drifting. A gaff rig drove her under sail. It was a beautifully built vessel, an open boat, with a cuddy forward. The doors to the cuddy were fitted with small stained-glass panels. Johnny picked up a discarded chunk of wood from a workbench. It was a cross-section of the mast, and it revealed its construction. The mast was round, but hollow inside. The sample he produced showed that it was made up from six separate lengths of wood, each interlocking the next in a unique pattern. It was a splendid example of workmanship.

Johnny was born in Devon, but acquired considerable knowledge of wooden boat construction from his work at the famous Smith & Rhuland shipyard in Lunenburg, Nova Scotia. He became their chief loftsman, converting architect blueprints into full-scale lines on the shop floor. These lines became the guide to building keel and frames for shaping the vessel by shipwrights. The walls of Johnny's living room displayed pictures of many of the boats he had some hand in building or sailing over the years. Among the photos was a replica of explorer John Cabot's the *Matthew*. Johnny had been mate aboard that vessel during a centennial of its historic crossing from Europe.

Wonderful achievements in life often are countered by crushing disappointment. So it was with the Walkers. A company with whom Johnny had worked for many years and from which he retired went into bankruptcy. While those at the top of the corporate structure cushioned their fall, those on the line lost jobs and those who had retired lost pensions. Johnny was one of them. Then, an elderly man on a fixed income, he had nothing—less than nothing. He was also left alone when his first wife of many years died.

Willy, on the other hand, had been married to a Dutch soldier, living in the Netherlands with him and her children until her husband died suddenly. Only then did she learn that he had neglected to change the terms of his will or the name of his next of kin from that of his first wife, whom he had divorced twenty years earlier; legally and inevitably, the first wife became beneficiary of his military insurance and heir to his estate. Willy was devastated when she and her children were turned away with nothing.

Later, Willy immigrated to Canada to start life anew. Eventually, she and Johnny met, fell in love, and married. In many ways, they still seemed like newlyweds. The gentle affection they showed for each other during our visit with them was remarkable and touching.

Johnny Walker had turned seventy-eight this year. His bald head and snow-white beard hinted at age, but his attitude didn't. He was remarkably agile and sharp intellectually. In the recent past he had begun to design canoes. He had been a founding member and a director of the Canadian Canoe Museum, and he insisted that we must visit the museum the next day. He and Willy would give us a guided tour. We would meet them at the Peterborough marina at noon. They would be waiting for us at dockside. We could not refuse, nor did we wish to.

Peterborough was fourteen miles away. The river was placid, and soft light filtered through the willows which hung over the water. Trees and marshland made up the rural setting through which we passed. The Otonabee River presented a pastoral picture, undisturbed until the wake of a fast-moving cruiser knocked us about and nearly upended a fisherman in an aluminum skiff near shore.

After we cleared the lock, a mile ahead, we bore off to port and entered a kidney-shaped body of water called Little Lake. The skyline of Peterborough crowded the lake's edge, and a few minutes later we pulled into the public marina. Johnny and Willy were waiting. They took us first on a car tour of Peterborough, which ended at Lock 21, the famous lift lock. Then we visited the canoe museum.

The Canadian Canoe Museum was impressive. Over six hundred canoes and kayaks were on display. They ranged from aboriginal bark canoes to Inuit skin-covered kayaks, from the large transport canoes of the French voyageurs to more delicate, modern, wood plank vessels, from former prime minister Pierre Trudeau's personal canoe to those manned by explorers and adventurers on historic voyages. There were West Coast dugouts used for whaling and East Coast canoes used for warfare. What made the visit most memorable, however, was Johnny Walker's vast knowledge of each canoe and the running commentary he provided as we wandered among them.

Outside the museum the Walkers posed for a photograph. They stood in front of a rear exit which faced a large warehouse. "There are four hundred more canoes in there," he said, pointing to the warehouse. There just isn't room to display them all.

We said our final goodbye to the Walkers and returned to the marina.

Black ominous thunderstorms rattled across the sky all afternoon, but each missed us. We walked uptown. It was a civic holiday in Peterborough. Some stores were closed. I searched out boat supply businesses for a particular chart I would need for the next stretch along the canal. To my disappointment, charts were still in short supply, some glitch in the supply from the Hydrographic Service or their printers. None could be bought locally, and none could be purchased at the locks, which usually had plenty in stock.

My inability to find charts for the next leg of the journey eventually forced me to search for used charts among local boaters. I passed from boat to boat like a desperate vacuum-cleaner salesman until one man considered parting with his charts. He wasn't sure, though. They had been a gift from his wife. He would have to replace them, but he couldn't decide on a fair price. He asked me to return the next morning and, when I arrived, we reached an agreement. Within minutes, Bob and I were slipping lines and motoring for the next lock.

Bob Zack handling the lines at the big Peterborough Lift Lock.

Lock 20 was a mile away at the head of Little Lake and, a mile beyond that, we came to the Peterborough Lock. The Peterborough Lock was like nothing I had seen before. It was like nothing I would have imagined before. It stood ahead of us at the end of our ribbon of water like a stalwart fortification. Two thirty-five-foot stone towers straddled the waterway. Between them rose a taller stone column with a square, red roof, capped with a staff streaming the Maple Leaf pennant. Linking the towers were what looked like black, steel walls. Earthworks rose up on either bank to meet the towers. Thickets of trees crowded these ramparts so that we faced what seemed an unassailable fortress. As we drew closer, the definition of the blackened walls became more distinct and revealed enormous steel vats in front of each of them. One vat was at water level; the other was suspended in air twenty feet higher. The blackness behind them was the wall of the dam which held back the Trent River. As we watched, the vats began to move, the upper one slowly dropping, the lower one slowly ascending, like external elevators on a modern skyscraper.

The upper vat sank to a level even with us; its gate opened; and we were signalled to enter. I put the engine in gear and slowly approached the mouth of the steel basin. Inside we lay against the inside wall and tied onto a metal grate above it. We now found ourselves in a huge steel bathtub filled with water.

The gate closed, and we began a slow steady ascent. We bobbed and sloshed from the inertia as it lifted boat, water, captain, and crew to the heights of the tower. All the while I stood on deck, holding white-knuckled onto the steel grate, wondering if the hinges or locks on the doors would burst, as they had once or twice in the history of the lock, and water, boat, captain, and crew would be flushed into what now was a precipice below. All the while, Bob and I grinned at each other through clenched teeth.

Eventually the gates opened as designed, and we spilled gently into the sleepy river once again. For several miles the passage was narrow and shaded with overhanging boughs, but then Trent University appeared. The river ran through the heart of it, and a bridge arced above to join both halves of the campus. Stone walls banked the shore. A terraced stone staircase led into the river. Several of the buildings rose from the water's edge. All were stone, monolithic, nearly windowless, modern, stark. The university had a severe, yet intriguing appearance, and we stared at it with nearly the same interest as we would at enormous granite crystalline shapes growing from the earth.

Two more locks came in quick succession. Cedars surrounded the lock grounds. Their scent was rich and sweet and hung like a veil in the warm summer air as we relaxed in the boat and watched the lock crews stomp like horses around a capstan to manually open and close the hundred-year-old water gates. When we reached the Otonabee Lock, the second one, we pulled alongside the stand-by wall and waited for downstream boats to clear. Then we pulled in and lay against the starboard wall. One of the lock's crew caught our lines and hauled us in.

"Are you the fellas from PEI?" he asked.

"Why, yes," I replied. "How did you know that?"

"Heard about you from a few of the boats that came through yesterday," he said. "Quite a trip you're on. We don't see many boats from that far away. Good luck."

Pines replaced the cedars as we steamed ahead. Three more locks. The town of Lakefield. Then a narrow channel through Katchewanooka Lake, very shoal and marshy.

Clear Lake was deeper and half a mile wide. A number of heavy cruisers passed us, some slowing to blunt the effects of their wake, others running at high throttle and oblivious to anything beyond the gleaming stainless steel rails on their own decks. Gradually over the day, the landscape changed. Banks grew steeper; their shale ledges gave way to the dense impregnable rock of the pre-Cambrian Shield. The meadows and farmland of Southern Ontario had disappeared, and white pine and spruce replaced the hardwood stands.

Hell's Gate lay ahead. It separated Clear Lake from Stony Lake, and it was where we would turn into a westerly channel. Hell's Gate was aptly named. It consisted of fifty to a hundred rock islands, some barren and some with soil enough to support one or two hardy trees, a gnarly shrub, and some tufts of grass. What we could not see were the many hundreds of rocks below the water's surface which lay between and around those islands. As we approached Hell's Gate, we passed one island hard on our port side. There was a long low building on it and a sign which read St. Peter's Anglican Church on the Rock. Here, it seemed, St. Peter stood guard at the gates of Hell as well as the gates of Heaven.

I had corresponded with a man who had cruised through here a few years before. Even though he was an experienced boater, he had an unpleasant moment when he failed to sight the next buoy in the series which would guide him through this region. It was understandable how something like that could happen, though. The scenery is wild and beautiful, threatening, yet alluring, and anyone could become momentarily distracted. For whatever reason, he drifted off the marked channel for a short distance. He caught his mistake and stopped dead in the water, but when he looked back to retrace his course, he could not determine which of all the buoys he saw behind him was the last one. With much anxiety about being holed by an uncharted rock but with considerable patience, he eventually was able to negotiate a safe return to the channel.

We stayed well inside the narrow buoyed channel which cut through the lower end of Hell's Gate. Strangely, even here in a region devoid of roads and inaccessible except by boat or hiking boot, a few grand summer homes peeked through the conifers.

We spent that evening at the Buckhorn Lock and left early the next morning, three days into August. The morning was misty. Light tints of pink, grey, and violet formed indistinct blotches on the horizon. I was still groggy from yesterday's heat. More of the same was forecast for today.

We encountered no locks for the next seventeen miles, but a swing bridge opened for us part way through the town of Bobcaygeon. We pulled into a standby area for the next lock and tied up beside a town park. It held picnic tables, shade trees, and a picturesque community surrounded it all.

Bobcaygeon was a tourist town. Sidewalks teemed with casual shoppers; boutiques were trendy; the price of most goods was premium. Bob headed one way and I another. We met up later at a sports store, which also sold marine charts. I needed two. They had one in stock. The remaining chart, an important one covering Lake Simcoe to Orillia, was unavailable. And I needed that chart tomorrow.

We had intended to rest in Bobcaygeon for just one hour, but it turned into two by the time we made lunch and dragged ourselves out from under the cool canopy of shade trees in the town park. Then we motored through another sweltering day under a withering blue sky until we reached the village of Rosedale.

ROSEDALE, ON

Bob was a sport fisherman, and he had brought a collapsible rod and a small kit of gear with him. We had passed many other fishers along the Trent-Severn Waterway, but Bob had noticed that few caught fish. Across the stream from our boat in the shade beneath a bridge, a pair of Asian fishermen cast their lines for three or four hours without luck. A local couple with their children dropped hooks off our pier. A few nibbles. A small rockfish was hauled up. Nothing more. In spite of that, Bob snagged, and later released, an eighteen-ounce big-mouth bass. Bob speculated that zebra mussels were causing the poor fishing. They were an exotic new species carried into the Great Lakes on the bottoms of foreign cargo ships within the last few decades. We had seen many clinging to the walls of the locks we'd traversed. They reproduced in large numbers, and they are reputed to clean out many of the micro-organisms which are an essential part of fish food chain.

Another lavender and grey morning greeted us. Calm water. Still air. At 0630 we started the engine and motored into Balsam Lake. Within two hours we reached Kirkfield Lift Lock, the same bucket-like lock we had used at Peterborough, except that this time we were at the top, looking down, over sixty feet. The Kirkfield lock marked the highest elevation in the Trent-Severn Waterway. As we stood there waiting for the lock to open for the day, we were 840 feet above sea level. That meant that we had climbed 766 feet above Lake Ontario in six days. From here to Georgian Bay it would be all downhill, and the *Arja D.* would now be considered an outward-bound vessel, and the channel buoys would reverse position from what they had been. In the end, the 50-foot drop at the Kirkfield Lift Lock proved not so unnerving as the experience at Peterborough, even though this lock was more than twice as high.

Since Hell's Gate, the terrain had returned to marshy lakes and narrow canals and low banks crowded with overhanging trees and undergrowth. Several low-hung swing bridges spanned the Talbot River, along which we sailed. The second bridge had just opened to let two cruisers, which were approaching, head upstream. Then the bridge swung closed.

We held our position for several minutes trying to figure out what had happened. The one automobile, which had been waiting, crossed the river. Then the bridge operator waved us forward. We motored ahead cautiously. Still, the bridge remained closed. He waved us on again. This time he was on the middle of the bridge, eyeballing the height of our vessel, and guessing at the clearance we might have. With the mast and boom cradled three feet above the top of the cabin, it was impossible for Bob or me to judge whether or not we would make it under the steel trusses of the bridge. We did clear it. However, only one foot or so lay in the difference.

Three more miles of canal brought us to Gamebridge, the last lock before Lake Simcoe. I chatted with park officials. I had been unable to get a chart for Lake Simcoe in Rosedale, and no charts were available at this lock either. The weather forecast called for southwest winds 10–15 knots with scattered showers and possibility of thunderstorms.

I took a final look at my last chart. Only a fragment of the lake appeared at the map's edge. That was very little to depend on. In the pool of blue, which represented that body of water, a note, printed in a delicate font, read, "Sudden storms are frequent on Lake Simcoe and every care and seamanlike precaution should be observed...."

Chance has not often been a trustworthy guide during my life. In spite of that, when I find myself in similar circumstances, I sometimes feel that I have been cast in the role of a tragic Greek character, listening stupidly at the mouth of a fortune-teller's cave for guidance...but like all such tragic characters, I am compelled by fate to ignore it. After all, what truth lies in the alignment of stars, the entrails of chickens, or the pattern of tea leaves? So, in this case, I trusted my own counsel: I would sail ahead with no chart. No charts were available, and none likely would become available. The sky was clear; the wind was fair; and the lake was crossable in three or four hours. I could take a bearing on Couchiching Lock which showed on my next chart and deduct a guessed-at number of degrees in order to point to the city of Orillia, our destination. At least, this would give me a half-assed course to steer by.

Most of the vessels which had cleared the lock with us remained at the rest area or headed for the small marina at Beaverton. We made for an island a few miles into the lake, skirted its edge, and then set our course. By mid-afternoon the north shore of the lake was prominent and not more than five miles ahead. To the west, however, clouds were piling up, and it became clear that we would not escape its dark outstretched hand. As the wind grew stronger from the southwest, so did the waves, and so did the rolling of the boat.

This was also Bob's first real encounter with bad weather on this boat and, although he had sailed before off San Diego, his confidence in the *Arja D.* was understandably shaky. We had donned life jackets some time before it struck but, as the rolling became more profound, we put on safety harnesses and snapped them onto either a jack line or a shackle in the cockpit. I also spouted some emergency tactics should the mast let go from its cradle or if either of us should go overboard. As the rolling of the boat heightened, I became more concerned with the mast, cradled above the deck. The forward support which sank straight into the mast's tabernacle in the keel was sound, but the aft brace which was fastened to the steel frame of the traveller was less rigid. So I bent a clove hitch around the mast for added stability.

ORILLIA, ON

The sky blackened, and rain poured down. The lake was shallow and the waves built quickly to five feet. I shifted course from Orillia toward the northwest shore of the lake. Near there, a point of land jutted out, and I knew that, in shelter behind it, waves would diminish.

The squall was uncomfortable, but short-lived and not a serious threat. Waves softened as we slipped east of the small cape and crowded the northern shore. Our altered course took us well off our bearing line to Orillia, out of the channel, and beyond sight of buoys or recognizable landmarks. So now we would have to feel our way eastward along the northern coastline like half-blind men.

Ahead a large shallow bay opened up. We followed a powerboat into it. Cottages lined the shore. Smoke rose near one house where a man tended a rubbish fire. We edged nearer the wisps of smoke and, when we were close enough, we hallooed for directions. The man feeding the burn barrel pointed to an island further east. We swung round and made for it, but a few minutes later he overtook us in his outboard and offered useful details about rounding the island and where to pick up the buoys.

Within an hour we entered Orillia. Early evening had set in by then. The marina was busy with boats and activities supporting a major powerboat show the next day. Nevertheless, we managed to secure a berth on the agreement that we would leave early in the morning. We were told that every berth for the upcoming weekend had been reserved for the big event.

The set-up already was well under way. Along the pier, thick black cables snaked around the media trucks; vendors with rolled-up sleeves assembled booths and positioned tidy stacks of promotional material; public-relations and sales men huddled in groups and honed their spiels; big cruiser owners boasted the finer points of their fine vessels; and within and around this mix of commerce and trade drifted clusters of curious tourists, local gawkers, covetous spectators, yachting aficionados, and a dapple of idlers. An air of restrained yet hopeful excitement cemented these disparate groups with one exception. Me.

I felt apart from it all. Not alienated exactly, just out of place. My beautiful blue wooden sailboat rocked gently back and forth in the light evening breeze. It was the only sailboat in a field of flawless white plastic and gleaming stainless steel. It seemed like a violet, invisible beneath the flourish of roses and lilies in a sun-washed garden, and that made me strangely sad.

The passage between Orillia and Lock 42 encloses Lake Couchiching, a stretch of water about seven miles long. A highway swing bridge spans the stream. Past the bridge stretched twenty miles of lakes and bays, dozens of piney islands and narrow corridors of ragged channel, all of which led us into a small basin leading to Big Chute, a marine railway and the most extraordinary of all the locks we would encounter. We tied up to the stand-by wharf which stood on the opposing shore. Our view across the basin, however, gave no indication of what we should expect.

An hour later we caught our first glimpse of the machine, which would carry us down to the next water level in the Trent-Severn Waterway. Its superstructure slowly crested the summit next to the lock headquarters. It was an odd-looking rig. It resembled a building in the early stages of construction: a rectangular base, open at both ends, and two side walls formed by half a dozen vertical and evenly spaced steel girders. The entire structure moved quietly on wheels over a rail bed. It continued its gentle descent toward the water, dipped into it, and submerged sufficiently for its cargo of half a dozen powerboats to regain their buoyancy, restart their engines, and float away.

As soon as it emptied, a loudspeaker broadcast directions to those of us waiting at the stand-by wharf. Our sailboat was called first. We manoeuvred toward the mouth of the railway car. A small framework clung to the outward edge of several steel uprights. This was the "wheelhouse," from which railway officials called out to us and gave instructions. They enquired about the nature of our keel and then directed us forward and over a spot where two heavy webbed straps lay below the water surface. When we were correctly positioned, the straps hydraulically raised and grew taut around the hull so that the *Arja D.* rested in a cradle.

After the remaining boats loaded in a similar fashion, the railway car began to move, propelled by a cable, like a carnival roller coaster or a ski lift. As the car rose from its submerged position onto land, the water within it drained out, and the boats aboard grounded on the machine's planked floor.

Not until the rail car hove alongside the lock building did I see the ravine into which we would descend, a steep fifty-seven-foot drop into the waterway below. A 60 percent grade, I would guess. Strands of terror crept up my back. My hands clenched both the cockpit coaming and seat as I awaited the inevitable tipping of the rail car, nose down like a plane in a power dive. I could imagine the cable parting, like an elevator scene in countless movies. I could imagine the straps, which held my boat in place like seatbelts, loosening and the *Arja D.* sliding forward off the car and hurtling into the bay below.

But none of that occurred. The rail car didn't tip as I had dreaded. The contraption remained perfectly level, and I was left in momentary bewilderment until I realized that the wheels of the machine ran on two separate sets of tracks. The set on which the front wheels of the vehicle moved was elevated higher than the set on which the rear wheels ran. The railway car descended into the gully as smoothly and evenly as each stair on an escalator.

PORT SEVERN, ON

At the bottom lay Port Severn and the last lock on the Trent-Severn Waterway and, after six days, we reached that milestone and passed through. We spent the night against the wall below the lock with two other vessels. Once again I went searching for charts, this time for Georgian Bay, the body of water we would reach tomorrow. The lockmaster mentioned a marina on the other side of the lock dam. They may have something, he suggested. So I set out for it.

The day was mellowing. Its pulse was fading into an ambient stillness. A soft murmur of Asians bearing fishing poles passed me on the bridge over the lock. Ahead the path became a road. A grocery store and restaurant on the right. The marina on the left. Bush Boat Livery was the name of the marina.

It was a business in the last throes of decay. A framework of slots for berthing or storing vessels was empty. The arms of mooring posts stretched out, withered by sun, blanched by weather, and bent with age. A footpath beat through a tangle of weeds that beset the place. Nearer the two-storey building that was the office and storehouse, the weeds gave way to a truck-worn, earthen swath that served as a parking lot. Puddles of rainwater pointed to the unevenness of that patch of dirt, and muddy boot prints led to the door of the one-time showroom. The door was locked. I knocked and rang the bell.

There was a holler from the second-storey window. The voice asked what I wanted. I said charts. The voice replied that it would be right down. Rich, or perhaps Reg, was his name, opened the door and invited me into the dismal showroom. Rich had inherited the place from his father. He apologized for its unseemly condition. A long ell-shaped glass display case stood near the door. Bins and cabinets filled the rest of the room. Lighting was poor. A dinginess hung about every corner. Stock had not been replaced or updated in decades. Parts of disassembled boat engines were scattered about or piled into corners.

Rich was helpful, though, and from him I was able to secure several strip maps tracing the eastern passage of Georgian Bay and a water-stained large-scale map of the region, each of them fifteen years old. We agreed upon a price of fourteen dollars for all three charts. Then I returned to the boat and mulled over them. When I emerged from the cabin an hour later, the evening sky was clear, black as ebony, and brilliant with stars.

Chapter 16

TECHNICOLOR TRAILS

Georgian Bay is 170 miles long, almost the size of Lake Ontario, and the largest bay in Lake Huron. It is separated from Lake Huron by the Bruce Peninsula and a group of islands which run northerly along the bay's western reaches.

We emerged from Port Severn at the southeast end of the bay. The eastern shore there is rugged. Glaciers had clawed and scoured this land to its bedrock. Sparse soils accumulated over succeeding millennia, but even now only pine forests and hardy wildlife thrive, amidst a rough-hewn beauty, both wonderful and daunting. A mid-twentieth-century Canadian art movement, called the Group of Seven, discovered in the landscape of this region an element of the national character—a region stripped of lushness and tempered with resilience, a place broken by the elements and renewed with hungry resolve, a land whose Puritan rigor severs need from desire and divides life's essentials from its excesses.

MIDLAND, ON

Yet one excess abounds along this bay. Islands. Countless islands. As many as thirty thousand lay in a thick spattering along the entire eastern shore. And perhaps twenty thousand of these are just lurking knobs of rock lapping the surface, wonderfully picturesque, but hazardous, and for that reason I planned to sail west to Midland, Ontario, and then northwest toward Manitoulin Island, rather than cruise the eastern coast.

We took the Tug Channel out of Port Severn, and passed through the Sawdust Islands. Green Island, and the swarm of islets, rocks, and shoals which surrounded it, fell along our starboard side. Then we struck an open two-mile patch of water before we entered the Middle Ground Shoal. Here the channel was tight and tortuous. But after we cleared Sturgeon Point the water grew deep, the seaway became clear, and Midland hove into view.

The town of Midland is tucked deep within Midland Bay. It held three marinas. One of them was a half mile past Midland. It was the largest and capable of stepping the mast which had been cradled above my deck. The fuel dock was just inside the entrance to the marina. We pulled in, filled our tank, and enquired where the lift boom was located. Then we wound our way through a neighbourhood of several hundred boats until we reached an inner wall and tied up next to the crane.

The marina's main building stood near the crane. It was broad, two storeys high, and loomed over the waterfront. In addition to the usual amenities found in a commercial, upscale marina like this one, there was also a large boat-parts and service area that doubled as the office, and this is where I asked about lifting the mast.

"Just let us know when you're ready to have it raised," said the clerk, "and someone will come out and operate the winch."

"I've operated winches before. There's no need," I replied.

"No," he said, "one of our operators has to do it. No one else is allowed."

"All right, then," I replied. " What do you charge for stepping the mast?"

He examined a listing behind the counter and said, "That will be one fifty-five."

"I mean what's the price for just the lift and drop. I do all the rigging myself."

"One fifty-five," he repeated.

I left the office somewhat stunned at the quote. At home in Beach Point, the fishermen's wharf is equipped with a small, do-it-yourself derrick and, with the help of one other person, stepping the mast takes ten to fifteen minutes.

One fifty-five rattled around in my head as Bob and I rove the main and jib halyards and the topping lift rope through the respective sheaves of the mast. Frank Murphy, prepping his nearby sailboat for a family outing, came over to help position the *Arja D.* below the crane. Murph was a local business owner, an ex-navy man, and reportedly the best sailor in Lake Simcoe. He has sailed competitively in the big annual race on Lake Michigan from Chicago to the Mackinac Bridge at the head of Lake Huron.

One fifty-five was still rattling around in my head when I returned to the service desk to arrange for someone to operate the crane. Somehow I couldn't reconcile fifteen minute's work on that machine as worth one fifty-five. Perhaps there was some misunderstanding that I hadn't perceived. So I pressed a clerk on the issue.

"Can you explain to me why it costs one fifty-five to lift the mast? That seems high to me."

He walked away, consulted with a grey-haired manager, and returned.

"Insurance," he said. "Liability insurance."

"That's odd," I said. "When I had the mast unstepped in Belleville, the marina only charged forty dollars. Sounds to me like you've got the wrong insurance company."

The clerk shrugged and said that an employee would be along shortly to operate the crane. We waited, but no one came. We waited some more. We lazed about at a picnic table next to the crane, while the grey-haired manager passed by. Still no one arrived to help.

Murph had finished stocking his boat for the family sail and strolled over to see how we were doing. I mentioned the delay in getting the crane operator.

"There's no excuse for that," he said. "I'll do it. I've done it enough times in the past here, and I have as much experience as any of them." With that said, the mast was up and in place within minutes.

I settled my account for the one fifty-five without further comment, even though it had been entirely a do-it-yourself enterprise. Then Bob and I turned our attention to rigging. We were only about a half hour into that task when the grey-haired manager stopped in front of us.

"You'll have to move your boat. There's another coming in to use the crane."

"We haven't finished the rigging, but we'll be done here in another half hour."

"You'll have to do it now. They radioed that they're coming right in."

Murph's boat was in a double slip. The other berth was empty. So pointing toward it, I said, "We'll slide her in there until we finish rigging."

"That berth is rented to someone. They might come back."

It was then that Murph piped in, "They're gone for the weekend."

"That doesn't matter," said the grey-haired manager, and he walked away.

Murph bristled. "Pull your boat alongside mine and tie her on. I rent a full half of this berth, and there's room for both of us on my half. So long as you're tied onto me, there's not a damn thing he can do about it." By the time Murph had cracked open an ice chest and passed a couple of beers over the cockpit to us, his voice had lost most of the petulance that had crept into it. "Stay as long as you like," he added.

Two hours passed. They were relaxed hours: a bit of conversation, a bit of work, and at the end of it, the rigging was complete: stays taut, boom shipped, sails bent onto the spar, and sheets coiled. It did not escape our notice that no boat had arrived to use the crane that afternoon.

When we were ready to cast off, we did so. I had no wish to remain.

The municipal marina was ten minutes away. That marina lay in the heart of the business district of Midland. The breakwater was broad enough to hold its office and related facilities, benches, several walkways, and covered picnic areas. On the shore side was a larger park area, backed by downtown restaurants and shops. What most caught the eye, though, was a waterfront industrial complex, perhaps a granary, whose silo-like structures were brightly painted with enormous murals depicting the history of the Hurons and missionaries and the earliest settlers in the region. Many other walls in the town also had become canvas for historic paintings.

Next morning began almost as the evening before had ended—at Uncle Roy's Chinese restaurant—this time for breakfast. Later I took a long walk uptown and uphill to St. Margaret's Church for Sunday services. One would expect that such a beginning would set the day's pattern as one of rest and relaxation but, little by little, this Sunday slipped into a drudgery of necessary chores. I topped up the water tank, scrubbed the deck and the companionway, and checked oil in the engine. As the sun grew warmer, I sought refuge under a covered rest area on the breakwater. On a large picnic table I spread out charts and pencilled a series of courses up Georgian Bay.

Nearby, a Canadian Coast Guard ship stood just outside the breakwater wall. At the foot of the gangway stood one of the ship's officers and a young woman. Bob had wandered over to look at the vessel. As he passed alongside, he overheard part of a conversation between the two who were standing there. It dealt with a crew member who had become quite shaken after a recent search and rescue mission. Three boys had gone missing after their boat capsized. The search had lasted days. In the end, the boys were found, each of them dead, floating in the northern part of the bay. They had worn life jackets, drifted a considerable distance from their boat, and probably died from hypothermia. Her husband had helped pull the bodies from the water. It had been a grisly task, and it had troubled him.

Bob called it *oh-dark-thirty*. I called it *too damned early*. The illuminated dial of my wristwatch read 0400. It was black outside, not yet a glimmer of dawn. I got up and showered. Afterward, Bob and I went to an all-night Tim Hortons coffee shop for breakfast. I filled my Thermos, and we left the wharf at 0530.

HAY ISLAND

The first leg of our course took us north-northwest. Beausoleil Island, part of Georgian Bay Islands National Park, lay to starboard, and Sawlog Bay passed on our port side. Then we turned northwest. Giants Tomb Island, sarcophagus-shaped in profile, rose bluntly out of the water. Beckwith Island. Hope Island. Then open water, deep water, for thirty-five miles. For four hours we were out of sight of land. But it was a fine day to be sailing: sun, a light southwest breeze, and calm seas.

We anchored off Hay Island at the northern approaches to Colpoys Bay. At the head of that bay is Wiarton, Ontario, the burrow of Wiarton Willie, the groundhog that forecasts Canada's spring weather.

The bottom surrounding Hay Island was stony and clear, and the water shoaled gradually. So we were able to set our anchor within a hundred yards of shore. Hay Island is a low island, less than two hundred feet above the water, and two and a half miles long. It is wooded to the shore, and its beaches are heavy gravel and stone. It was a quiet and comfortable anchorage and the surrounding water was placid enough to break out the cook stove on deck and make a hot meal: bratwurst, fried onions, and beef vegetable soup. Bob fished unsuccessfully that evening. I read and listened to the radio until the gentle sway of the boat and the soft lap of the water against the boards led me into a restful sleep.

We hauled anchor and resumed our course up the east end of the Bruce Peninsula. A 15-knot southerly breeze followed us, and we took that opportunity to raise sail. Two hours later we rounded Cape Croker. The wind freshened. We reefed sail. The sea kicked up three-foot waves. There was heavy spray and, as our course shifted more northwest, the wind veered northwest as well, so much so that sailing became untenable. Consequently, we doused the sails and fired up the diesel.

We cruised outside of Barrier Island with our nose pointed toward Lion's Head. Lion's Head is a formidable outcropping halfway up the Bruce Peninsula. It protrudes in a box-like fashion, two miles square, into the bay. Although not much higher than Hay Island, the face it presents is more dramatic, for it rises one hundred feet sharply from an incline of rubble, boulder, and rock, rising out of the water. A band of conifer took root in this detritus and hid its meagre hold on life under a swath of green the length of the cape. Out of the grey rock and green band of spruce rose a sheer, craggy cliff, another hundred feet higher, where it flattened into a desolate, unassailable plateau. Lion's Head was a striking landform and, as we skimmed along its base, we studied it with both wonder and caution.

In a crook formed at the base of the Head there is a small cove. We put into the marina there to refuel and walked into the village to stretch our legs and gather fresh food. Then, after an hour, we set out again.

WINGFIELD BASIN

Our next stop would be an anchorage at Wingfield Basin, sixteen miles distant, on the northern extremity of Bruce Peninsula. Here, the end of that peninsula splays out like the head of a well-hammered cold chisel. The west end includes the town and port of Tobermory, Ontario; the eastern end, devoid of villages or marinas, has only Wingfield Basin for cover.

As it happened, we would need the protection of Wingfield Basin, almost immediately, for rounding Cabot Head on the Bruce Peninsula was like rounding a corner on a city block and coming upon some repulsive and alarming sight: two drunken men lurching at each other with bloody knives, or an incensed mob spilling out with flailing arms and curses spat out in our direction. But for us the danger and the dread issued from natural, not human, sources.

The northwest horizon had been obscured for some time by the cape, but now we saw a sky more menacing than anything we had seen thus far. A thick, low gathering of black and purple cloud had massed on the lands north of Georgian Bay; it was tinged with slate grey and murky green; and it was moving swiftly. Soon it rolled over all the northern terrains and blotted them out like a black avalanche. Against the dark wall of cloud, lightning ignited and broke into glowing splinters which radiated in aberrant patterns.

The lightning was more than occasional, more than frequent; it was continuous and manifold; not a sector of the sky was without illumination, and each flash transformed black to momentary purple and reverberated with the rumble of a rolling barrage in a military engagement. It was a frightening spectacle for a yachtsman, and the only thought which preoccupied my mind was whether or not we could make the tiny cove at Wingfield Basin before the storm struck.

The basin was just a mile away, but the storm was nearly upon us. Already it had engulfed much of Manitoulin Island; and it had swept over half of the open water north of us. The leading edge of the blow was clearly visible: a thin, white wisp, semi-detached from the great dark mass, like a vaporous tongue lapping unquenchably at the recoiling waves.

We blew through the two lips of sand that formed the tiny mouth into Wingfield Basin with less caution than usual. Already ten other sailboats and power craft cowered there. The cove was a small oval shape, not more than a quarter mile in length, and the vessels that swung at anchor, nearly filled the navigational portion of the cove. The choicest spots had been taken but, as the wind stiffened, we found a tolerable piece of water and dropped anchor. To our dismay, the anchor didn't dig in, and we began to drift toward a marsh. While I manoeuvred away from shoals and other vessels, Bob hastily hauled up the anchor line. The anchor flukes had fouled in thick vegetation from the seabed. Bob hurriedly cleaned them off. I swung the tiller for a pass at an alternate location. With eleven feet of water beneath us, I signalled to Bob. He let the anchor and chain slip through his fingers and payed out seventy-five feet of rope. It caught, and it held. Then the sky broke open with torrents of rain and driving winds. We skittered below and closed the hatch and, as I peered through a cabin porthole, another sailboat entered the basin.

The storm was tumultuous, but not long-lived, and the little cove in which we laboured at our mooring was a secure one. As the remnants of light faded, the storm dissipated. Some light showers chased the tail of the thunderstorm but, as evening deepened, the sky cleared. The night became exceedingly pleasant. The semi-luminous shadow of a new moon passed through a sea of stars above. They reflected themselves in the placid waters below, and then blended with dancing anchor lights, the glimmer from other cabin windows, the murmur of quiet conversations, and fragrances of brandy and wine.

The small collection of boats around me seemed strangely quiet and vacant, and the sound of my engine became an offensive breach of the stillness when we departed at 0615. Beyond the cove the water was unsettled, and the sky was ambiguous. I steamed north for a while, testing the water, testing the weather, and testing my resolve to continue on to Killarney, my destination on the north shore of Georgian Bay, fifty miles away. With little cover between here and there, I sought some surety for a safe voyage, at the same time fully realizing that surety at sea is merely a convenient self-deception. Still, in this odd way, duplicity becomes an engine to venture onward.

Clarity came soon enough, however. As the sky dulled, the sun disappeared like a wary cat. Ahead, a mass of variantly grey cloud, low and dense, grew over the rim of horizon. A thin line at first. Then a hump of headless shoulders muscling up out of a restless sleep and catching the scent of day. Neither Bob nor I caught any subtlety in this forerunner. It looked ominous and potentially as dangerous as its weather cousin yesterday. So I swung the tiller and returned to Wingfield Basin.

We had more leisure to search about for a good anchorage this morning than we had the previous evening, and we found a secure corner. It was close to the north end of the cove where the rise of land and trees offered a better windbreak and less exposure to waves. An hour later the front reached us. Strong wind gusted, and rain drove down hard. Clouds scudded across the basin, so low that their mist enveloped the middle bluff southwest of our anchorage. In the face of this, I went below and took a turn in my bunk. I had a good sleep, woke to more showers and wind, slept again, and rose finally at 1100 to the sound of an engine. One or two boats were moving out as the front cleared, it seemed. I flicked on the marine radio for a weather update. It was not favourable. Thunderstorms were forecast. A small craft advisory had been posted. I might risk leaving for a short jump to another port, but to head north, as we had planned, was not something I'd chance, and all of this brought to mind the three teens who lost their lives a short time before. They too had ducked into Wingfield Basin to avoid nasty weather, but sailed away before a system had fully passed.

By early afternoon the sky had cleared. The wind was still up, and there was a bit of sea running, but inside the basin it was quite pleasant. The bow of *Arja D.* nosed up toward the northwest as it bobbed on its mooring line. It also faced the only visible structure ashore, an old stone house or cottage set back among the conifers. In the water west of it lay the partially sunken hulk of *Gargantua*, a cargo schooner which had been converted to a steam tug. Its deck had rotted; its ribs stood bare through gaping holes in the wood hull; iron plates and bulwarks corroded with rust. It remained the only visible wreck of several others which had died in the basin over the past hundred years.

Staring at the stone edifice and the grounded boat aroused my curiosity and sparked a desire to explore the shores of Wingfield Basin. So I broke out the inflatable raft, blew it up, and Bob and I rowed the short distance to the western shore. The forest floor was soft underfoot; the air was rich with the scent of cedar and pine and birch. It was only a short hike before the woodland was broken by a lane. We followed it until we neared the stone house. At an outbuilding close to it, an elderly man split blocks of hardwood. His axe rang dully in the summer air, and he was too busy at his task to notice us until we were upon him.

He and his wife were a retired couple, but this was not his cottage, he told us. It was a bird-banding station for the Cabot Head

Provincial Nature Reserve. Once a private hunting lodge, the buildings and land now are owned by Ontario Parks, and they are a favoured location for bird watchers, naturalists, and scientists. The couple on site were volunteer caretakers of the station. We chatted for a short time; they took us through the lodge, restored and remodelled from its earliest uses. The side, which faced my boat, was open and airy with much glass. Heavy wood beams girded the ceiling, and softwood planks formed the interior walls.

Morning darkness cloaked the basin, not yet a hint of gloaming. Somewhere beyond the veil of night, the wind loosed a battery of deep-throated moans that lifted the sea and dashed it onto the shores of Georgian Bay. The sound of that unseen display of power was dismaying.

I had risen with the hope of making an early getaway to Killarney. That would not be possible now. So I waited until there was enough light to make out sea conditions visually. With binoculars and standing on the cabin sole, I fixed my sight on the waves beyond the low entrance to the cove. The sea was running high. The wind had not eased.

The weather forecast, however, was more positive than our present reality and suggested that conditions would improve. Winds would shift from northwest to northeast, and they would diminish to between 10 and 15 knots. That was encouraging. So we waited.

By 0930 the wind had slackened, and I had a mind to leave. We weighed anchor, and I swung the boat about, motored down the cove, and lined up the entrance to the bay. Seas were running high. Waves were spilling into the gut with a force that flooded over the lips of sand and stone on each side. I put the throttle down hard and drove toward the mouth of the cove. I didn't want to lose way against the force of breakers pressing in against us. The *Arja D.* slowed a bit as it crashed into the waves, but it was a heavy boat and had momentum enough to lift itself over the hill of water and muscle ahead, through, and out into Georgian Bay.

Outside, conditions were poor. The spray was heavy. The sea was running in confusion. Waves up to six feet surged out of the northwest. Then, suddenly, two or three rollers would rush us from the northeast quarter and nearly lay us down. I found something of a pattern in the madness and, by keeping a sharp eye several waves ahead of those which were upon us, I learned to anticipate the rogues and swing the bow to better engage them. Steering in this fashion was tiring, though, and it lasted for nearly four hours. Fortunately, I was able to maintain a good heading for Killarney, and by the time we cleared Lonely Island, the waves had moderated. Two hours later they dwindled almost to nothing, glassy ripples and shallow rollers.

The craggy north shore of Georgian Bay loomed by mid-afternoon. Then the lighthouse on Red Rock Point hove into view. Killarney lay west, along a corridor formed by George Island nuzzling the mainland. The passage was short and narrow. Land rose sharply, exposing slabs of rock, red and yellow limestone, and swaths of white silica. We found a berth at Gateway Marina in Killarney, a village of 280 residents.

"Our grains of sand weigh two tons," laughed the manager of the marina in his commentary on local boating hazards, "and our mud is solid," he added. Our conversation turned to weather, and I talked of the storm which kept us in Wingfield Basin for two days.

"Killarney suffered badly in that blow," he said. "That same thunderstorm spawned a tornado. The funnel touched down... destroyed some barns in the area...then lightning struck a tent in a campsite. It killed a visiting Ukrainian professor...missed his two sons. They were left without a parent...in a strange country and all. Sad. But you can get a meal at the restaurant in the building behind us, and there's a phone booth outside," he finished. Afterwards we made a quick tour of the village.

The grey morning mist condensed on my face and dampened my hair as I clambered over the planks of the floating wharf toward the low-slung marina office and purchased a chart of the North

Channel. Afterwards, I returned to the boat, repaired a VHF connector, and replaced the light bulb over the chart table.

A steady, heavy rain accompanied our departure from Killarney, and it showered or drizzled for most of our twenty-two-mile sail to Little Current. Visibility was poor, and the dreary veil of weather we slipped through reduced the pretty islands in the Lansdowne Channel to mere contours, bled of colour and dulled in texture.

Over the morning I grew increasingly wet and cold and found that my rain gear leaked. Eventually, my clothing clung; my skin recoiled at the touch of clammy sweat; and a cool, dank, northerly flow chilled me. A general discomfort numbed any wish to move, any desire to think, or any urge to engage in human discourse. And I sensed that Bob felt the same. So conversation fell to a trickle, and then vanished as each of us sank into a self-absorbed solitude. For several hours I huddled in my damp burrow of oil clothes, hand on tiller, and gazed woodenly through the droplets of water tumbling from the brim of my sou'wester, while a vague, grey, disinterested world looked back.

LITTLE CURRENT, ON

Part of that world, Manitoulin Island, had been at the visible rim of our nautical world for several days now and would be for several more. It's the largest island of an archipelago which forms the western barrier of Georgian Bay and the North Channel which straddles the US-Canada border, and at eighty-one miles long, Manitoulin Island is also the largest freshwater island in the world. After four and a half hours, we arrived at Little Current on Manitoulin Island.

The waterfront at Little Current extends the length of the town and consists of one long continuous wharf busy with boats. The wall of a brick municipal building screens out the main street which runs parallel to the waterfront. A pretty, wooded park area next to it stretches for a lengthy distance down shore. A walkway rambles among its scattered benches and shade trees and past a marble monument to the island's war veterans. Restaurants and cafes, pharmacies and gift shops, craft stores, and miscellaneous offices line main street, and each of them is housed neatly in series of conjoined, two-storey, wooden buildings with flat roofs.

By mid-afternoon, the rain had stopped and the ceiling of cloud lifted and, as it did, so did our spirits, and so did our appetites. The Anchor Inn Bar and Grill was on the corner nearest our boat. We stopped there for a late lunch of whitefish.

Later that evening Bob and I returned to the Anchor Inn. There was a tavern upstairs. It had a dark cast to it. Light flickered from a TV screen above the mirror behind the bar. Three or four sat on stools and nursed draft beers. In another corner two couples leaned over tables toward one another in intimate conversation. The volume of talk at the bar fell off when we entered but returned to its previous level after we moved to the pool table at the back.

A woman brought our beers a few minutes later. She was part of the large Indigenous population on the island, made up of Ojibwa, Ottawa, and Potawatomi tribes. Manitoulin Island was unique among Canadian aboriginals because its land had never been ceded by treaty to the Crown.

Bob and I dominated the table for an hour or so. Part way through one game a hand slipped out of the surrounding darkness and placed coins on the ledge of the table, a challenge to the winner of our game. As usual, Bob won. He beat his challenger, Chancy, as well as a subsequent challenger, Aaron. Then Bob, worn-out after a long day, returned to the boat and left me to continue the match.

Both Chancy and Aaron were Ojibwa. Aaron was younger than Chancy. Perhaps twenty. More grounded. Pleasant. Strong, slender build. A construction worker, he said. He had a manner which put me at ease, and he spoke freely about himself and his island home.

Chancy was the bigger of the two, standing about six-foot-two. He was rugged, strongly built, and dressed only in black. He didn't walk. He swaggered. And he did so in a manner which devoured more of the room than anyone in the tavern. His temperament was spirited, almost unnaturally so, like a bad actor's; and sometimes his attention faded to a faraway space. A jukebox cranked out a string of country tunes and rock songs. Chancy sank a ball, missed another. He stood erect, raised his head toward the ceiling as if to address God.

"I love that song," he said. "I love it." He spoke with an uncharacteristic ardour and piety that was disturbing. All the while, the eerie, plaintive whine of Jim Morrison singing "People Are Strange" pumped out of the speakers. Chancy's eyes grew distant. He fed more money into the jukebox between games and brought back a fresh beer.

Chancy's demeanour had made me somewhat guarded. Both alcohol and pool can unchain the most unpleasant human responses. Tonight he was on the losing end of several pool games, and on the upward spiral of a drunken high, and I wondered whether the descent would send him reeling into meanness or a smiling placidity, paranoia or drowsiness, cruelty or stupor.

I would never know the answer. Chancy lost two of the three games we played and, then, suddenly he vanished on some errand of the night.

MELDRUM BAY

We made Meldrum Bay late in the day, nearly 1900, some fifty-four miles behind us. It was a three-mile run into the small marina. Its breakwater had been fashioned out of a string of large, filled, metal containers, sunk just off the entry to the wharves, and fixed there by anchors. All the containers were canted, having been pressed upon by ice floes driven by fierce, northerly, winter winds.

We enjoyed two visitors while we ate dinner in the cockpit. The first was a newlywed couple from Michigan who wanted a picture of our boat. The second was skipper of a 36-foot Beneteau sailboat nearby. He had been a naval officer aboard a Canadian destroyer, but his thick glasses very much reminded me of the near-blind cartoon character, Mr. Magoo, and, sadly, that was all I could focus on as he kindly showed us his charts and the approaches to Drummond, the US Customs checkpoint we would clear tomorrow.

The village of Drummond is situated on the northwest side of Drummond Island, two islands west of here. It forms part of the North Channel, and it is US territory, part of upper Michigan. In spite of the fact that Drummond Island appears on my Canadian chart, that portion of the chart which shows American waters contained no hydrographic data—no water depths, no indication of navigable channels, no record of shoals or rocks, nothing. As the evening progressed, I learned that I could only get the information I needed from another chart, an American one, and it could not be purchased locally. So I was forced to take what bearings and notes I could from the generous Mr. Magoo and hope that they would be accurate enough and that the weather would remain kind enough for me to require nothing more.

If I did need anything more than verbal directions, it could not be got at Meldrum Bay, for Meldrum Bay is neither town nor village, neither hamlet nor community. Its one road in and one road out deny qualification even as a crossroads. Only a few accommodations and conveniences attached themselves to the place. One, of course, is the marina. It contains a dozen boat slips and an office. Its nearest toilet facilities are a pair of outhouses next to a couple of rustic cottages, a stone's throw from the office. A hundred yards north is Meldrum Bay Inn, a stately place, built at the turn of the twentieth century, and stopping place for salmon fishers, tourists, and boaters weary of their own bunks. Across the road from the inn is a collection of tents and camping trailers. At the campground a cement block building holds a shower and bathroom for campers and boaters staying at the marina.

It was well after dark when the narrow beam of my flashlight led me to that shower room. In the deep shadows beyond, a campfire here, a campfire there. Each blaze flared and quivered; and each pulse of flame illuminated a different set of faces in a circle around it. Several guitars plunked out old folk ballads and popular country tunes. A harmonica. A banjo. Children chased one another and laughed in taunting rhythms. And voices sang out half-remembered lyrics to near-forgotten songs. Melody and mirth drifted further in the night air and even reverberated pleasantly within the concrete confines of the shower room. By the time I finished my shower and left the building, however, the gathering had lost momentum. Guitar players were less strident and the interim between their songs more empty; childish laughter had flattened to a few simpers and whines; and the voices of the choristers had grown thin and isolated and discordant. Small groups were moving to their tents and trailers, and they were bedding down.

For many at the campground, sport fishing was the great thrill of their vacation and, as they readied themselves for an early start, they undoubtedly envisioned a day charged with sport, challenge, camaraderie, and success. Perhaps they would even dream... dream of the snap of nylon line...the spastic flex of fibrous rod...a leaden tug...a shower of spray...a flash of silver green...thumping sounds...shimmering shapes...shouts and shuffling feet... fumbling hands...and fevered grins. Perhaps I would dream with them...dream of the snap of jib...the flutter of sail...the shriek of ratchets on hauled sheets...the unknown well-met...and three thousand miles by the boards.

DRUMMOND, MI

After we climbed out of Meldrum Bay, we headed for Drummond Island in US waters. The wharf at Drummond was not large, but bustled with activity. Tourists with children tugging at their arms gawked and pointed. Transient boaters busied themselves moving vessels, adjusting lines, loading supplies, filling water tanks, or fuelling up. Some seasonal, semi-permanent boaters were tanning on their decks, lounging in chairs, nibbling on sandwiches, nursing barbeques or sipping beer. Little of the village of Drummond was visible, the wharf being surrounded by a number of outbuildings, small warehouses, and a marina office which doubled as a customs clearing house, gift shop, and marine supply centre.

Inside, I purchased an American chart which would lead us through upper Lake Huron as far as the Straits of Mackinac, the entry to Lake Michigan. The woman behind the counter was tall and sturdy and had an air of ownership about the place, as she juggled half a dozen customers. I enquired about customs clearance, and she passed me a form, asked me to fill it out and produce a passport or other photo identification. I occupied a space at the counter and began to pencil in the information, but I found it hard to concentrate. My mind buzzed with the busyness around me: the clutter of people, the clamour of voices. I took what seemed an extraordinary amount of time to complete the page.

A self-assured voice at the end of the counter caught the woman's attention. "Give this to the boys on the dock. They were very helpful," he said and passed her a ten-dollar bill.

I pushed my information sheet and passport toward her. She examined it, confirmed that I was the person in the photo, and said, "Welcome to the United States."

Is that it? I wondered. I had assumed that she would pass my information on to some uniformed customs officer who would run me through a battery of questions, and search the boat for illegal booze or drugs or explosives. After all, this was the post-9/11 expectation, wasn't it?

"My boat's at the wharf out front. Doesn't anyone want to look at it?" I asked. I can't recall whether there was more surprise or disappointment in my voice.

"No need," she said cheerily. "The customs agent is busy right now. But you're okay to go. Have a nice day."

Bob and I walked outside. I squinted. The sun was bright. We grabbed a couple bottles of pop from the vending machine outside the door and wandered up the wharf to stretch our legs before we set out again. The customs agent strode toward us from the opposite way. His badge glinted. He stared at us with professional interest. Then he smiled and waved and continued by. Ten minutes later we were aboard and on our way.

It's four miles from Drummond village across Sturgeon Bay to the end of Drummond Island. Beyond that point is the De Tour Passage, the main water link between Lake Huron and Lake

Superior. We were less than two miles out when we spied an outboard motorboat gaining on us from astern. It slowed as it came alongside and signalled. There was a man and a woman aboard. I recognized the man as the ten-dollar tipper from the marina. He hollered again, and we drifted to a stop.

"Your card?" he said, waving something in his hand. He was difficult to make out above the sounds of the engines. The woman's higher pitch carried farther.

"Did you leave your credit card?" she asked. She passed a plastic card to me over the washboard, and yes, it was mine. I had left it on the counter at the marina office after I bought the chart. I thanked them. They smiled, waved, and sped back to Drummond.

The weather remained fair all morning, and the afternoon promised the same. We turned south into the De Tour Passage. Three or four freighters navigated through the mile-wide channel. Drummond Island lay to port; mainland upper Michigan lay to starboard. Ahead was Lake Huron. Behind, the De Tour Passage turned into the St. Mary's River, and forty or fifty miles up the river Sault St. Marie stood at the entrance to Lake Superior.

DE TOUR VILLAGE, MI

The village of De Tour was the end of this day's travels. The marina was well-constructed and new. Slip fees were reasonable. The village was pretty, and we arrived early enough to call home, enjoy a good meal at a restaurant, and shoot pool in the adjacent bar room. The decor there leaned heavily toward themes of patriotism and the military, not unlike any Legion hall. But this wasn't a Legion hall. The plaques and pictures, posters and flags, pennants and memorabilia reflected a bit of the history of the man behind the bar. He had served with the 101st Airborne, the Ranger Battalion. Now he worked in the effort to find and return those soldiers still listed as missing in action during the Vietnam War.

Back in my boat, I lay on my bunk on the verge of sleep. Then I heard voices.

"They're from Prince Edward Island in Canada. Can you imagine that!"

The pair of voices passed through the night and by my boat like a slow bird in flight. The unrhythmic clack of their footsteps on the wooden planks faded. And then it was morning.

Three miles down the De Tour Passage, we entered Lake Huron. To starboard stood the De Tour Reef Light, four storeys high on its square concrete island a mile off the point. A covey of fishing boats had gathered in the mix of waters further out. We bent west, open water to port. Upper Michigan lay to starboard and, from that shore, chains of islands reach out into the lake like the detached finger bones of a fleshless hand.

We took a bearing on Mackinac Island and followed the freighter route toward the head of Lake Huron. We encountered little traffic on our crossing but, as we closed on Mackinac Island, water traffic abounded. We sighted several freighters, numerous powerboats, a handful of sailboats, and several high-speed ferries which sent up plumes of water as they carried boatloads of passengers to Mackinac Island.

The number of ferries that ran from Mackinaw City to Mackinac Island proved that the island still was a popular destination. During the Victorian era it had gained renown as a summer retreat, and since then it has maintained a Victorian flavour in architecture and transportation. An old fortress and a governor's mansion were clearly visible from our vantage point, and still the only vehicles used by visitors and the island's five hundred permanent residents are bicycles and horse-drawn carriages. Cars, buses, and motorcycles are prohibited.

MACKINAW CITY, MI

Ahead, the Mackinac Bridge spread out unobstructed before us. The bridge, a three-and-a-half-mile span completed in the 1950s, joins Michigan with its northern peninsula and it's the gateway to Lake Michigan. Because we had made such good time from De

Tour, I decided to make for Mackinaw City, a port on the south end of the Mackinac Bridge. The town bustled with tourists. Streets were crowded. Shops and restaurants were full.

After dinner we returned to the marina. A border patrolman, this one armed, moved methodically like a hound through each line of boats noting registration numbers and whatever other details might be telltale of an illegal entry or a contraband runner.

"Where are you from?" he asked. He was young, business-like, and deliberate.

"Prince Edward Island, Canada," I replied.

"How long have you been here?"

"Just a few hours...today."

"Have you cleared customs?"

"Yes."

"Where?"

"In Drummond," I said.

He nodded, hesitated, made a mental note, smiled slightly, and moved to another boat.

I returned to sorting the chart work for tomorrow's cruise, but conflicting currents of mood distracted me from my work. Something—emerging perhaps from my military days—gave me reassurance in seeing someone doing a job well, even a routine one. Yet something else wishes it needed not to be so...wishes that guardedness had not become routine...and that safety had not been garrisoned.

PART THREE

Chapter 17

TRIPPIN' THROUGH AMERICANA

"Are you going to leave without paying?!"

The words were shouted from the walkway above, and the man who shouted them struck a defiant pose behind the railing. He was middle-aged, contentious, and seemed smug as a shopkeeper nabbing a twelve-year-old thief.

"I paid yesterday," I said.

"There's no record of that. You can't go without paying!"

I went up the stairs to the office and produced my receipt for the berth. He was not convinced, and he continued thumbing through his registry. I pointed to the name of my boat on a page. It seems that a previous clerk had listed it by a different berth number than the one it was occupying.

"I paid. I'm leaving."

The duty clerk muttered, but he apologized for neither his rudeness nor his error.

We slipped under the Mackinac Bridge and felt the southwest wind freshen. The deep blue colour of Lake Michigan was a sharp contrast to Lake Huron's green, and its rich blue seas rose with the wind. On account of the course we sailed, waves beat on our starboard and sometimes close to our beam. Over a period of hours the constant drumming became an irritant.

CHARLEVOIX, MI

The deep blue stretched for endless miles in all directions, but the Gray Shoals were near. Our passage through them would take us south toward Charlevoix, Michigan. A lighthouse and breakwater guard the entrance to Charlevoix and, inside it, a river passage narrows and bends for a short distance.

Charlevoix seemed the prettiest of all the pretty towns I have seen. An extensive park runs the length of the harbour front. Main Street lies behind it and exhibits the usual restaurants and shops and bars, and several art galleries too. As we walked up from the marina, we heard music, and saw a crowd gathering on the grass which sloped toward an amphitheatre in the centre of the park. Some, especially the elderly, had brought chairs; most people just reclined on the lawn or a blanket. A community orchestra had assembled in the band shell. They opened their performance with the "Star Spangled Banner" and then filled the early evening air with traditional marches, popular classical pieces, and a nautical medley.

Bob and I stayed and listened for a half hour before we struck out to see more of the town. Further along Main Street we crossed the bridge under which we had passed an hour before. Several resort hotels crowded the riverfront on both sides of the bridge, which marked the end of the commercial district. A US Coast Guard ship was at its berth near the bridge and inside the basin which formed Charlevoix Harbour. At the east end of the basin was the bottleneck entry to Lake Charlevoix, the third-largest lake in Michigan.

At a bend in the road past the bridge, we turned down one of several avenues which intersected Main Street and entered a residential neighbourhood, which made me feel as though I had stepped into a different world, one that I remembered from many, many years ago. This was the place where likeable characters from '50s television shows like *Father Knows Best*, *The Adventures of Ozzie and Harriet*, or *The Life of Riley* would have lived. The avenue was broad and the sidewalk generous enough to allow several couples to pass one another comfortably side by side. Most of the homes were solid and almost stately, wood or stone single-family dwellings, built fifty to seventy-five years ago. All were well-kept; all had lush lawns and tended gardens and shrubs. And all maintained a respectable distance from both street and neighbour. Most had front porches, reminiscent of times when neighbour knew neighbour, and people would relax on their verandas in an evening and call out to passing friends or wave to acquaintances. Maples and oak trees rose high above the houses. Their trunks were too massive to lock one's arms around and their sinewy limbs interlocked one another in a canopy which stretched across the breadth of the street. Splotches of sunshine trickled through the foliage, and shadows fell in cool pools of darkness on the pavements and greenery beneath them.

The most striking feature of the place, however, was the quiet. Tranquility existed there, and it embraced the neighbourhood like a child in its mother's arms. One or two pedestrians passed on footsteps scarcely heard. One or two cars navigated the avenue with puttering engines muffled by murmuring trees. Birds seemed muted and distant; dogs seemed more content to whimper than bark. Voices seemed lulled into subdued tones. All sounds seemed hushed, deferential, respectful, slow to rouse, and more pleased to charm than to thrill.

At 0530 we topped up our water tank from a hose at the fuel dock. Several vessels already stood in the channel waiting for the 0600 lift of the bridge. Their running lights glowed red in the ebbing darkness, and in the middle of the basin another half-dozen boats rested at moorings. Their anchor lights scribed small white ovals with each gentle rock of a mast.

Once we cleared Charlevoix, I turned the helm over to Bob and went below to study the charts and fix some waypoints to our next destination, the town of Leland. Our opening course took us westerly across the mouth of Grand Traverse Bay. As we approached

Cat Head Point, at the bay's western extremity, I was amazed to see small dunes and sandy beaches, unusual features for a freshwater lake, I thought. But, as we rounded the point and headed south along the coast, these dunes became more expansive and sharply defined and, a few hours later, they reached wondrous proportions.

I am familiar with many of the beautiful beaches in Atlantic Canada, but these were especially striking. They had surprising depth, reaching miles back from the shore and making them seem more than just a deposit of sand from centuries of storm and wind grinding away at a sea coast. At times they looked like a series of great rolling mounds of sand. At other times they shaped themselves as towering bluffs, over four hundred feet high, with precipitous sandy faces dropping toward the water. Their colour varied from the yellow of bare sand to the light green of grasses knitting together the delicate soil. At higher elevations the green darkened with bush and stubby trees. And the wondrous spectacle of these dunes ran along the coastline for forty miles, at least.

FRANKFORT, MI

The town of Leland, our destination, had dropped behind us earlier in the day. We had been making such good time, a comfortable 6 knots with a following wind, that we pressed on to Frankfort at the southern end of the most spectacular of the dune formations. The sailboat *Cygnus* passed us on our final leg to Frankfort. It looked to be a 36-footer. It raised its main sail and motor-sailed out of sight. Point Betsie Lighthouse rose fifty feet above lake water and slipped past our port side.

Two long breakwaters jutting from the shore at Frankfort, drew together, and formed a large cup-shaped basin shielding access to the town. A small coast guard station stood by itself just inside the harbour and, further along the northern curve of shore, we spotted a marina. We pulled into the fuel dock. An attendant caught our bow and stern lines.

"How much is a berth here?" I asked while he topped up my fuel tanks.

"Forty dollars a night," he replied. This was more than I had spent at any marina in the last 1,800 miles.

"Is there a municipal marina in Frankfort?"

The attendant pointed up the bay.

"Is it the same price as here?"

"Close to the same."

"No difference?"

"It might be a few dollars cheaper," he said, when pressed.

I thanked him and paid for the fuel. He didn't push out the bow as we prepared to cast off. Instead, he took a few steps back and turned away, looking as if he'd just laid hands on a soiled rag.

The attendant had been right. The municipal marina of Frankfort was a few dollars cheaper, twenty dollars cheaper, actually. Several idle men there rushed over to catch our lines. One of them had been exercising his chocolate Lab but, when he saw us coming in, he cinched the dog to a post and joined the others. After our boat was secure, they evaporated back to their own boats, except for the man with the dog. He was captain of *Cygnus*, now at anchor among one or two other sailboats.

"I couldn't believe how fast you were moving along!" he said. "I had difficulty catching you, and I have a fifty-horsepower diesel."

We chatted a bit more. Then he and his dog shoved off in their tender and rowed to their anchorage.

Later Bob and I went to an uptown restaurant. Balls clicked on several tavern-size tables. A solo musician pounded his keyboard for the dwindling number of evening diners. Then he pounded his keyboard more enthusiastically for a growing number of late-night customers. The place grew busy; then it grew crowded. Pretty women filed in, groups of two or three. Some glanced coyly about; others aired a practiced indifference. The men were young and muscular, many of them posted at the coast guard station or in the reserve unit. They struck aloof poses against the bar, boasted believable lies, and laughed with the robustness of proud young men. All the while, the sound of Gordon Lightfoot, Cat Stevens, the Beatles, and James Taylor rose above the growing murmur.

Weather news the next morning reported an approaching front. That was enough cause for a day off, a light-duty day at least, and I leaped into it by tackling a few maintenance problems which had been building. I tightened the belt for the water pump and generator; two new stainless steel rods bedding down the engine mounts had stretched. I tightened them as well. Of the two bilge pumps, one was not working. The exhaust hose of one had fouled the high-water switch of the other. I checked the crankcase oil and water level of the engine. The coolant was down a quart. So I topped it up. I had also gotten lazy with the ship's log the past few days. That needed tending, and I finished it all just before noon.

Bob disappeared in the morning, and I didn't see him again until late. For that I was glad. I needed to clear my head. Advertisers have popularized sailing as an effortless and liberating pastime, but for me it has always been a demanding pursuit in which vigilance, prudence, and good judgment don't close their eyes and lie back on a tanning deck. Consequently, after many days at the work of sailing, my body was tiring and my spirit was wearing down. I felt as if I were being swept away. Perhaps the length of the trip was beginning to tell on me. At any rate, I needed solitude. I needed to empty my mind and let my spirit draw from whatever spring fed it.

The patter of raindrops on the cabin top swelled and ripened into one great rustling blanket, a soothing sound that drew me into a numbing sleep. At 1330 I finally awoke, roused myself, and emerged from the cabin. The rain had stopped. The sky foretold more showers but, for now, I could wander the town dry, free of care, and without purpose.

Showers began after dark. Stormy weather followed. Hundreds of lightning bolts lit the cabin, and long rolls of thunder kept sleep from gaining a strong foothold. Heavy rain poured down, and the wind piped up. The *Arja D.* rolled uneasily in the breeze. It was a nervous, quirky movement, grown from a rolling lift of wave and the taut snap of the mooring lines as they fell away. The boat fenders creaked incessantly and chaotically. Water sloshed in the half-filled water tank in the fore peak. Eventually the weight of sleep forced itself upon me at some late hour, but it wasn't restful, and it soon soiled itself in a cavernous nightmare from which I roused myself at 0300.

My shadow was the only one which splashed a dark human form on the paved walkway to the washrooms of the marina. The lamps overhead cast a vaguely yellow hue. In the distance, lightning flashed silently. After I returned to the boat, I poured myself a large brandy. I was missing home, and I was missing Brenda, and I was tired of the daily grind. I sipped the brandy until the showers began again at 0400. By then they had grown lighter, and the wind had settled. Sometime near dawn, the air grew balmy, and I fell into a deep slumber.

I woke at 0700, much earlier than I wanted or would have expected after such a restless night. It may have been the sound of engines that disturbed my sleep. A stretched-out line of boats was retreating up the harbour, returning from a brief attempt at sport fishing. The charters had left Frankfort just before dawn and met with long high-rollers offshore, but with the break of day conditions deteriorated even more. The southwest wind veered north, bit into the rollers and turned the seascape into a chaotic scene of whitecaps and confused seas, five to eight feet high, and breaking from unpredictable directions.

The sky remained threatening for the remainder of the morning, and sudden gusts peppered the harbour and marina. In the afternoon, Bob and I walked through town past the coast guard base and the resort community fronting the lake. The breakwater, a hundred yards beyond this point, protected the shore, but the waters of Lake Michigan still beat against its steel and concrete ramparts with great lumbering force. Every swell struck with the witless momentum of a madman, but each spent itself in a fractious leap of water and gasp of froth and, in the end, did no more harm than slinging splintered planes of water across the barrier and roughing the surface of the inner basin.

In spite of the tumult of sea and wind around us, the weather was improving. The cloud cover had risen and was coming undone;

glimpses of blue and galleries of light shone through fissures in the grey masses above. The next morning, Saturday, might be fair enough for a departure, but it would have to be a short, quick run, because more bad weather was forecast for tomorrow afternoon.

It was black at 0550. Sport and commercial fishing boats were moving out of the harbour. A steady low hum of engines filled the air. Red and green running lights moved against the pitch backdrop, forming a thin line, and gliding toward the mouth of the harbour. We merged into the parade of lights, and they gradually drew us into the expanse of Lake Michigan.

There we saw a beautiful spectacle. Over a hundred boats spread themselves across several miles of water. They hovered somewhere between the black sky, the black horizon, and the black sea. Only their running lights or masthead lights marked their position and course, and sometimes even these glimmers would blink or disappear as a vessel dipped into a trough or became eclipsed by the hull of another vessel.

We turned south. In time, the numbers of lights around us dwindled and grew faint as we put a few miles between us and the fishers. Other lights took their place. Lightning. And multiple bursts of it illuminated the pre-dawn sky far to the north. We would escape that mess of weather, but our turn still might come. Severe thunderstorms were predicted for the central Michigan coast later in the day, and winds of 60 mph were expected. So, our plan was to make Manistee, Michigan, before noon. It was a twenty-three-mile sail and, barring a sharp change in weather, it should be a safe one.

MANISTEE, MI

It would not be a dry one, however. A heavy, steady rain began about twenty minutes out of Frankfort. Winds were 10 knots southwest, enough to churn up one- to two-foot waves and a handful of spray.

I hurried into my rain gear and stayed on the tiller. I sent Bob down below, there being no sense in two of us on deck in poor conditions, and I stayed on the tiller for a few more hours. New rain gear kept me dry and warm, and I began to feel snug and contented enough to watch the showers fall and to feel the *Arja D.* slip between grey water and sky as we approached Arcadia, then Pierport. Manistee lay ahead.

We arrived in the port of Manistee at 1030. By that time the showers had ended but, after we left the registration office, the skies once again grew threatening. Cumulonimbus clouds piled to towering heights in the east. Packets of black and grey cloud moved close to the ground out of the north. Although the skies cleared in the afternoon, the winds were up, and the sea was up, as well.

A river cuts a notch between Lake Michigan and Manistee Lake, and the land on the southern side rises steadily. The town of Manistee spans both banks, but most of the community lies on the southern incline, and it was about a mile's walk up that hillside to St. Joseph's Church, where I attended Mass on Sunday morning.

By the time I returned to the boat, Bob had gone off somewhere. I chatted with several local sailors, explored the streets of the town, and relaxed in what was a pleasant, sunny day on shore. It was deceptive weather, though, because the terrain above the marina had baffled much of the wind. Offshore, it was blowing quite strongly.

A number of people cast fishing lines into the river from the sterns of their boats or off the tip of one of the piers. Bob was among them. He had landed a three-pound small-mouth bass and gave it to a couple of less fortunate children fishing from the deck of *Chump Change*, a 40-foot-plus cruiser lying a few berths west of us.

After supper, we visited Sandy and Nikki on *Bitter Sweet*. Sandy had been a submariner in the navy. Later he had worked for International Harvester until there was a change in ownership resulting in the loss of his pension. Now he works as a millwright and a part-time instructor at a community college. We sat around the galley table aboard his 30-foot boat, nibbling cheese and crackers, grapes and peanuts, and working our way through several beers. Intermittently, Bob or Sandy fired a satirical barb aimed at sinking the reputation of the other's branch of the Armed Forces. It began with Sandy's disparaging accusation of Marines being "jarheads" and Bob's slur about sailors being "seagoing bellhops." More inventive remarks and more vulgar ones followed, a familiar repartee among former servicemen.

Eventually, the chatter turned to where I would lay up my boat for the season. Phone calls to marinas in upper Illinois for their rates brought responses starting from a thousand dollars and ranging higher as one got closer to Chicago. However, Sandy suggested another alternative—the Great Lakes Naval Training Station, northwest of Chicago. Even though it's a military base, it maintains extensive recreational facilities, including a marina for current and retired Armed Forces personnel. It would be considerably less expensive than commercial marinas, he said. Since both Bob and I were former Marines, there should be no problem, he thought.

That evening's reminiscence of days in military service continued after Bob and I returned to the *Arja D*. The early years of Bob's military career were with the Marine Corps band. He played trumpet with them in San Diego, Cherry Point, and Hawaii, and in the evenings he played local nightclubs, backing up popular crooners of the time, including the Ink Spots, Julie London, Andy Williams, Gogi Grant, and Teresa Brewer. But by 1967 the music grew stale. After he closed the Pat Boone show in Hawaii, he laid the trumpet down and didn't play for fifteen years. He retrained as an electronics specialist, and during the Vietnam War he set up communications outposts for infantry and artillery units in country.

For me war was more elusive. It seemed to drift in front of me one moment, and then slip away in the next, like an unsettled apparition. My first brush with it occurred while stationed in Okinawa with the 3rd Marine Division. I requested transfer to serve as military observer attached to Vietnamese troops who were then fighting Viet Cong. My request was turned down. That quota had been filled. Months passed. Then, in the spring of '65, my tour of duty in Asia was over. I was transferred stateside. Days later, however, the crisis in the Gulf of Tonkin had changed everything. The role of US personnel in Vietnam switched from an advisory one to a combat mission, and 3rd Marine Division, the one I had been with for thirteen months, boarded ships bound for Vietnam. I missed that deployment by a little over four weeks.

During the next year I was stationed with the 2nd Marine Division in Camp Lejeune, North Carolina. For six of those months I was motor transport officer for the 2nd Marine regiment until orders came for transfer to the 8th Marines. While waiting for the date of my transfer, the platoon I commanded was put on standby. There had been an insurrection in Dominican Republic. Just after my transfer became effective, my unit was mobilized, formed part of a larger reinforced battalion, and was sent to quell that rebellion.

I did get to the tropics a few months later with the two-eight, as part of the permanent Caribbean fleet. The action in the Dominican had cooled, but it heated again. We steamed offshore, fully expecting to land there, but the unrest on that island subsided, and in June of '66, my enlistment up, I became a civilian once again.

I knew many who served, suffered, or died in Vietnam. And this realization has generated a conflict that I have never fully resolved. I felt blessed to have been spared the ugliness of war; but I also felt guilty that some went where I felt I ought to have been. As a result, each of these emotions, poles apart and incompatible by their nature, still tug on my mind like needy children craving attention might tug on my shirt sleeves.

On Monday morning the sky was overcast, and there was a bit of a breeze along the waterfront. Several boats pulled out of the marina and headed north despite the forecast of poor weather. So their departure surprised me. Had I missed something? Perhaps. I turned on the VHF radio and tuned into one of the marine weather stations, but, no, conditions had changed little from yesterday's prediction: strong winds and severe thunderstorm warnings continued; waterspouts were likely; and this was the outlook for the northern and central portions of the lake for the remainder of the day.

Bob and I had a late breakfast. By the time we returned to the marina, several boats which had made an early departure had come back. *Chump Change* had been one of them. It had been chewed up by the weather. Steaming north against the swells, its bow had burrowed into waves, and blue water swept its deck, leaving family members shaken and the skipper strained, so much so that he oversteered on his return to port, struck the wharf, and mangled a section of bow rail.

Next day we cast off at 0600 just behind *Bitter Sweet*. There was not yet a hint of dawn as we followed the navigation lights and the drone of sport-fishing vessels. Several fishing boats began a pattern of trolling just outside the breakwater, and one of them created a hazard by trolling across the breakwater entrance, temporarily blocking the channel, and slowing the string of vessels lined up to exit.

Light northerly winds developed in the morning and generated one- or two-foot following seas. The sky was blackened with rain clouds west and north toward Frankfort. Puffy grey clouds gathered to the east over the land, but they were too loose in structure to worry about.

Both Sandy and I headed for Muskegon. Both of us raised sail soon after we had cleared Manistee. It was a wonderful wind for it. Foresail and mainsail set wing on wing. Both drew strongly, and our speed lifted to 6.3 knots. Sometimes it surged as high as 7.4.

In late afternoon, however, winds became variable and light. Sails began to baffle. We jibed twice when a following sea caught our stern. The lines of the main sheet slackened, the double blocks and rigging drooped, and snapped taut in light puffs. Twice the blocks jammed. Since there was little hope in getting a fair wind, we took in sail and motored the remainder of the distance to Muskegon, a port which we made by 1800.

MUSKEGON, MI

The channel from Lake Michigan into Muskegon Lake was about a mile long and ample in width. We passed two moored vessels along that water route. The first was the *McLane*, a 1927 coast guard vessel, built for the war against bootleggers during the Prohibition era and rearmed for the bigger war against Japan. The *McLane* and her sister ships were 125 feet long, something which prompted their designation as "buck and a quarter class" vessels. Just past the *McLane* lay the submarine USS *Silversides*. That boat hit the water for the first time one week after the Japanese assault on Pearl Harbor. It served its war career in the blockade of Japan and racked up the third highest count of enemy vessels sunk during the war. Now, both *McLane* and *Silversides* are retired floating museums.

Bob and I met up with Sandy and Nikki on the wharf of the Great Lakes Marina in Muskegon. They had been having stern gear problems on their sailboat and needed a mechanic. As it turned out, because of those repairs, we would not see them again for another year.

Bob and I ate at the Cafe USA up the road and gathered a few supplies. While I stowed the groceries, Bob took a bag of cans and bottles to a trash bin at the end of the wharf. It was a long dock, about seventy yards long. Bob had not quite reached the trash bin before a large German shepherd emerged from the shadowy slot between two boats, stood in his path, and began to bark just like it had treed a squirrel. That noisy confrontation drew Bob to a standstill. It also roused two curious heads above the deck of a nearby boat.

"Captain!" one of the heads shouted. Bob looked up. The dog's ears twitched.

"Come here!" demanded head number two. Bob scowled at being ordered about by strangers. The dog retreated.

"That's *his* name...the dog's...Captain...Captain Morgan," said head number one, "and sorry about his behaviour. Gee, he's never like this." Bob noticed that the name of their boat was *Captain Morgan* too.

"Well, almost never," said head number two, outlined against the fading skyline. "He's a bit of a drinker, 'f ya know what I mean. Ha! Ha! He enjoys a sip or two. Har! Captain probably thinks you got rum in that bag of yours! Har! Har!"

At the sound of his name, the dog's eyes brightened. Captain's tongue, lolling from his mouth, swept smartly across his snout. Boundless optimism coursed through his brain. Heads one and two both chuckled and snorted at the sudden attentiveness of their animal. Bob laughed too, but for another reason. He took the sack of garbage he had been carrying, opened it, pulled out and held up an empty bottle that read, "Captain Morgan Original Spiced Rum."

The stern wave fanned out in a long unbroken vee, until its tip touched the walls of the channel and stroked its sides with a gentle and continuous motion. It rippled only when startled by the hulls of *Silversides* and *McLane*, which lay warped against their concrete final resting places. Looking at both of those ships, especially *Silversides*, awakened a feeling of sadness in me. I suppose I saw in them some fragment of a scene I vaguely remembered from childhood: a patriotically decorated Memorial Day stage exhibiting a frail Civil War veteran bent into a straight-backed chair; a wheezing Marine from Belleau Wood; and a Medal of Honor dangling from the neck of a Second World War corporal. Each of them seemed bound by obligation, but distant; each seemed ill at ease with ceremony and vaguely embarrassed by tribute; each seemed burdened by disappointment and distracted by memories. Each seemed so alone.

SOUTH HAVEN, MI

The engine reverberated with a sharp ring against the banks of the channel. Outside, in the lake, the sky was clear and a fair wind blew steadily out of the northwest. Once again we raised sail and bent onto a course for South Haven, a distance of fifty miles. It was a wonderful sailing day—the wind astern, mainsail spread wide to starboard, foresail filling fully to port. And a following sea.

The experience was exhilarating, and it was rhythmic, and it captured the grandeur and surprise of a symphony with every sweep of sea which overtook our boat. Although my attention was directed forward, hand on tiller, eyes on course, I could feel the pressure of water with each wave that built from behind; I could sense the stern lift lightly, and then forcefully heave up with an accelerating thrust. The sea swelled around us. It seemed it would engulf us. Then it parted like two strong arms, one along each quarter of the stern, and it held *Arja D.* as powerfully and firmly as Nureyev catching his ballerina's waist in her great leap above his head.

The moment which followed that lift seemed to suspend itself in time.

Then the sound of the rush and the froth of the whitening water washed past the vessel's boards. The boat surged ahead and down the watery mound. The stream of air generated by that swift headlong rush dampened the following breeze and then, wonderfully so, the four tons of wood and lead, canvas and steel, of which the *Arja D.* is made, sank into the trough of the wave as softly as one's head lands on a pillow. And on and on, the pattern recurred. And this was the measure of our day for many hours.

We arrived at South Haven around 1800. It was a short dogleg up the channel to the municipal marina and a steep walk uphill to the main street of town. We picked up a few things at a supermarket and, on the way back, we stepped out of the heat of day and into a cool dark tavern. The beer was cold and the pool table toward the rear of the bar would have been tempting if it had not been covered over and converted to a temporary utility table. A cake and sundry foodstuffs covered the table; party decorations hung above the mirrored panels behind the bar; and the attractive woman drawing draft beer from the tap was flirtatious and festive. It was her son's birthday. He was a soldier. She had not seen him for months since his enlistment, boot camp, and subsequent training. But today he was coming home. Tonight there would be a party. Next week he would join troops heading for the war in Iraq.

At the end of the bar nearest the door sat three young men: a drummer and two guitarists. They were friends of the woman who owned the tavern and were playing that evening for the birthday of her son. The drummer wore a T-shirt with a blues theme. That was reason enough for me to strike up a conversation, and that led to a good chat.

The drummer said that his band had played Legends in Chicago. Legends, owned by Buddy Guy, is probably the most well-known blues club in the Midwest, and Buddy Guy, together with B. B. King, both in their late seventies, are the last of the big-name Chicago bluesmen.

"Did you meet him?" I asked the rhythm guitarist.

"He wasn't there when we started our sets," he said. "I think he was playing with Clapton at some concert that night."

We ordered a couple more beer. Then he continued: "Buddy didn't come in 'til late. He had a cute young blonde hanging onto him. The place was crowded...no place to sit. Buddy walked off somewhere...to do something...and left her standing...just standing. The bands have a couple of reserved tables up front. So I thought I'd be polite and ask if she wanted to sit at our table until Buddy got back. She didn't say anything...just stared...maybe she was too drunk or stoned. Anyway, a little later Buddy comes over... lays his big arm across my shoulder...and starts talking. I didn't know what he said. He was pretty drunk...mumbling...incoherent... but the tone was clear enough. He thought I was trying to hustle his woman. So I made myself disappear for the rest of the evening. I didn't want trouble."

Bob and I waved goodbye a short time later and headed for the door.

"The party starts at nine," shouted the pretty lady behind the bar.

"We'll try," I said, but my promised effort was more than half a lie.

My parting remark was a lie, but a kind one. I knew that tomorrow we had a challenging day ahead of us, and that was to make the run across the lake from South Haven, Michigan, to Great Lakes Naval Station, Illinois. The distance was seventy miles.

GREAT LAKES NAVAL STATION, IL

Of course, there was no light at 0300 when we woke. So I had to make coffee and toast by flashlight. However, by 0400 we had cast off, moved slowly into the main stream, and slipped between the more profound darknesses that shaped the banks of the channel.

The hour was too early even for the fishing fleets. There was no traffic on the water. So we had the lake to ourselves, and shared it only with the moon which emerged from a nest of cloud and cast a sheen of light all round, and, as predicted, a light southeast breeze puffed up and spilled over our port quarter.

After two hours of sailing, the few lights we glimpsed along the Michigan coastline disappeared behind us. Above, the vaulted sky was patchy with stars and constellations, but diminished in grandeur by light wispy cloud. Ahead and more southwest, a grimy yellow glow hovered above the cities of Chicago and Evanston, Illinois.

During the pre-dawn hours we made 5 knots. I had taken the first turn on the tiller. Bob came back up on deck around 0630, camera in hand, and took a string of photographs. It was an impressive sunrise. A little later we raised the main and continued to motor-sail. We picked up a half-knot of speed, and the filling sail seemed to stabilize the boat among the waves which began to build as morning wore on. By noon they had grown two to four feet. They struck on the port quarter, slewed our stern to starboard, and that made it difficult to hold our course.

For eight hours I could see no shore ahead or behind, just open water. No vessels hove into sight. In fact, only a bird or two, water and wave, and the dance of sun and cloud filled the emptiness around me. It was a lonely landscape. And against such a backdrop the ordinary sometimes transforms itself into the extraordinary. And it did so that day in the form of a monarch butterfly.

The butterfly appeared after we were many, many miles from shore. Its delicate flutter of orange and black stood boldly against the bland palette of colour around it. It seemed with difficulty to overtake the *Arja D.* and, after finally doing so, it circled the boat wearily and in an eccentric pattern. Sometimes, it fell away and then, with a burst of energy, regained position like a runner in a marathon. Other times, it drifted, sometimes disappearing entirely, but returning, hovering uncertainly, and lighting for a moment upon some part of the boat—the mast or the lee of the mainsail.

Occasionally, when the monarch disappeared for long periods and I was convinced that it had flown off forever, then I discovered that I missed it very much. It was a pretty distraction, yes. Most of all, however, I admired the wonderful spirit that dwelled within such a fragile thing: heroic strength, remarkable resolve, and singular beauty radiating from one simple creature. Certainly, it was one of nature's works of art. Perhaps it was also one of the archetypes on which ancient men and women modelled their own works of art, their assemblages of words, clay or pigment, things easily scorched, marred, or broken but also capable of moving hardened souls to feel and leading stony minds to imagine.

So, whenever the butterfly reappeared, I was both relieved and pleased. When it finally vanished, though, I sensed the loss. That happened mid-afternoon. By then we stood about fifteen miles from Illinois. The shore was still a ghostly line but, out of it, one could perceive indistinct shapes which eventually solidified into grey sky-scraping buildings near Skokie and Evanston. At the ten-mile mark a large squat building took shape on the horizon ahead on our compass heading toward Great Lakes, Illinois. The end of this year's voyage was within sight.

It was 1730 when Bob and I entered the harbour at the naval base and slid alongside one of the piers in the marina. The dock master was in a building that, in any city in the US, would have been recognizable as the armoury of the local military reserve unit. It was a large, rectangular, two-and-a-half storey, stone block structure. Each corner of the building was buttressed by a turret which rose above the lowest pitch of the roof. The lines were clear, simple, and strong. The building may have had other uses in other times, but now it housed offices, supplies, and storage areas which supported recreational boating activities for base personnel.

It took some time to sort out the administrative details: proof of identity, military background, ownership of the boat, and boat-insurance papers. Later, additional bureaucracy would allow us to come and go as we pleased on the base.

For now, however, the next few hours were devoted to preparing the *Arja D.* for winter storage—at least the initial stages of it. We bagged clothes and boxed leftover canned goods and perishables. We bound up the charts and papers. We unbent the sails and stuffed them into their respective sailbags.

We had moved the boat from the pier to one of the finger docks where other sailboats were tied. It would remain there until the end of September when all of the boats were hauled out and stored for the season. That task and the final winterizing of the boat were jobs that I entrusted to Bob.

We cooked our final meal on the boat that evening. Afterwards we scrubbed the decks, cleaned the icebox, and opened all the compartments below deck. Everything else had been boxed or bagged. Nothing remained but the wait for Bob's wife, Barb, and his son, Peter, to arrive. In the meantime, we lay back on the deck of the stripped-down sloop and reminisced about the voyage. Our words dropped onto the still evening air through tired minds; the name of one port blurred with the image of some other port.

Below us, the *Arja D.* seemed naked and twitchy as it nudged the dock, its spars and decks bare, devoid of sheets and halyards, anchor and rode, blocks and running gear. And it acted like a sulky dog that knows you will not take it when you leave.

Since she was built thirteen years ago, she had never been out of my sight or care, but for the next eight months I would trust her to others and that was disquieting. Through my mind raced a stream of scenarios depicting circumstances leading to either damage or disaster to my boat. A poorly tied knot, an undrained hose, an unstable jack stand, no engine anti-freeze, dry rot from moisture, mould from poor ventilation, chafing from unsecured canvas. And so on. Nevertheless, the situation was out of my control. There was no alternative. She would stay in the United States, and I would return to Prince Edward Island and Canada.

On the other hand, I knew that Bob would be diligent in winterizing the engine and securely covering the boat. He had good attention to detail. I knew too that security in the marina was second to none. The base was closed to itinerants; armed guards were posted throughout. And Sandy, wherever he was now, would at some time return with his boat to this naval facility and, as he assured me, he would keep his eye on my boat whenever he checked his own.

Each of these convincing arguments ran through my mind, and the outcome was that I grew less anxious than I had been. I would never be completely assured, but at least now I could lean back against the mast and feel some confidence in what would be.

My mind also reflected my last two seasons of sailing: the dream that had propelled me forward, and the path it laid out for me in '04—the calamity of bone-chilling cold, endless fog, mechanical failures, near collisions, and vicious weather that snarled and snapped at my heels for nearly one thousand miles out and back. Those hardships were unexpected and crushing, but they may have been the forge which steeled me to try again the following year.

And that next year was different. As I reflected on the past two months, I recognized a change within me: something had quieted, and something had awakened. Neither of those things had yet clarified themselves in my mind. Yet I felt stronger; I felt more positive; I felt more hopeful of success in my unusual venture. Only minor discomforts or inconveniences had arisen over the past two thousand miles. Stumbling blocks had fallen only in the road of others. *Setback* was a word not spoken.

My fortune had changed, I thought, and I gave that idea time to age and mature in my imagination like a choice wine.

My fortune has really changed.

The light of day dimmed. The soft shadows lengthened. The air was warm. Boats moved imperceptibly to the touch of the water around them and, on the blue sail cover of the boat lying next to us, a monarch butterfly quietly rested its wings.

Chapter 18

CHI-TOWN AND THE BIG BARGE BLOCKADE

After arriving at Great Lakes Naval Station on August 25, 2005, I spent a week at my cousin's home on the Fox River just south of Chicago and booked my flight home. It would be a troubling week. First, Hurricane Katrina struck Louisiana. When the levees broke there, many communities were flooded, including New Orleans and Slidell on Lake Pontchartrain. Some called it the greatest natural disaster ever to strike the United States, and millions who watched it on TV were horrified. For my cousin Bob and his wife, Barb, it was a horror born out of fear. Their son, Mike Zack, and his family live on the shore of Lake Pontchartrain.

Mike, a retired US Coast Guard commander, now a lawyer with the US Army Corps of Engineers, is also my godson. His family evacuated just before the storm made landfall, but it would be days before they would learn the fate of their house. In the meantime, Bob was packing to head south and help with the cleanup.

The second troubling episode occurred two days after we landed. I badly twisted my ankle and was whisked off to a local emergency room. After a three-hour wait and an X-ray, it proved to be a bad sprain. Still, a walking cast and crutches made it quite difficult to shift luggage and navigate airports on my return to Canada.

At home, I realized that all was not well there, either. While I had been away, nearly everything which can break down mechanically had done just that and had done it several times. The lawn mower three times, the car twice, and the truck once. While my wife is quite resourceful in many regards, these inconveniences were beyond her expertise, and the frequency of them was beyond her patience. Anyone who is married knows where I am going here.

I was not yet in the doghouse, but I learned that she had acquired several kennel-building how-to books from our local library while I had been away. A new leash dangled from a hook near the front door. It didn't belong to our pet beagle. So I became wary.

In hindsight, I should have grown smarter when younger, but a pocketful of Boy Scout merit badges and a hatful of university degrees don't prepare one for a *cum laude* in marital relations. And my learning curve, when it comes to women, only rises as steeply as a Kansas mountainside.

Ironically, one of the questions boaters along the way most frequently ask me is this one: "Does your wife sail with you?"

"No," I reply. "She would like to, but she has a bad case of motion sickness. As a matter of fact, she gets dizzy if I back the car up too quickly."

"Ha, ha, ha!"

"No, it's true," I insist.

At one time, Brenda enjoyed water and boats. Her father was a commercial fisherman. She grew up in a fishing village. She had been aboard lobster boats many times. She had even sailed with me in the early years of our relationship. Somewhere along the line, however, she lost her sea legs. Now, even the thought of taking the twelve-mile ferry ride from Prince Edward Island to the mainland is a circumstance that leads to anxiety and the popping of a Gravol tablet or two.

And often there is a follow-up question: "What does she think of you going off sailing alone?"

The first time I was asked, I laughed and tossed back some stock, cliché response. It was probably not until I had heard the same question three times that I sensed an emerging pattern. Perhaps they knew something that I had not learned in the four years I had spent at an all-boys Jesuit-taught high school.

Frankly, the thought of asking my wife if I could go on a long sailing trip by myself had never occurred to me. Never. With that said, some may think me incredibly naive; some may think me insensitive; and others that it is just a man acting like a man. I don't know. I may have to confer with my wife on that one.

Mea culpas notwithstanding, the fact remains. I had begun the voyage. Now I had to continue, and that conclusion eventually brought me back to Illinois in the spring of 2006.

It was 0630 on the thirtieth of May when Bob, Barb, and I left their home in Chicago. We arrived at the Naval Station two hours later. We cleared the security check at the main gate and drove slowly through the base toward the marina. Sailors in crisp white uniforms moved toward their mess hall; oaks and maples and chestnuts rose on thick trunks toward a grey sky; large buildings of brick and stone nestled among clusters of trees and faced parade grounds and lawns and avenues still wet with dew. Severe thunderstorms had beaten a line southeast from Wisconsin yesterday evening. As a result, the harbour had churned itself brown, and quite a bit of debris floated within the breakwater.

Fog obscured most of Lake Michigan but, by 0930, it was lifting. So we cast off. Seas were calm, and the wind was light. We turned south toward Chicago, five or six hours away. There would be no sailing on this leg of the trip because our mast would not clear the fixed railway bridge in South Chicago. So, as we had done through the Trent-Severn Waterway, we built a carriage above the deck. On it rested the mast and boom, and there it would remain until I hit Mobile, Alabama, on the Gulf of Mexico. The forward support for the mast also served a second purpose. Several extra fuel containers were lashed to it. Ordinarily, I would have tied a canvas boot around the mast post to shed any rainwater. I hadn't. Now, however, it looked like rain.

Bob offered to install the boot and went forward to do so. I turned around to gauge how much distance we had made from the naval station and, as I did, I saw disturbing weather. Black, heavy clouds were tumbling out of the north. Ominous things. They travelled low to the ground and drove wisps of white cloud before them. Just as Bob was about to loosen the cord tying the fuel cans to the post, I shouted.

"Bob! Hold it! Leave the cans!"

He looked at me. He looked beyond me, spotted the clouds, and scampered back to the cockpit. We rushed into our rain gear, double-checked the lashings holding the mast in its cradle, and secured anything loose in the cockpit. Then we waited.

The clouds were ugly. They moved quickly. We braced ourselves. And soon they were upon us.

Then, that which was most unexpected happened. Nothing. Other than a light gust and a rippling of the water, nothing. Nothing at all. The storm swept past. The episode was almost grotesque in its anti-climactic nature. Like some bully's threatening fist replaced by a mocking laugh and a "see-you-again-soon."

We escaped with only a wasted flurry of energy, but bullying weather had struck another vessel tragically on September 5, 1860, not far from here. On that date, the side-wheel steamer *Lady Elgin* was struck by the two-masted schooner *Augusta* during a heavy gale. We sailed over her watery gravesite just after noon, a few miles off Winnetka, Illinois. The dead numbered between three and four hundred, making that collision the second-worst nautical disaster on the Great Lakes.

The sinking of the *Lady Elgin* also became a weapon in the battle over states' rights and slavery, issues that reached a feverish pitch in Wisconsin, the home state of the *Lady Elgin*. On the eve of the 1860 presidential election, some of that state's legislator's had moved a resolution to secede from the Union and declare war on the federal government if it didn't end slavery. They went so far as to poll the four state militias on where they would stand on the issue. Garrett Barry, captain of the Milwaukee Union Guard, one of the militias, said that he opposed slavery, but to secede would be treason. Because of his stand the legislature revoked Barry's military commission. Then they disarmed and disbanded the Union Guard. The guard refused to disband, though, and with the help of the local Democratic Party organized an excursion to Chicago to attend a political rally and raise cash to re-arm. The *Lady Elgin* returned them to Chicago, but on their trip to Milwaukee, Barry and most of his guard were drowned.

The *Augusta* made it safely back to shore, but the captain of the *Augusta* was accused of being an *agent provocateur* of both the Confederacy and pro-Confederacy Britain. Mobs gathered, the captain and crew fled, and their fate is written only on smudged pages of history.

The history of our day's progress on the *Arja D.*, however, trailed in our wake. It fanned out in ever-widening ripples behind us, becoming less distinct, and disappeared finally into an imperfect memory. Fog persisted, not dense, though, but enough to spoil the horizon and the shore. As we closed on Chicago, the skyscrapers of Skokie and Evanston rose from their foundations as dark-grey fingers on a leaden curtain. Chicago itself was a disappointment, the tops of its tallest buildings embedded in a thick roof of fog.

Our primary landmark for the city was the Navy Pier. Originally built in 1916 to serve Lake Michigan freighters, the Navy Pier converted to military use during the Second World War. After the war it became a college campus, and today it's Chicago's most-visited attraction. At 1430, however, it was just a grey smear on the horizon and, if indeed it were a tourist magnet, we would never have known. Even the navigation light at the end of the pier was obscured by mist until we were a mile from it.

We rounded the pier and located the lock that connected Lake Michigan to the Chicago River. I hailed lock control over my VHF radio but received no reply. In the meantime, I let the *Arja D.* drift out of the main channel. I called again. Still no reply. Eventually, the doors to the lock opened. No vessel was inside. I took that as an invitation, put the boat in gear, and drove in. We tied up against the starboard wall. No one appeared with instructions. In fact, we saw no one at all. We waited for the rush of water draining out as we had at so many other locks along the St. Lawrence and Trent-Severn Waterway. It seemed like a long wait. Then the western door swung open.

"Is that it?" I asked no one in particular.

"Ya know," said Bob, "I think the water level may have dropped a few inches or so since we came in."

I would have noticed a six-inch drop of water in my bathtub, but in a basin great enough to hold ten or fifteen barges, such a drop was too subtle, especially when the mountain range of concrete buildings just outside the lock's doors commanded so much of one's attention. I put the engine in gear and crept timidly out.

Welcome to Chicago.

No subtlety here. No weaknesses. It's bluff and bold. It's brisk and busy. And the poetic words of Carl Sandburg describe this city's glimmer, even more vivaciously, when one sees it and hears it and strides through it:

Come and show me another city with lifted head singing
So proud to be alive and coarse and strong and cunning.
Flinging magnetic curses amid the toil of piling job on
Job, here is a tall bold slugger set vivid against the little soft cities;

And Sandburg's energy comes to life, as the gears engage and the engine growls, and the bow of the *Arja D.* presses softly forward as if it were joining a great parade. The parade route is a watery one, and it passes through the core of the city. The banks of the Chicago River turn to quarried rock. They rise high on each side of us, and then they blend with the sides of immense buildings of stone and steel, mortar and brick, glass and concrete. Even on such a dull day as this, the walls of glass and panes of windows gather light, and one building bathes the other with its own luminescence, a strange reverberation, an echo of light.

It's a strange experience sailing through the city, virtually alone, for there is no river traffic except the occasional tour boat or police cruiser. For a few moments, one feels privileged, special, yet still in awe of one's surroundings. The debutante presented. The new director introduced. We pass small docks at grand hotels; wharves for the *Sun-Times*; ramps for tourists to board sightseeing boats. And we pass under fifty-four bridges in five miles. We pass buildings tall, rectangular; structures square and formidable; buildings historic, ornate; the modern and showy; buildings like onyx, others of marble; buildings that reflected only the images of the others around them, like chameleons.

The allure of the city is an allusion, of course. Its power of seduction is glamorous, heady, and compelling, but surrender to it often leads to an unpleasant end. The debutante undone. The new director ridiculed. My first inkling that Chicago was more philanderer than friend came just after my thought: *Wouldn't it be a treat to stop for half an hour, find a nice restaurant—The Berghoff maybe—and just enjoy the moment, here, in one of the world's great cities.* It was not until then that I began to notice the small, discreet, blunt signs along the docks and banks: No Stopping; No Loitering; Private Landing; Guests Only. They might just as easily have said: "Keep movin' right along, Kiddo. It takes real dough to play in this game."

In hindsight, perhaps I overreacted. Perhaps I've become defensive and jaded. Still, I could not shake the feeling that the broad shoulders and big open arms of Sandburg's Chicago, had closed tight-fistedly around the lure of capitalism and the lusty feel of money.

If I couldn't negotiate a smoked meat sandwich and sauerkraut at The Berghoff, then I could at least be content to snack on a few sour grapes. Later I washed the sour grapes down with a tepid cup of Thermos coffee. Behind me, the skyline of Chicago grew distant, dwindled in proportion, and diminished in stature. I had already slipped out its back door.

Backyards of homes can be venues for celebration and friendship; for garden and rest; for reflection and play. Sadly, they can also be depositories for refuse, plots of abandonment, and cemeteries of hope, screened from the public gaze as guardedly as the minds of those who tend them. The backyard of Chicago is not pretty, and it has a long and shameful history.

It began in the mid-1800s when the burgeoning city began to use Lake Michigan as the toilet bowl for its wastes, both personal and industrial. We should remember that Chicago was not only "hog butcher of the world," but it was also butcher of almost every longhorn steer roped and driven across the US plains. Where the trail drives ended, railroads began, and an unending stream of cattle cars rumbled north to the Chicago stockyards. In their time, the beasts were slaughtered lickety-split. And the slaughterhouses had to flush the offal somewhere. As often as not, that somewhere was Lake Michigan.

Eventually, city fathers and engineers violated a fundamental Boy Scout principle: don't piss upstream from your campsite. The recurring plagues of typhoid, cholera, and diphtheria killed thousands. Over the next fifty years smarter engineers constructed two canals to link Lake Michigan with the Chicago River, an engineering feat that reversed the flow of the Chicago River and allowed the Chicago River and Sanitary Canal to carry waste water away from the city. On the positive side, the typhoid death rate fell dramatically. On the negative side, reversing the flow of the Chicago River started the draining of Lake Michigan. That made Canada unhappy. Another effect was a surprising increase in the sightings of "brown trout" and detached cow parts far downstream. This made St. Louis, Missouri, unhappy. Lawsuits followed.

By the 1890s successive generations of smarter lawyers and even smarter engineers had solved the problems by ordinances and statutes and by sewage tunnels and flood plans but, as I sailed along the Chicago River and Sanitary Canal, I gradually thought of it more and more as the Chicago River and Anal Canal. I was convinced that all was not well there. In spite of public relations' attempts to pump out water-quality news with a smiley face, I could still find a homegrown newspaper article or two which dredged up new failings in the water system or the river itself. In addition, Illinois has published advisories against eating fish caught in the river because they may be contaminated by PCBs and heavy metals. Another report said that Chicago has one of the highest lead-contamination rates in the country. Most telling for me, however, were the small metal signs posted at regular intervals along both riverbanks that warned not to drink, not to swim in, and not to bathe with the water. The caveat that stirred up the most dread was the last: Avoid any contact with water. To be fair, I have to admit that I never saw any "brown trout" in the murky green-brown water, and I never spotted any three-eyed fish. We did see a fawn, and Bob pointed out a beaver, but I thought it looked more like a wharf rat and, while I didn't press the point with Bob, at the same time I recalled that he had mistaken an osprey for a golden eagle last year.

Despite failings past and current, downtown Chicago remains a strikingly beautiful sight. In fact, it was so engaging that, when I passed through, it displaced a grim memory of an event which had taken place there. Only now, as we sailed through this troubled waterway did it recover and come to mind once more. And that vagrant recollection involved a vessel named *Eastland*.

Engineers and naval architects designed *Eastland* as a fast, shallow-draft freighter built to haul cargo from the eastern shore of Lake Michigan to Chicago. The cargoes of freight in its holds increased stability. Then came the tinkers.

In the case of the *Eastland*, one tinker shortened the vessel by sixty feet, making it less buoyant. Another tinker added a deck, making it more top-heavy. Also, because of the *Titanic* disaster additional lifeboats, weighing ten to fourteen tons, were stored on the top deck of the *Eastland*. All that tinkering left the boat, when loaded with cargo and passengers, with as little as twelve inches above the waterline. The *Arja D.*, by comparison, has twenty-three inches of freeboard.

On July 24, 1915, twenty-five hundred Western Electric employees gathered to board the *Eastland* for their annual picnic excursion to Michigan City. The vessel was docked at a wharf next to the Clark Street Bridge. There was no cargo in the hold, but the weight of incoming passengers made the *Eastland* unstable. The ship listed. Then it rolled. Over eight hundred were trapped and drowned. That incident became the greatest marine tragedy in Great Lakes history and, ironically, on a ship which never left its dock.

Four or five miles below the lock control on Lake Michigan, the number of bridges under which we sailed dropped to one per mile. Skyscrapers were a memory. The terrain changed from urban to scrub land. Ranks of spindly trees crowded the water's edge. The stream flowed lazily toward the Mississippi on a waterway that was more canal than river. The channel was dredged. Both banks were built of stone. Only fifty feet of water flowed between them. On the one hand, it seemed the picture of contentedness, and one could conjure up a pastoral sensibility, if contamination of the river were not so fresh in mind.

Mile after mile of stone wall framed the channel, but now those stones—blackened limestone blocks, hand-hewn, and hand-laid as much as a hundred years ago—acquired the look of antiquity, disrepair, and disregard. A buoyant spirit might have perceived quaintness in the scene, like coming upon the stony ruins of an Irish chapel or the moss-grown remnants of Hadrian's Wall. But buoyant spirits are delicate things, like butterflies, and we were entering a twenty-mile stretch of river that was the back alley of Illinois commerce and industry, places where beauty and charm would shrink like frightened children. It was not a place of wickedness necessarily, but without question it was a place of ugliness and a cause for dismay.

Soon hundreds of wharves sprang from the shore. Behind them lay generating plants, factories, processing plants. Fabricators, recycling depots, grain silos, and warehouses. Squat tanks of petrol and diesel fuel glinted dully in the late afternoon light. Gas flares burned from vents, and chimneys pumped a limp breath of smoke. From them, aromas sweet or worrying, familiar or mysterious brushed our cheeks and left unpleasant tastes on our palates. When no great factories packed against the shore, we found great manufactured expanses. Mountainous stockpiles of coal ranged across hundred-acre fields. Dunes of stored gravel or sand grew into deserts. Most troubling of all, however, were the fields of scrap metal, square miles of rusting, dismembered, and junked carcasses, many storeys high, over which trundled yellow, track-driven machines, plucking here and there, like carrion-feeding insects.

The common thread feeding most of this industry is the tugboat and the barges they pushed. Tugs were the working elephants which transformed the central United States from a farming hinterland into a manufacturing and business stronghold, especially in the last century. They are inexpensive to run, and they carry enormous loads. One tug, pushing fifteen barges, three across and five deep, transports 2,300 tons of material. It would take 870 tractor-trailer rigs to do the same job but, to do so would burn eight times the fuel used by the barge. Even railroads can't compete with barges for economy.

On the upper reaches of the Chicago River, their loads are smaller because there is so little sea room for two approaching tugs to pass safely. Several work boats already had gone by us, but so far we had seen nothing bigger than a one-by-four, a single line of four barges, pushed by a tug.

As evening came on, I began looking for a place to moor the boat. Deep gouges in the stone embankments attested to barges having ground against them in an attempt to navigate the narrow canal. That observation discouraged any notion of laying against the bank and tying to a tree. On the other hand, travelling at night can be hazardous too. No navigation lights mark the channel or the banks and, although tugs rumble through after dark, they do so with powerful searchlights scanning hundreds of yards ahead of them in order to illuminate bends in the river, abandoned barges rusting along old wharves, or other obstructions. The lights are blinding, and their glare would kill our night vision.

MILE 299, ILL. RIVER

An alternative was to find a slip. The slips on the canal were pond-sized bodies of water which led off the main channel. They allowed tugs and their tow loads to leave the canal and access a wharf where their cargoes could be loaded or unloaded. These slips, of course, were privately owned and privately guarded in most instances and, therefore, off-limits. At 1930, just when light was beginning to fade, we passed four industrial slips. One was active. Another was packed with barges, probably inactive, but, in case someone had to hook up or drop off a barge during the night, we decided not to stop there. One of the slips, however, was empty. Inside, we glimpsed a wharf and several buildings rusting into disrepair. This became our best option. So we motored in, moved to the farthest side of the slip, and dropped anchor.

After night had set in darkly, and after we had retired for the evening, the shudder of a big engine and a disturbing flash of light illuminated our cabin and sent us spilling onto the deck. We saw a line of barges lumbering toward us. I started the engine. Bob rushed to haul the anchor. I edged the boat north, away from the slow-moving hulk. I couldn't be certain where the vessel intended to go, but it seemed to be lining up with the old wharf. Then a voice hollered from the deck of the forward-most barge.

"You're okay where you are. No need to move." A flashlight lit his silhouette. "We're going to lay against the wharf."

I hollered back an acknowledgement, but I continued to edge the *Arja D.* to a northerly spot in the slip, where we dropped anchor, still just twenty yards from the barge.

We watched, as best we could on a moonless night, as the shadowy string of vessels crept into the slip. It was slow; it was tedious. A much more time-consuming task than I would have expected. From my position, I guessed the total length of tug and barges came close to a hundred yards. The entire string of them was fixed together as one composite unit. Because of its length, the vessel could not swing into the slip. So, to negotiate the turn, the captain had to break apart his rigid line of barges somewhere near the middle, leaving the forward barges coupled to the aft ones on one side only, like a hinge. The hinge allowed a couple of forward barges to be forced through the slip's entrance while the other half remained in the channel. Once the forward half was nudged into the slip, the tug nosed the remaining barges around, closing the hinge, and entering the slip as a straight load once more. It was a delicate job, done as gently as an astronaut docking a shuttle to an orbiting space station. Unfortunately, it had all been done in vain.

I had tuned the VHF to channel 14. The chatter on the marine radio revealed that the load was too long for the slip. The tug's stern still jutted into the canal. It was a futile position. Consequently, the process of getting the vessel into the slip had to be reversed, and tug and barges had to be withdrawn. Their retreat from the slip proceeded as slowly as their entry. Then they disappeared in the night leaving in their wake a fading rumble of engines and a dwindling flicker of searchlights.

Shortly after we left Slip #2 the next morning, we passed a boat heading upstream. Not only do riverboats push heavy loads, they also push volumes of water. This boat pushed three barges, and those three barges displaced a lot of water. The bow wave was not large but, as we passed, it knocked us about with surprising severity. In such a narrow canal, the waves reverberated against the riverbanks like echoes in a cave or like a jug of water knocked on its side. Instead of a firm roll or two, the *Arja D.* snapped back and forth so violently amid the clash of waves that I feared for the security of the mast in its cradle above our heads. After the tug passed, I stopped and checked the mast. The force of the disturbance had driven the spar about a foot back from where it had been tethered. We repositioned it, relashed it, and then we moved on.

Our travels would take us along the industrialized sector of the river until we reached the Brandon Road Lock at Joliet, nine miles ahead. In the meantime, we passed countless railroad spurs and access roads which led to industrial parks, refineries, grain elevators, asphalt plants, warehouses, and storage fields for various substances. One depot stockpiled enormous heaps of some vivid blue mineral; others stored gravel or sand. Alongside one wharf at a sand depository lay the *Mallard*, a tugboat. One of its ship's officers stood on deck. He leaned against the rail outside the vessel's bridge and puffed a cigarette. He eyed us curiously as we slid by.

"Nice boat," he said with a wave.

Three more miles separated the *Mallard*'s *salut* from the Lockport Lock and dam. When we reached the Lockport Lock at 0905, we had a wait. The *Pamela Dewey* was "locking-down," in other words going through the lock and heading downstream. There was ample room for us to lock-through with *Pamela Dewey*, but we were forbidden from doing so because it was carrying something nasty in its cargo. It could have been caustic soda, benzene, or hydrochloric acid, chemicals which would dissolve you. Or it could have been gasoline or fuel oil, or other such chemicals which might toast you. At any rate, vessels with dangerous cargo must lock-through by themselves.

I discovered that this was not always a simple process. The *Pamela Dewey* was 128 feet long and 42 feet wide. It worked out of Paducah, Kentucky, where the Ohio River meets the Tennessee. The load it was pushing was a two-by-five, a joined load of barges, two abreast and five deep, too long to lock-through as a unit. In such a case, then, the load is broken in two. Each part is locked through separately and reassembled after both had locked-down. As a result, the transit of the *Pamela Dewey* meant a three-hour delay for Bob and me.

It was midday when we received clearance to enter the lock. The water level dropped forty feet, yet it was a surprisingly smooth transition, not like the turbulent St. Lawrence River locks. The next lock, the Brandon Road Lock, lay five miles downstream on the south side of Joliet, Illinois. Halfway to the lock, the Des Plaines River and the Chicago River merge to become the Des Plaines River. Just past that juncture lies Joliet Correctional Center, former home of gangster Al Capone, as well as Alvin Karpis, ringleader of the famous breakout from Alcatraz. Joliet was also the location where crews filmed the first season of the popular TV thriller *Prison Break*.

We reached the Brandon Lock in half an hour and radioed lock control that we were standing by. They said there would be a bit of a wait. *Pamela Dewey* was locking-down ahead of us. They would call when the lock was clear, they said. So we gnawed away at the next hour by drifting and steaming, drifting down toward the lock, steaming a mile upstream, drifting toward the lock, and back again, and again and again. As we paced back and forth in my boat, we must have passed the River Club a dozen times.

The River Club was a two-storey, flat-roofed, cement-block building. Its back door led to a square of patchy grass, a picnic table or two, and a riverfront wall which seemed to beckon each time we floated by it. Eventually, we pulled in and tied up to that landing.

We tried to enter the club, but the door was locked. We peered through the glass panels of the double door. The interior had a vintage look, a lot of woodwork, heavy-gauged and polished, not stylized like the trendy new bars. There were a couple of pool tables and a number of slot machines too. A Coke and a sandwich would have hit the spot, but there was no sign of it opening. There was nobody about. In lieu of that, it would be a treat to stretch one's legs, maybe even go for a quick walk up the street. The latter thought was put to rest, however, when we discovered that street access was gated off. We couldn't leave these small grounds. So we made lunch on the boat and waited. By this time, I was beginning to feel imprisoned, a kind of house arrest, benign but frustrating. Surely, it couldn't be much longer before we got a green light for the lock.

"It can't be much longer now, Bob," I said. My words spoke what my thoughts had been repeating like a mantra. Already we had waited three hours. It was 1500. Bob's head nodded without conviction.

It was about that time that I heard a shuffling metallic sound. The patio door of the River Club slid open on its track. A large fat man strode through the portal and stepped into the green square of the backyard. He saw us, walked halfway across the grass in our direction, and stopped. He seemed to gasp for breath.

"We're open," he said.

"Yea, we tried the door earlier, but..."

"Well we're open now. You can come in. We've got beer...food... whatever."

"Thanks. We've been waiting for the lock. It's been three hours. I think they'll be calling soon."

"Aren't you coming in?"

"Maybe later...once we've heard something."

"If you aren't coming in, then shove off," he spouted. Then he turned his back to us, lumbered through the doorway, and disappeared into the shadowy recesses of his empty club.

Apparently, we had not grasped the fact that our presence at an empty wharf behind an empty saloon next to an empty parking lot was spoiling his business. So, with his curt reminder ringing in our minds, we cast off our lines and edged into the channel once more. We continued our motorized version of pacing back and forth, waiting for a message which never seemed to come, until we spied a rusting hulk of a barge tied to the shore next to what looked like a scrap yard. We pulled alongside the barge and tied to it. It was a shady spot, a couple of hundred yards north of the River Club. The arms of several trees splayed out over the barge. The rustle of leaves was soft and murmurous, and the foliage shielded us from the late afternoon heat. And the day stole by in idleness and inconsequential chat.

Then, after a long silence, Bob suggested, "Maybe you should call the lock and see what's happening."

"That's probably a good idea," I replied and lay back across the bridge and let the dulling warmth of the sun ease me more deeply into my comfortable, untroubled listlessness.

Finally, at 1730, almost five hours after our arrival, I radioed the lock.

"Lockport Lock, Lockport Lock, this is pleasure boat *Arja D.* We request an update on our status to lock-down, over."

"Pleasure boat, this is Lockport Lock. You can lock-through. We've been trying to get you on the radio, but there was no response, over."

"Strange...we received no call..." A long pause. "Anyway, we're heading down now. *Arja D.* out."

We hadn't left the boat; the radio had been on. The rush of elation, which ordinarily would have sent me happily on my way, collided with a contrary desire to kick at something or someone responsible for the unnecessary delay. In the end, each emotion cut the legs out from the other and, as I motored toward the lock doors, I felt nothing more than a peculiar buzz of euphoric consternation.

MILE 278, BIG BASIN MARINA

After we transited the lock, there were ten miles to Big Basin Marina, our objective for what remained of a much-wasted day. Along the way and for the first time since the Great Lakes, we saw navigation lights and buoys. We were heading downstream. Outward-bound. Daylight was dwindling as we neared Treats Island, south of Joliet. The river bent west. Ahead, Smiths Highway Bridge, I-55, spanned the river. The Big Basin Marina lay just beyond that span. But there was a problem. An obstruction in the river.

A half mile from our destination, the river was blocked. A tug and about four hundred feet of barge lay broadside across the channel. The rig had been trying to turn into a slip along the river when the manoeuvre went sour. The vessel went aground; and it was my nemesis *du jour*; it was the *Pamela Dewey.*

Once in a while, I become heedless. This was one of those times. The cape was red; the matador was haughty; and I was going to bull my way past. Bulls, of course are brazen creatures; however, they are not stupid. Crossing the bow of the tug convoy would have been stupid, and I had not yet fallen so low, even though I knew that deeper water lay there at the head of the string of barges. On my port side, however, the *Pamela Dewey* was pushing and puffing and grunting, and its screws were churning up sludgy brown water from the riverbed. Its stern spewed a plume of froth and a ferment of water. But that's where I pointed the bow and that's where I chose to go—around the tug's grounded stern.

As I did, the depth sounder began its slow, numeric descent. I reduced speed. I steered the boat as close to the riverbank as I thought safe and as far from the stern of *Pamela Dewey* as I thought prudent. The *Arja D.* shuddered at the force of water the tug was kicking out. The depth shrank to three feet...then two feet. I held my breath. I heard a thump. It was a brushing sound. The sound of thick mud. The boat rose an inch or two in the water...the hull slowed... and the keel of the *Arja D.* eased. It had found some water. After that, the depth sounder began a steady, reassuring, numeric ascent.

The tavern at the Big Basin Marina, where we spent the night, opens at 0600. Bob, a more gregarious morning person than I, had wandered off early and found the doors open. Inside, a growing number of pensioners had gathered for a morning pick-up of Bailey's and coffee. Bob joined them for a chat. Today was Bob's last on the *Arja D.* He had signed on for three or four days of sailing, and he had done that. At 0830 Barb arrived, and they began their drive home.

The junction of the Des Plaines and Kankakee Rivers marks the beginning of the Illinois River, which leads 270 miles southwest to the Mississippi. I cleared two locks during the day's passage. Dresden Lock was first. After that, the banks of the Illinois become low and slope gently toward the water. Tall, slender groves of trees line the shore, and a rural, isolated feel takes hold of the landscape. Where there are signs of commerce, one is more likely to see a grain elevator than a chemical plant, and the most frequently seen man-made structures are not cottages, but duck blinds, weather-beaten lean-tos or shacks, curiosities rather than eyesores, and no more out of place in the wooded terrain than thatched huts of aboriginal tribesmen in the outback.

Being alone, though, led me toward introspection, and the remoteness and serenity of this rural scene provided an ease that supported quiet reflection. So my thoughts naturally turned inward, as they did from time to time, to take stock of my small odyssey. Naturally, they turned to the first year. That, of course, had been gruelling, but I worked through it and, as a result, I felt that I had matured in experience and skill. My second year, however, began on a more timorous note—with unvoiced concerns, insubstantial ghosts of the past—but as momentum of the trip set in, much of that doubt evaporated, and confidence slowly buoyed until I became sure that my extraordinary bad luck had slipped behind me for good. This year would be no different. I knew it. Success has a way of growing from the ash of failure.

MILE 240, OTTAWA, IL

I arrived at Marseilles Lock at 1445. Barge crews were uploading a "double." It meant a delay, but so what? The spiritual retreat into my thoughts and hopes and fears had a healing effect. I felt mellow. The current above the lock was lazy, and the day was warm. So I lay back in the cockpit, and I drifted slowly with eyes closed and let the world float with me until lock control eventually radioed. They directed me to approach and standoff near the lock doors in front of another tug and barge waiting to lock-down. When the lock doors opened, I remained another half hour until the job of winching-out the uploading barges concluded. It was 1650 by the time I passed through the Marseilles Lock, and it was suppertime when I arrived in Ottawa, Illinois.

The town of Ottawa lies in the heart of Illinois's corn and soybean farmland, where the Fox River joins the Illinois. Ottawa had been a major stop for runaway slaves on the Underground Railway, and it had hosted the first debate between presidential contenders Abraham Lincoln and Stephen A. Douglas in 1858. On Ottawa's Fox River side, the city established four or five slips for transient boaters. A wooded bluff conceals the slips from the city and provides a degree of privacy for boaters. Only a pedestrian walkway winds along the river's edge.

A light mist hung over the Fox River the next morning. A few bass-fishing boats cruised slowly down the stream toward the Veterans Memorial Bridge which spanned the Illinois. Their bows split the glassy surface of the water, and their wakes radiated vee-shaped ripples, which fanned out and faintly stirred the hull of the *Arja D.* at its resting-place along the dock. By 0700 the dock was a memory, and the morning evolved from an uncertain mistiness to an energetic blue. Well-being and optimism hovered in the air and followed my trek to Starved Rock.

Starved Rock is a lock and a dam, a state park, a former French fort, and an important place in Indigenous history and legend. Native American culture found a home there as long ago as 8000 BC. The explorer La Salle built a fort on top of Starved Rock and called it Fort St. Louis. Its purpose was to protect their Illinois allies from their arch-enemy, the Iroquois.

European politics changed, and the fort disappeared. Local Native American politics changed too and, when in the 1760s Pontiac, a great Ottawa chief, was murdered by an Illinois native during a tribal council, that death led to war. Several battles ensued. The Ottawa tribes drove south. An Illinois tribe, the Illiniwek, tried to hide on Starved Rock in the hope that an Ottawa war party, the Potawatomi, would pass through and not discover them, but the ruse didn't work, and they found themselves trapped without food or water atop that 125-foot limestone butte. Some tried to escape, but they were killed. Those who remained and would not surrender wasted away. Ever since, the site which marked their death has been called Starved Rock.

I cleared the lock within half an hour. The shores of the river below were lined with fishers, mostly families or small groups. The south side of the stream, almost in the shadow of the massacre two centuries before, was more heavily fished. White bass were abundant; crappie, wall-eye, and other bass were snagged occasionally; catfish and stripers were hooked more rarely. The fishers on the south shore mostly were American Indian natives; those on the north shore mostly were not. The yellow cliffs of Starved Rock glinted in the sunshine; a verdant green plain disappeared into the opposite horizon.

Gradually over the next hour, both shores assumed a lower profile. Riverbanks scarcely rose above the water, and the land beyond them dressed in vegetation which hinted at a capricious marshy environment that would surely flood in spring.

Out of the fresh look from the shore came an enlivened pulse from the river itself. The *Arja D.* moved briskly downstream at over 6.5 knots even though I had only throttled the engine up to 1800 rpm. A few towns passed quickly. Peru was the first. It had a rough industrial face to its waterfront, and its Water Street looked dingy. Below Peru, the *Thurston Morton* was pushing a two-by-four loaded with benzene and wood chips upstream. Between the grain elevators of Spring Valley and Hennepin, the river meandered between low areas and shallow lakes, and by then the stiffening current was carrying me at 7 knots. Although it was early afternoon, I already had travelled forty miles. That held promise of a great day's run and, if I brought my engine speed up to 2500 rpm, my normal operating speed, I could get 8 knots, maybe more. That promised an extraordinary day's run. So I pushed the throttle down.

A real thrill accompanies the release of pent-up energy in a powerful engine, any engine for that matter, whether it's the sharp whine of a remote-controlled airplane or the raucous lineup of a NASCAR rally. It's a thrill one remembers in the bones; it's a kick which endures from youth to old age. Perhaps it reminds men of the roar which broke from the throats of our cave-dwelling ancestors as they hurled themselves into tribal battle or pitted themselves against some great beast and which we replicate in the machines we create and use today.

My motor revved. My boat surged. My spirit skipped with excitement. And the thrill was as empowering for me with my thirteen-horsepower diesel as I'm sure it was for Orville Wright and his twelve-horsepower airplane.

My engine growled like a cranky bear. Then, it gasped. It baffled like some blow had struck it in the belly and knocked the wind out of it. It sounded hurt and weak. It faltered. I yanked the throttle into neutral. I turned the engine off. For a moment I hung motionless, hunched over the long arm of the tiller. Desperation settled on me like a cold, dark shadow. All around me was an isolated region of river—wooded islands, shallow lakes, sloughs and levees, no villages, and few boats.

I shifted the rudder and let the boat drift outside the main channel. I didn't want to be surprised by a tug with a dozen barges rounding the bend and bearing down on me. Once clear, I went below and inspected the engine. Oil level. Okay. Water level. Okay. Burning smells. None. Leaks. None. Engine temperature. Normal. I returned to the cockpit and restarted the engine. It turned over quickly and sparked to life, just as it always had. Then I extended my head and shoulders over the vessel's side to check the exhaust. Cooling water was pumping out the exhaust port, just as it should. Everything was operating routinely. So I put the engine in gear and eased down the throttle. No problem arose until the engine cracked 2500 rpm. Then the engine spit and coughed and choked up a second time. When I reduced rpm, the engine ran normally once more. I couldn't determine what caused the breakdown, but it seemed to cause no harm to run at low engine speed. So I steamed ahead at a cripple's pace until I reached Henry, Illinois.

Chapter 19

THE GREAT RISING UP OF GREMLINS

"I wish I knew a hit man," Joyce said.

She wasn't smiling. Her eyes burned a hole in the ground she stared at. Perhaps she was talking to herself. A curt soliloquy, I thought. Then she glanced up at me for a second longer than I felt comfortable. Joyce was the first person I met at Henry, Illinois.

It was mid-afternoon when I arrived. The current was brisk. My engine was flagging. I hurled a coil of stern line onto the wharf on the outer breakwater to the marina and jumped after it. The long line fouled, but I managed to snag a bight around a cleat on the dock and reined the *Arja D.* back. The line grew taut. I braced myself against the strain like some cowboy roping a stray. The line groaned maliciously until the *Arja D.* threw her shoulder against the fenders of the dock and came to rest.

The outer breakwater at Henry was an ell-shaped peninsula, a man-made one. Running parallel to it and about thirty yards offshore was a short island. Together they made up the remnants of what had once been the first lock and dam on the Illinois River, a historical happenstance that allowed droll locals to declare Henry the "best town in Illinois by a dam site." The lock was gone; the dam was gone. Now the slot between the island and peninsula served as a temporary dock and a refuelling station.

From the water's edge the land was too high to see either town or marina, but I did hear voices, and I climbed the steep embankment toward the sound. Three overall-clad workers cut and burned brush that had grown up near a rusting, corrugated metal silo at the head of the arm of land. Broken concrete slabs and other rubble from a long-demolished building were scattered about. A short distance from the men, two women stood near the open rear hatch of a station wagon. One of the women directed the work party.

"I'm Joyce, and this is Jenny," she said, after I had introduced myself.

I explained my difficulty. She listened attentively and popped open the cooler in the back of the car. A dozen or more bottles of water, soda, and juice bobbed in a sea of ice.

"Like a cold one?" she asked and handed me a drink. "A diesel mechanic. That might not be easy today...Saturday and all...but let me see," she added, pulled out a cellphone, and made a string of calls, all to no avail. "There is Dershell, though. He's good with hot rods...or he might know someone," she said, and pointed beyond the boats and docks, enclosed within the arms of the peninsula, to the marina clubhouse and restaurant on the far shore.

Joyce was secretary of the Henry Yacht Club and a past commodore. She was energetic, coy, pleasant, and efficient. She was trim and daintily business-like. She was also recently divorced, bitter at the yet-unresolved property settlement, frustrated at her now-blunted lifestyle, and charged with a rancour which she occasionally levelled and fired off during conversations involving her former husband, Rick.

Rick was a man in his fifties. He had an imposing stature and an affable, easygoing demeanour. His silver hair and silver moustache gave him a distinguished appearance. He had owned a car dealership but lost the business. Now he had just two obvious assets: a thirty-six-foot cabin cruiser which he lived aboard on weekends, and a smile that would have charmed the most hardened nun in the parochial school he once attended.

Rick was at the club that evening. So were a couple hundred others. On weekends, local boaters, sundry residents, and yacht-club members from out of town or out of state return for what amounts to a three-day party. The restaurant and bar, named Henry Harbour Landings, was privately owned, but it was the social centre of the yacht club, and on this Saturday night, every stool and table in the bar was filled. In fact, every square foot of standing room was occupied. And in the adjacent restaurant a blues rock band had set up, and a large area had been cleared for dancing.

That afternoon, I became acquainted with at least a dozen people, a number of them being boaters who had gathered to catch my lines when I moved into a permanent berth. Randy and Connie were among them. They owned a cruiser which lay opposite my boat, and they too were at the Landings in the evening.

Randy is some kind of doctor. Connie is a businesswoman. Randy believes that the destruction of the World Trade Center was planned and directed by President George W. Bush and a company of others determined to lead the country into a war against their oil-laden, Arab arch-enemies. Connie believes that the US Constitution guarantees freedom of speech to all citizens, whether they glean their convictions from the *Washington Post* or the *Daily Blogger*. Randy is also manic. Even in his most relaxed and reflective moment, that period just before his first morning coffee, Randy's spirit races like an old truck with a jammed throttle, and by Saturday night he redlines. He becomes lead strutter in the Conga line, baton major in a parade of willing fools, choirmaster of bawdy song, class clown, and zany wit. The rest of us become lords and ladies, attendants and servants, pages, and torchbearers, in other words, props to support his dramatic flourishes. Connie, on the other hand, quietly stands the watch, becomes the mooring that brakes the flurry of his abandon, and allows him to come finally and safely to rest.

When not involved in one of Randy's improvisational scenes, I played pool with Rick and Motor at one of the tables in the back corner of the bar. Motor was a businessman—the old-fashioned kind: crusty, blue-collar-bred, plain talking, hands-on.

"They call me Motor," he said the next day. He slouched back in a lawn chair on the shaded deck of his houseboat. He gripped a beer bottle in one hand and fixed his gaze on the marina entrance and the town's bridge beyond it. "It's short for motor-mouth, if you hadn't guessed already. I run my mouth off a lot."

His nickname had as much to do with his delivery as it did with his continual streaming of words. An uninterrupted brusqueness underscored every phrase, so as to say "this is the way it is." No metaphors, tarted-up facts; none of his expressions had secret compartments; none of his beliefs had been scrubbed and starched with "political correctness."

He nodded his head toward the cruiser next to him. It was Rick's boat.

"He drinks too damn much, and he spends too damn much. He and his wife both. That's why he lost the business. They're divorced now, y' know."

"I met Joyce yesterday. She said something about that."

"I think he ran up a big debt...to some questionable people too. Sometimes he acts skittish. There was a big red Cadillac driving around looking for him. It was here a few times. I told him about it, but he never said a word, not one word."

"What did he do?"

"He disappeared for a few days. Y'know this boat of mine has never left the dock...ever. I just like to sit here, drink beer, and look at the water...no desire to go anywhere...it's relaxing. Everything I want is right here. This is perfect. Perfect." This was as poetic as Motor would ever become.

Motor had recommended J. R. He said that J. R. was honest, did a day's work, and charged a fair wage for what he did. J. R. was the mechanic who owned the garage at the head of the bridge a few hundred yards from the marina, and he agreed to take a quick look at the engine the afternoon I arrived. When he got to the boat, he checked the valve clearances and the injector timing, the usual suspects, and said he would be back Monday morning. He didn't work on Sundays.

At the beginning of the week J. R. returned to the boat at 0845 as promised. J. R. said little and, when he did speak, he spoke slowly.

His was a mind tuned to cams and rotors, valves and bushings, racks and pinions, all those devices which are measurable, predictable and fixed, all those things which words are not. I never minded the long silences, though.

"If it doesn't need saying, then it makes no sense to say it," he might have said, and I would have agreed and, despite the fact that he was not a diesel mechanic, I liked his methodical approach to problem solving.

J. R. reset the valve clearances, and we took the boat for a short run along the main course of the marina but, as soon as load increased, the engine balked again. So we returned to the berth.

"I have to take the head off," he said, "but I have another job to go to now. If you want, you could strip off the exhaust and some of the hoses. This one, this one, and those two. I'll be back tomorrow," he added. He sensed my limited financial situation from the spartan nature of the cabin. His parting suggestion was a polite way of telling me, by rolling up my own sleeves, repair costs would drop.

I had turned to the task before he drove out of the parking lot in front of the Landings. It was not an arduous job. It took a few hours. By then it was after noon. It was hot below deck, and I was ready for a cold drink.

Rick was seated at the bar at the Landings when I arrived. He was eager for company. No one else was in the place. So I joined him.

"Engine fixed?" he asked.

"Not yet."

"Get a mechanic?"

I filled him in, but Rick wasn't impressed.

"Get a real diesel mechanic," he argued. "Get somebody who knows what they're doin'. It'll be cheaper in the long run and quicker."

"You may be right, but I think I'll stick with J. R. for the time being. See how things go. Besides, there's no marine diesel places around."

"I'll tell you what...I'll drive you to Peoria...It's an hour away... Gotta be one there."

It was a generous offer, and I was tempted to accept, but two thoughts held me back. First, I was convinced that the engine problem would prove to be a simple one. Second, I was paralysed by what I imagined would be an enormous repair bill from a fancy diesel shop. I muttered my thanks but no thanks. At the same time, there was comfort in knowing that, despite Rick's shortcomings, he had a benevolent spirit.

"What happened to your arm?" I asked, changing the subject. His right elbow was badly swollen, puffy with fluid. It was a bad fall, he said. A drunken one, I thought. No, he hadn't seen a doctor, he said. He probably would, he added, but not convincingly.

Rick had the bearing of the well-to-do. He had the appearance of money. He owned some toys that money provided. In reality, however, Rick was broke, and he had no money for a doctor, none that he was willing to spare, anyway.

That was the conclusion I reached and, while I was doing so, I thought back to my sprained ankle from last summer. I had been treated for the injury in the outpatient's clinic of an Illinois hospital. In Canada, the same hospital services and doctor's care would have cost $250. Of course, Canadians don't actually pay. The government covers it entirely, and the Canadian government, true to form, paid the US hospital $250 for the services it provided. A few months later, however, I received an invoice for $1,200, the balance for what that Illinois hospital insisted I still owed *after* Canadian reimbursement. At the time I received that letter, a voice inside my head muttered dumbly as if it had been clipped by a car. Then, shaking off its addled thinking, the voice rose in anger and shot out a volley of epithets, and created such a racket that it gave me a splitting headache. I would have taken a Tylenol 3, but that remedy would have cost $150 at an American health-care facility. So what was the use?

Denial. Anger. Bargaining. Depression. Acceptance...Acceptance? No, I hadn't quite reached that stage of grieving over my loss of money. Neither had Rick. His eyes glazed; his mouth drooped. His mind whirled through a depressing pack of scenes which he feared might come true for him, and he would have wallowed there if he had not pictured Joyce in one of those scenes. That image re-fortified him and propelled him back into a lively juggling of denial, anger and bargaining, all those things which make the wheels spin wildly even if the truck is not moving. A tight-lipped monologue poured forth like acrid smoke, and at the end of it...

"I hate that woman!" He spit the words out like he had bitten into a wormy apple.

Then he added, "If only I knew a hit man..." His voice trailed off after that, and in the silence which ensued, his mind ground to pulp a few more of the ugly fantasies which had taken root there.

My encounter with Rick had tumbled me into a blue funk of sorts. Rick ordered another beer, but I left him at the bar. I had to get away. So I retired to the boat and rested for an hour on my bunk. I was tired. The cabin was hot and stuffy. I couldn't sleep and, when I finally roused myself, I found that I had no energy to make supper.

A placard I'd seen at the Landings gave me an out, though. It had announced a Chamber of Commerce fundraiser: Spaghetti. $6. All you can eat. Tonight. My plan to escape the doldrums, therefore, was this: to eat somebody else's deliciously prepared food and enjoy the ambience of a company of strangers who seemed, on the surface at least, content with their lives.

But Joyce's was the first face I saw. She stood near the door in some official capacity at the dinner. She smiled, at least feigning good cheer, and introduced me to several people as "this is the traveller I was telling you about." Eventually, I made my way to the buffet line, loaded my plate with pasta, salad, and rolls and, as I searched the restaurant for a small table, an older gentleman approached.

"Joyce tells me that you sailed from eastern Canada," he said. "Do you mind if I join you? I'd like to hear more. My name's Larry."

Larry was a transplant. A long-time Chicago resident, he ran a printing company until his retirement. Then he moved to Henry, why I never learned, and he assumed the role of terrier in a struggle to burrow through the complacency of Henry's citizens and drag them out and into a renewed social consciousness. Henry was probably the only liberal, no doubt the most vocal one, in this conservative, Republican, small town.

During supper Larry leaned forward with twinkling eyes and an eagerness to know about my voyage. He was so full of questions that I could scarcely punctuate my responses with a fork full of spaghetti. He had to know about this or that detail of the trip.

"Would you join me for some wine?" he asked. "I have a couple of good bottles at my house. I could drive you there and bring you back later." Larry drove me across town in his 1929 Model A Ford convertible. It was a beautiful automobile, Sherwood green in colour, and complete with a rumble seat and a trunk-like storage box strapped above the rear bumper. Larry's house was a small bungalow about a mile from the marina. We chatted around the kitchen table. A Chagall broadside decorated one wall, and several shelves held African artifacts. A while later Larry's girlfriend, Carole, arrived. She brought Joyce with her. The wine was Cabernet Sauvignon from a Napa Valley winery owned by a special friend of theirs.

Larry was a well-read and well-informed fellow, and between dialogues about the war in Iraq and local politics, I learned that Larry had been in the Army Air Corps during the Second World War. After university he was commissioned a lieutenant and went to flight school in Texas where he flew P-40s and P-47s. The P-47s were rugged fighter-bombers and, as many pilots described them, "unbreakable."

Larry was apparently unbreakable too. I did the math. He was eighty years old, but "old" was not a fitting word to describe him. He was more spry and alert and active and interested in the world around him than almost anyone I knew, regardless of age. Among his other undertakings, he had run for town council once, lost, and planned to run again. He sang in a barbershop quartet, and he chaired a local public-affairs discussion group that met once a week at The Coffee Cup uptown.

I met up with Larry the next day and most days after that while I waited for the engine to be repaired. Over the following week my relationship with the engine deteriorated from problem to dilemma. J. R. inspected the head. The valves seated well, and the pistons were tight. Then he removed the injection pump and injectors and sent them to a repair depot for testing. They were found to be somewhat wanting. So they were rebuilt. J. R. reinstalled them later in the week, but the engine still blew out black smoke and balked at higher rpm, just as it had all along. He adjusted shims; he reset clearances; he checked for blockages; he scratched his head; and he inventoried his dwindling options. Finally, he called the mechanic at the depot which had rebuilt the injectors and asked him to look over the engine. He would, the mechanic said. On Monday.

I had led Larry and Carole to expect that my engine would be repaired and that I would be on my way by the weekend. To commemorate my leaving, therefore, they invited me to dinner at the Landings. A going-away dinner. My not-going-away didn't dissuade them. A seafood buffet and wine followed and, as usual Joyce and a few others joined the group. After dinner tables cleared, a DJ began to set up for the weekend crowd. We retired to the bar and, soon the place bustled with club members returning for the weekend.

Showers began Friday evening and lasted until the following day. The temperature dropped to fifty degrees Fahrenheit, and boaters hunkered down in their cabins. All of this muted the gaiety of the waterfront. I had tried to hook up an electric space heater, but my extension cord needed a special adapter. Frank, a neighbouring boater and electrician, loaned me one. As a result, the cabin was toasty warm that night, but it would be cold again the next day because I had to return the adapter. Joyce saw me fiddling with the cord after Frank returned home. She had been chatting with her girlfriend on the boat "next door."

"I know where there's an adapter," she said.

"You do? That would be great!" I said. "Where?"

"On Rick's boat."

"Oh?" I tried to assess what trouble I was stepping into as she pursued this potentially reckless course of action.

"I know where he hides the keys."

I winced. In my mind I imagined some alarm going off, the police arriving, trespassing charges laid.

"I dunno. That sounds kinda illegal to me," I said.

"Nonsense. The boat is still half mine," she added.

I further imagined a cold dank cabin. I envisioned the feel of a clammy blanket. I foresaw my breath fogging up the porthole windows.

"Well, if you think he wouldn't mind..."

Joyce brought me the adapter. It worked. And I spent the last night of the weekend quite comfortably warm. No adverse consequences followed the questionable borrowing.

In fact, during the sweltering week which had just passed, Rick had made me an extraordinary offer: "Why don't you stay on my boat?" he said. "I'm not going to be here all week. It's got air-conditioning, television, whatever you need. It's too hot to stay in your boat. The keys are..."

And during the even more sweltering heat of the week following, Joyce made a remarkable offer: "Why don't you stay in the cottage behind my house? It's got air-conditioning. Nobody's renting it right now. It would be more comfortable than your boat in this weather. Why don't you think about it?"

I declined both offers, tempted though I was, and told each of them, separately, the truth: "I really appreciate your thoughtfulness...but living aboard my boat is part of the adventure. Odd as it may seem, it's...fun...sort of..."

It was also true that I wanted to remain neutral. I liked Rick. I liked Joyce. And I didn't fancy becoming tangled in the throes of their volatile, dying relationship.

I had a lot of time to kill in Henry. When I wasn't looking over J. R.'s shoulder or lending him a hand, I wandered about town. Once a day I walked the lane which led along the river. It was town parkland. Green lawns, mature shade trees, a scattering of benches and one or two picnic tables or fire pits made it an accommodating and relaxing environment, and I spent hours reading there or listening to the murmur of leaves or watching barges fill themselves from the grain chutes at the southwest end of the park. A library and a municipal pool stood on a ridge above the common. Beyond them the land levelled.

A town square stood in the heart of town. All town squares are cast in a similar mould. They form a restful swath of greenery in the centre of the village. A bandstand is erected for political rallies, speakers at civic holidays, or concerts. Walkways intersect each other and connect with adjacent sidewalks, and there are benches for the old, the idle, and the dreamers. Several blocks of businesses and restaurants and offices and shops surrounded the square. The buildings were pretty, Victorian, and neatly cared for, but many were vacant, and the businesses that once enlivened them had been supplanted by malls which clung like leeches to the outer limbs of Henry, just as they do in nearly every other town and city in North America. Beyond the languishing business district, blocks of quiet streets and neat old houses spilled out in every direction.

On a corner of the square was the town's only public telephone. Every few days I could be found there calling Brenda, updating her on my progress, and having her coordinate with my son, Finley, who had planned to meet me in Cairo, Illinois, for a week's voyage on the river. By then, thanks mostly to Larry and Joyce, I seemed to have met half of the townspeople in Henry, and Brenda found it quite amusing that, on several occasions, our phone calls would be interrupted by some passing motorist honking the horn, waving, or shouting, "Finley...you still here?"

And in a similar fashion, whenever I stepped through the front door of The Coffee Cup, a block from the town square, Paula, the owner, would greet me: "Hi, Finley. Your engine not fixed? You're having an awful time with that, aren't you? What can I get for you?

Oh, have you met my children yet? This one is..."

Over two weeks I had the opportunity to meet not only her children, but also her husband, father, mother, brother, sister-in-law, and several other relatives. In addition to them, and among the regular morning customers, was Barb, a seventy-eight-year-old divorcee, who enjoyed a chat, sipping coffee, and catching up on news of the day. Sometimes, sitting with her would be Joyce, sorting invoices or tallying a ledger for one or another of the organizations to which she belonged.

Thursday morning was a special time at The Coffee Cup, for it was on that day that Larry hosted his weekly discussion group. They were informal gatherings at which members shared opinions on world news or local troubles. I was able to attend two of the meetings. Each time, three or four tables were strung together to accommodate the dozen or so participants. The mix was different each week and included an off-duty police officer or two, a local politician, a few retirees, so-and-so's visiting cousin from Sometown, itinerants like myself, the odd business person, and even a high-school student with parent. Larry always brought a folder of newspaper clippings and read them one at a time until a particular topic sparked enough interest to earn comment and counter-comment, and that exchange would flicker on until the fuel of controversy burned itself out.

As my stay in Henry began to feel more and more comfortable, my confidence in the resurrection of my engine grew more and more feeble. Monday's mechanic arrived from the shop which rebuilt the injectors and injection pump. J. R. was with him. Neither could find the fault with the engine. All it could be, thought Monday's mechanic was that the injector pressure had been improperly set. So he whisked them back to his shop for a re-test. In the afternoon J. R. returned with the results: the injectors were perfect. Maybe it's the fuel cam?

J. R.'s mind was not on mechanical work so much any more. His father was suffering from throat cancer; then doctors discovered a blood clot. He was dying. So, while J. R. spent more and more time taking care of his father's needs, I tore the engine down to the camshaft. The fuel cam was worn a bit, but both J. R. and I knew that wasn't the problem. Still, he considered replacing the fuel cam until I learned that the part would have to be ordered from Japan. Shipment would take four weeks.

J. R. had reassembled the engine by noon on Friday. That afternoon I settled my account with him. Just as Motor had said, J. R. "charged a fair day's wage for what he did." In fact, the labour costs he totalled up were considerably less than I had anticipated. The reason for that, I surmised, was a dent in his professional pride, his inability to isolate the problem with my diesel engine. As a result, he wouldn't charge for what he couldn't fix.

I should have felt disappointed, frustrated even, that I was no further ahead after two weeks but, in fact, I was relieved. At least now it was clear what I must do, and that was to lay up the boat for the season and go home. Yet it became a challenge to achieve even that modest goal. First of all, there was limited boat storage at the marina. Second, I didn't have a trailer to haul my boat. Nor would I likely find a suitable one. Third, the Henry Yacht Club was more club than marina. It had no facilities to haul a boat out, nor security or permanent staff to keep an eye on my boat until next season. My only alternative was towing the boat to Peoria, thirty-two miles downriver.

Joyce offered to do the job. Larry and Carole would join her tomorrow, Saturday, she said. Joyce was excited to help, but I had misgivings. Her boat was a small runabout. I didn't believe that it could handle my sailboat. So I turned down her offer. Fortunately, a second offer came from Rob and Cindy.

Rob and Cindy were an unlikely couple. Cindy was tall, blonde, willowy. She could have been a model. Rob was younger, mid-thirties, shorter, more sturdily built. Their attractions to each other must have run more strongly than their contrasting appearances, however, because they married. Then, like most everyone else I had met in Henry, they divorced. As fate would have it, their six-year breakup proved unsuccessful.

"We finally realized that we couldn't live without each other," said Rob. Cindy nodded. "So we got married again."

"We go to Peoria every weekend for a trip," said Rob. "So hauling your boat down there is no trouble for us. As a matter of fact, you'll save us a hundred bucks in gas by making us drive slower. Six miles per hour instead of twenty-six," he joked.

Rob was a blue-collar kind of guy. He came with no frills, and he put on no airs. In many ways he was like Motor, but without hard edges and without examining life through black-and-white spectacles. Benevolence and empathy balanced the colours of his spectrum, qualities which set him apart and qualities which probably grew out of his upbringing. He had been raised by a two-parent family, but both his father and mother had been completely blind from birth. The difficulties which that family faced are scarcely imaginable. They struggled financially, of course, but self-sacrifice, humility, love, and resolve enable families to succeed, where money cannot.

Then, like many young men out of high school, Rob drifted from one job to another until a car dealership took him on as an apprentice mechanic, work he enjoyed very much. Rob's life changed, however, on the day his boss wanted someone to take an upgrading course in body repair. Rob didn't want to go away for any course. Neither did the other mechanics, but Rob, having the least seniority, had no choice and grudgingly agreed to take the course, some new technique on removing hailstone dents from autos without damaging the original finish. A few years later he started his own business doing just that...and found success.

"I've had good luck. Now I have the chance to make life a little better for my parents. They deserve it," he said quietly.

Rob and Cindy arrived dockside around eleven on Saturday morning. Joyce arrived about the same time to see me off and give me a case of bottled water for the trip. A small collection of club members eased the *Arja D.* out of her berth and held her with lines from their stations at the tips of the docks, while Rob manoeuvred his cruiser to take me in tow.

Rob's Bayliner packed more horsepower and wielded heavier displacement than Joyce's vessel. Rob caught my tow-line, cleared a nearby string of boats before we drifted on top of them, and slowly dragged me through the narrow harbour mouth and into the Illinois River.

It was 1600 when we arrived at the Eastport Marina, across the river from downtown Peoria. The route from channel to breakwater was a zig-zag, and the wind forced Rob to leave me on the outer extremity of the string of wharves inside the marina's enclosure.

At the marina office I arranged to store the boat for the season. Later I met up with Rob and Cindy. They planned to attend the Riverfront Festival in Peoria that night and asked me to go along with them. We crossed the river to Peoria in Rob's cruiser and tied up at a busy wharf on Riverfront Park. A floating walkway ran along a high retaining wall of the riverbank. We followed it until we reached a ramp and ascended to the parkland above. We heard noises first—energetic, excited, musical, rhythmic sounds. Then a sprawl of carnival amusements spilled out before our eyes. Food stands and beer concessions and trinket booths abounded. Fortune tellers read customers' hidden wishes, face painters masked their flaws, and men of question promised luck in their games of chance. Mechanical rides rolled and twisted, snapped, spun, and tossed delighted youngsters and white-knuckled parents. Musicians and songsters took a turn at entertaining a crowd in the park's amphitheatre. The smells of beer, corn dogs, cotton candy, and french fries hovered above and wove within the throngs. Hucksters hooted; babies cried; children whined with disappointment or wailed with glee. Girls flirted; boys strutted; and grey heads with pained eyes limped toward hard benches. After a few hours, the press of the crowd and the din of the games grew tiring. So we left the carnival grounds, returned to the river and the boardwalk, and chatted with a few other boaters, some of whom we recognized from Henry.

Fireworks that had been scheduled for the evening had been cancelled because of the high winds but, as the night fell darkly over the water, a scheduled parade of boats began. Their procession was slow and stately, one by one, past the reviewing stand, past the loudspeakers, past the chirping emcee and beyond the park. The boats were illuminated with lights and torches, decorated with flowers and crepe, cardboard and fabric, and crewed by costumed merrymakers, and the boats espoused themes silly or sublime, commercial or comic, those worthy and those worth less.

After that, we boarded Rob's boat, but we didn't head back across the river to our marina. Instead we sailed at a listless pace downriver. The sky was a murky black above, but the river, which moved below us, glistened with the reflection of lights. In fact, we were surrounded by lights. Some lights were gaudy and brash and illuminated a casino boat, where luck recklessly tumbled across green felt tables. Channel buoys glowed in gentle, rhythmic pulses, and we slipped between them on our winding course south of the city. Headlights of cars flickered like strobes as they sped behind the steel balustrade and latticework of the bridges under which we passed.

On either shore, pinpricks of light marked breakwaters of marinas and boat ramps and sundry landings. Other lights illuminated the work at large commercial docks and terminals. They burned bright and bold, and sent a pale sheen across a great plane of water.

The river glowed, and from it emerged reassuring warmth. One could sense a headiness, like that which follows a glass of port wine at the end of a fine meal, when all cares scatter and flee. A river has the power, it seems, to do that more easily than either sea or ocean. Seas are restless and temperamental; rivers are steady. Seas challenge; rivers inspire. Seas are brackish and saline. Rivers quench. Rivers cleanse. Rivers heal.

For Rob and Cindy the Illinois River is their healing spirit. It's their church, and the thirty-odd miles between Henry and Peoria is their parish grounds. Every weekend, they make a pilgrimage from their home port to the dam's head and back again, and on the evenings like this, they linger, grow lyrical and introspective. Cindy peers into the black shimmering depths of the river and speaks wistfully of her dead father, his ashes not so long ago strewn on these waters. She revisits his deathbed pain and helplessness. She remembers her sadness and his kindness. Now, in the strength of this river, she sees his strength and, in the stride of this river, she sees his soul journeying.

And Rob?

As Rob's hands grip the boat's wheel, his eyes lift up and drink in the turbid black sky. He speaks of the peace and contentedness he feels here on the river, his love of the river. As he speaks, he doesn't look at me. He doesn't look at Cindy. His words flow like a monologue, and his eyes fix at some empty space above. Perhaps he thinks of his sightless parents. Perhaps, like them, when he stares through such murky blackness, he sees something other than resignation and emptiness. Perhaps he sees hope and fulfilment. Perhaps he sees a kind of redemption.

Chapter 20

THE BANANA PEEL SCHTICK

I had strapped my diesel engine down onto the deck of my van and driven it two thousand miles home in the late summer of 2006. There, it worked well enough when bench-tested by my Canadian mechanic. However, it would not work when returned to Peoria and installed in the boat. If I were superstitious, I would have sworn that the engine had been cursed.

An Illinois company that repairs diesel trucks took a crack at fixing it. Wrenches turned, and gauges tested, and mechanics pondered. Their thinking cut deeply, so much so that, after three weeks, my little engine lay spread out across their long metal worktable, as neatly taken apart as a cadaver dissected by a second-year medical student. The death certificate came in the form of a two-page printout of parts which needed replacement. The total cost would near $3,500.

"There are other options," suggested the shop foreman with the subdued air of a funeral director.

"We could price a factory-rebuilt job..." said a mechanic.

"That'd be around $10,000," added the foreman.

I grew pale.

"Or we could rebuild that diesel we got in here as a trade last year," said the chief mechanic. "We could do that for..." His fingers tapped a cheerful rhythm of keyboard calculations, "around $3,000...complete."

I nodded.

The resurrection of the second engine began almost immediately. Problems occurred almost immediately as well, and each week after that a new one surfaced to take its place. They formed a never-ending succession. In spite of that, I managed to keep a cheery outlook. Because the resumption of my trip always seemed just one more week in the future, hope burned softly away at doubt. But then, toward the end of the 2007 sailing season, the mechanics agreed that a part would have to be ordered. It could only be got in Japan, and it would take a month to arrive.

I went home again.

Over the autumn and winter months which passed, I believed that work would continue on my engine. But little of that happened. When I arrived in Peoria, launched the boat, and started the engine in 2008, my ready optimism shrank at the sound I heard. The engine either screamed out of control or collapsed and stalled. So, my second season in Peoria rapidly degenerated into a repetition of breakdowns and failings similar to those in the previous year and the year before.

May and most of June slipped by. Violent thunderstorms swept through every three or four days. Tornado warnings were common. The Mississippi, a two-day's run south, had flooded its banks, spilling disaster across most Midwestern states. News headlines labelled it a Hundred Year's Flood. My consolation was in the fact that the Mississippi was closed to all boat traffic. Even if my engine had been working, the broken levees and topped-over locks would have made it impossible to navigate.

It was not until the end of June when water levels on the Big Muddy began to drop, and it was about that same time when my mechanics said that the rebuild was completed and the second engine was ready to go.

I was elated.

The engine was reinstalled and, on June 30, I set forth on a trial run. The day was mildly warm, and the sun was muted behind a high veil. It was a lazy day. As I cleared the marina breakwater, it seemed strange to be sitting at the tiller and holding the throttle again. I felt nervous—like a novice driver. But when I turned the bow upriver, suddenly I felt free, as if chains had dropped from my body.

It had been two years since I sailed these waters, and heading upriver was like reeling back time. I sensed my past excitement at being completely on my own and not knowing what adventure might lie around the next bend. I had missed that. But I also found myself becoming more reflective as my thoughts turned to the many friends I had made in Peoria during the past two years. I would miss them as well.

Dennis was one of the first. His boat had been in a berth near mine at the outer extremity of Dock A, the transit dock. I had just emerged from my cabin and was about to phone my wife when he called out and introduced himself.

"Saw your boat pull in. Liked it," he said. "Don't see many wooden boats anymore. Where'd you get it?"

"Thanks. I built—"

"Friend of mine had one. Long time ago. Twenty-four foot. How long's yours?"

"It's—"

"About the same I s'pose. That's mine." He pointed. "Twenty-nine-footer. Crank-down keel. Chrysler. Outboard."

"My engine—"

"All the power I need. Original one too."

Dennis was a short, stocky man in his fifties. He had a truck-driver's paunch and scant hair. His voice was raw and raspy.

"Things growin' on my vocal cords," he said. "Had them removed once before. Doc says I might lose my voice...for good. Su'm'bitch. Didn't like the sound of that! Runs in the family, ya know."

"Have you?"

"Got them on the kidney too."

"Gotta go," I said, after the conversation stretched on for another twenty minutes. I had to call home. The nearest phone was a two-mile hike up the highway. If I waited longer, my wife would not be home. So I started down the dock.

"Runs in the family," he said again. By then I was ten yards away.

"Gotta go," I repeated.

"Father had them. An uncle too."

I half-turned and shrugged at fifteen yards.

"Might take 'er out for a sail...'s makin' up a breeze."

I nodded vigorously at twenty yards.

"Droppin' the water level tomorrow." His voice was scarcely a whisper, scarcely indistinguishable from the rush of wind.

I waved goodbye at forty yards. I neared the end of the dock. He said something. I don't know what. Then he disappeared from sight as I strode up the ramp to the marina complex, along the access road which led toward the highway to East Peoria.

Dennis enjoyed talking more than listening. Conversations were mostly monologues. Perhaps he thought that someday soon the surgeon's scalpel would cut away too much of the cysts growing on his vocal cords and his voice would be imprisoned forever within his thoughts. I don't know. Anyway, having plenty of time on my hands, I learned to listen to him much in the same way as the wedding guest listened in Coleridge's gripping *Rime of the Ancient Mariner*, and I learned many interesting things about the man.

Dennis grew up amongst a parcel of brothers who were drinkers and brawlers. Some of that rubbed off on Dennis. There were brushes with the law as well as a few head-on collisions. But he grew out of the worst of it. In the 1960s, he married. It was an unhappy affair. In the late 1960s, it ended.

"It was a bad couple a weeks all 'round," he said. "I got the final divorce papers at the beginning of one week. Damn if'n I didn't get a call from the draft board at the end of the next week. I asked them, 'How in hell did ya know I wasn't exempt? I just got divorced a few days ago.'"

They said, "Your wife called us. You've got thirty days to report to the US Army recruiting station at..."

He paused for a moment, and then added, "That su'm'bitch. She tried to kill me."

Dennis avoided his draft into the army by enlisting in the US Navy. There he learned to operate heavy equipment with the navy's

Construction Battalion, known as the Seabees. He drove a bulldozer in Vietnam, and he recounted surviving an attack on one of their work sites while his unit was building a fortification.

They had come under direct fire. A VC rocket blew the top off a Marine tank; machine-gun fire dropped a Marine rifleman close by; Dennis raised the blade on his bulldozer; bullets ricocheted with a snap and a whine off the curved steel, and he backed the dozer into a more covered position.

"I only had to pull a gun twice in my life," said Dennis. Well, maybe three times. I think that's pretty damn good."

In these instances, Dennis was talking about peacetime in the Unites States, not the war in Vietnam. The first incident occurred in the Deep South. He had been hired to run a dozer at a construction project in Alabama. He was working alone, when four or five local men came up on him.

"You a union man?" one of them asked.

"That's right."

"Where y'all from?"

"Illinois," Dennis said. Two of the men slowly moved around the bulldozer to the other side.

"We don' want red-neck Yankees down heah. Y'unnerstand? Yer takin' jobs away f'm us."

The circle of men around the dozer began to close. Dennis's hand reached forward and felt inside an open compartment under the dash of his cab. He grasped a small .38 pistol.

"Y' know...I think it's about time now for you boys to start movin' along," he said. The .38 rose slowly from its resting place in his lap. The barrel pointed out the direction of the nearest town.

Another episode took place in New York City late at night. Dennis was in his sailboat half asleep at a marina. He heard a commotion and poked his head out his cabin door. An elderly man and woman were crying for help. They were being mugged and robbed. Dennis reached back to an overhead rack, grabbed his 12-gauge shotgun, and fired a volley which cleared the heads of the thieves. The robbers fled; the couple was thankful; but local police criticized Dennis for shooting. Dennis stuck to his guns, his legal right to use them in such circumstances, that is.

It was difficult to fill months of idleness in East Peoria. When I wasn't hunched over, peering down a hatchway, watching one of several mechanics tune up or tear down my engine, I read. Novels mostly. I like to read slowly. So I finished only about eight books per season. And most of my reading took place on the sprawling covered deck of the marina's complex of offices, banquet halls, laundry facilities, and restaurant lounge.

The deck had a commanding view of the Illinois River and the skyline of Peoria on the distant bank. During the day, the vista is impressive but, as evening draws near, it becomes magical. Small puffs of cloud turn orange and woolly, low on the horizon. The sky slips into a deep soft red and, after a brief intermission of twilight, the big Midwestern sky becomes a luminous, sterling blue and etches the city's profile in crisp black.

The skylines of New York and Montreal are bold and spectacular, but the skyline of Peoria is simple, balanced, proportioned, and irresistible. Two bridges frame the boundaries of the city and, between them, something compels the eye to shift from tower to aircraft beacon, from high-rise to church spire, from strings of light to solitary glows, from the lumbering pace of navigation lights on tugboats and barges to the quick track of wing lights in the sky above. Altogether a most alluring sight, almost hypnotic, and one from which eyes can scarcely pull away.

Often at midday the heat rises into the nineties. To sit on the deck of the boat is impossible. To retire below reduces one to a sweating stupor. Even to sit under the cover of the marina's deck became intolerable. It was impossible to read anywhere. So, during those times, I would walk north of the marina to a small park. Beyond it, a path led through a wooded area along the river. There, a canopy of trees screened out enough of the sun's heat for me to gain some relief.

The trail meandered through much of what was a flood plain of the Illinois River. It was a narrow strip, sometimes less than a hundred yards wide, sandwiched between the river and a busy highway. Yet it abounded with wildlife and, each time I walked it, I was delighted with something new and surprising. On several occasions, deer foraged nearby and eyed me warily; once, a pack of raccoon cubs frolicked in the undergrowth of ferns, playfully pushed each other about, and ignored me entirely; blue birds, indigo buntings, cardinals, vireos, and thrushes darted through the high foliage, and I became familiar with their calls, even when I could not see them. Rabbits grazed in shaded grassy patches, and squirrels harped and scolded at my intrusion into their territory.

The trail ran a mile or more before it ended at a small marina. Sometimes I would turn back there, but sometimes I would turn up to an access road which led to an industrial park. There I would find Doug Forester at work in his cabinet-making shop. Doug was another good friend of mine.

Doug and I met at the marina. Like many others, he had been drawn to the quaintness of a wooden boat. As it happened, Doug had rebuilt several wood boats himself, not sailboats, but antique Chris-Craft speed boats. Now he was building another powerboat, his own design, from scratch. He had lofted it in a separate bay attached to his shop and had the sleek, classic appearance of 1930s runabouts. It looked to be about 24 feet long and held a double cockpit. The mahogany planking of his boat rounded up aft until it formed a bullet-shaped, overhanging stern, and this characteristic made it quite different from traditional Chris-Craft designs.

Doug was a dark-haired, trimly built man in his mid-forties. He married his high-school sweetheart. Later they divorced, but he still managed to remain friends with her and with her new husband. He was a good-looking man. If he were an actor, he could have played the romantic rival on an afternoon TV soap opera. In fact, several of the times I visited his shop, I would find dreamy-eyed attractive women who had dropped in "just to chat," having found themselves somehow "in the neighbourhood."

Not just women found themselves in the neighbourhood. Many others were drawn by Doug's easygoing demeanour and wide range of interests as well: contractors leaned against saw stands with small packets of plans and tossed out jokes; craftsmen from nearby industrial shops sipped on coffee and traded gossip; businessmen with a penchant for boats and engines dropped in with invitations to lunch.

Jack Ryan was one of the frequent visitors. He was a boating enthusiast. He had seen the *Arja D.* a few weeks before I met him. He was very interested in my plan to head down the Mississippi to the Gulf, and he was astounded at the string of setbacks which had delayed me in Peoria. He was retired and had a boat of his own at another marina.

Later, Doug told me about Jack's twenty-two-year career with the FBI. He had had an outstanding record of service which included the recruitment and management of nine high-level Mafia informants. But eighteen months before retirement, he found himself faced with a crisis of conscience, one which would change the course of his life.

It was the mid-80s, a time when the US military had intervened secretly and not so secretly in Central America. In protest to these

Doug Forester and Dennis (right) chatting at the Peoria marina.

activities which many labelled violent, immoral, and illegal, one Chicago activist group, Plowshares, went on a total hunger strike in a non-violent protest against violence. The group was made up of Second World War, Korean, and Vietnam vets, and others. A few of their members went a bit further than they should have and jammed up the door locks of eleven military recruiting centres. They were found out.

Ordinarily, their action, illegal though it was, might have resulted in a vandalism charge, a fine, or probation. However, the FBI's Terrorist Task Force escalated the seriousness of the matter by describing them as "terrorists" in an "organized conspiracy to use violence to coerce the United States into modifying its direction." This meant that the activists, if convicted, would spend many years in prison.

Ryan knew that the activists were not violent terrorists, but political pressure on the FBI to prosecute them as dangerous subversives put him in a conflict of interest. A 1983 US Bishop's Pastoral Letter on War and Peace caused him to reassess how he should respond to orders which were against his conscience. As a result, he refused to assist with a malicious prosecution and asked to be reassigned. Instead of a transfer, the FBI fired him, and he lost his pension. Years would pass before court proceedings would rule that the FBI discriminated against Jack Ryan on religious grounds and that the Bureau was wrong to require blind obedience to its orders.

During my first season in the East Port marina, I could replenish my boat's food stores only by taking a local bus the two-mile ride to the city centre and the supermarkets. There, I would gather up half a dozen bags under my arms and take the bus back to the marina. By the second season, the bus drivers recognized me, smiled, and said "hello" just as they did to all their regular customers. I told Doug that this was a sure sign that I had been in Peoria too long.

Doug said, "Why don't you take a car?" He meant that he was offering the use of *his* car. He owned six of them. My favourite was the Jaguar. It was a gleaming, wine-red sedan. Doug had installed a high-performance Corvette engine under its hood. It could stand up on its rear tires when asked. My mouth slid open dumbly. I stared at the Jag much the same way as my beagle stares at the last forkful of meat rising from a dinner plate. It was like an apparition. I began to salivate. I licked my lips. I swallowed.

"Take the Land Rover," he said. I blinked. My mouth went dry.

Nevertheless, the Land Rover opened up new possibilities for me. I could get groceries, sure. But now I could also go to the library or have dinner somewhere besides on the deck of my boat. I could run for boating supplies, paint, varnish, caulking, and so on. It also allowed me to head across the river to Dave's Good-Time Pool Hall, where few of the twenty-odd tables were not in use.

Dave's Good-Time Pool Hall had an old-time, risky feel to it that I liked. It was darkly lit; the scent of stale beer floated below drifts of blue cigarette smoke. The door to one washroom read, "sticks"; the other read, "pockets." Dusty trophies and autographed photos covered one wall. The counter of the bar stretched along another. In the dim reflection of the mirror, I saw street-smart grey heads lean over bottles, watch intently, speak in low voices about the money game at a nearby table, and wager a side bet among themselves. Occasionally, someone would discreetly glance toward the table where I played and try to size up whether I was a hustler from out of town or the amateur that I appeared to be.

Many recollections like these streamed through my head as I sailed up the Illinois River on that last day in June. I thought of Sean and Doc and Ty hauling boats, Liza chatting behind the bar, Captain Scottie and his tumultuous love interests, Uncle Bob's eccentricities, "Aunt" Ginny's pluck, Candy who imagined I was her father, and her husband, Tim, who predicted my future. There were many others, too, whose names I have omitted, forgotten or never knew, and I would miss them.

Meanwhile, the engine growled proudly as I passed up through the narrows at McClugage Bridge and met the riverboat *Spirit of Peoria* on her trip down. Her passengers gazed from the rail; some waved; some pointed cameras. Her great side-wheels churned the water as she swung around the last bend for Peoria. Hamm's Marina was about three hours upstream. I had expected to stop there for lunch, but construction work in the approaches left little room to manoeuvre. So I drifted quietly, made up a sandwich from ship stores, and let my mind churn with apprehension and exhilaration at the fact that, in a few days, my journey, undoubtedly, would resume once more.

Three hours later I tied up at my berth at the East Peoria marina. I felt myself curiously saddened at the thought of leaving Peoria. I had begun to feel comfortable there, almost lethargic, as dreamlike as any of the lotus-eaters among Ulysses's crew might have felt. So I struggled to steel myself for the journey which lay ahead, and whatever adventures or misadventures that may hold.

The future is ephemeral, though. It is not always what one expects. It is not always what one hopes. I found that out when I pulled the dipstick from the engine that evening and checked the oil level. The engine was down a quart of oil. I called the mechanics. A dye test showed that oil was seeping from the rear of the engine. That meant that the rear seal most likely was pinched when the engine was rebuilt. Days passed. The engine was pulled out of the boat and benched at the diesel repair shop. The mechanics attacked it vigorously. More days passed. The leaking seal turned out instead to be a crack in the backplate which holds the seal. So the backplate was sent to a tank welder for specialized welding. Another week passed. While this was being looked after, the mechanics noticed that the bearings, those which had just been replaced, were showing unusual wear. This suggested that the power train was misaligned somehow. This meant that the mechanics would have to...

Finally, I had reached the end of my tether. I felt the rope tighten against my throat.

"I've had enough," I told the diesel shop foreman. We sat opposite each other like two prizefighters awaiting the ring of the bell for round one.

"Just five more days. Give me five more days," he demanded.

"I want my money back. The engine's no good. It's not working out."

"You won't give me five days? You won't give me just five more days?!!" he shouted. He sat back in his chair, arms crossed, head cocked at a queer angle, like an animal alarmed by a strange noise.

"I've already given you five days...and five days...and five days... for two seasons!"

"We've worked in good faith! It's cost us thousands!"

"You've worked in good faith unsuccessfully, and it's cost me thousands to return here again and again. Enough!"

He shouted.

I shouted.

We both shouted.

Despite appearances, though, I was not really angry. I was resolute, yes. I was determined, yes, but my show of anger was just that, posturing, and no more substantial than the pretentious haggling that buyers and sellers act out over the price of a trinket in an Asian marketplace. It was, however, effective and, in the end, we agreed on a suitable refund.

"Fair enough," I said.

We stood. I offered my hand. He looked surprised, hesitated, but shook it.

There was a short awkward moment, and then a cloud passed over his countenance. His head canted forward. His lips moved slowly as if they were about to give up some ghastly secret.

"That engine..." he began. The words hissed out like an escaping demon. "It was...It was...a *fucking*...nightmare."

I nodded solemnly, like a priest in his confessional.

I have never resolved whether or not to believe in the existence of fate, divine intervention, or luck. There were times when I have felt the presence of God over my shoulder gently nudging me this way or that. Other times, I have been content to accept the belief that my will to do this or that was helped or hindered by unlimited other causes bent on their own set courses. I felt like one of millions of human targets in a cosmic and chaotic game of dodge ball. And even in those moments or periods of my life when I have flirted with one or another of these philosophical views, I remained sceptical of the degree to which they affected people's lives.

Once again, however, my mind churned over these ideas, ones perhaps too grand for a humble mind. The circumstances which ignited my thinking were these: I had spent two and a half years trying to repair one and then another engine. Numerous mechanics had taken a crack at it. None were successful. My tribulations and frustrated expectations had already added several verses to the book of Job. Even at that, a dark cloud persevered, stalked me, and rained down a packet of mechanical calamities, the magnitude of which defied an explanation as simplistic as bad luck.

I never expected to end my voyage in Peoria, Illinois. But that is precisely what happened. Ending a voyage in Peoria has the same cachet as closing a musical comedy in Scranton. As a sailor, I would prefer to have been shipwrecked on a remote Bahamian island; and if I were a playwright, I would have wished for at least a brief off-Broadway run. But the ending of a memoir cannot be rewritten. As a result, the *Arja D.* and I danced at one end or another of a Peoria wharf for two seasons and, at times, I grew to feel like one of Mack Sennett's Keystone Cops—dangling from the open rear door of a careening police van. Helpless. Pathetic. And bewildered.

It was mechanical problems, not willpower, which put a stop to my trip and an end to my old dream. I offer that in my defence. Nevertheless, I accepted defeat. I resigned myself to the fact that I could not complete the last half of my voyage. I made that decision on a Monday. Tuesday morning I walked out of the diesel repair shop with little more than a slim hope of finding a way to get my boat home. And that was a worry. I couldn't afford to ship my boat home. Perhaps I would have to sell it, I pondered. But there was no market for sailboats here, and I couldn't bring myself to sell it, anyway. Perhaps I would have to store it for a year or two. Maybe longer. But that thought provoked visions of it rotting away in some dry dock, the fate of other orphaned boats.

What happened then seemed almost miraculous. Doug and Dennis had uncovered a couple of promising leads and, before the sun had set that day, I had found a big-engine cargo van and a tandem boat trailer almost without effort. Both cost less than I could have imagined and, before week's end, I would be on the road and heading home.

Was it fate? Divine intervention? I don't know. But the circumstances which prevented my voyaging further downstream were many and unstoppable. Some would say they were uncanny. On the other hand, the ease with which I found the means to return home was extraordinary. Some would call it auspicious.

In the end, I was left more than half-believing that something never meant me to sail past Peoria and that I had been too stubborn or too foolish to accept that different path.

In the few days which followed, both Doug and Dennis helped me prepare for my return to Prince Edward Island. Doug gave me a spare tire for the trailer. Dennis offered his trucker's advice on hauling eight thousand pounds of boat two thousand miles across the continent. He showed me how to conserve fuel and suggested a route with fewer mountains.

He also offered some other advice.

"You've had a lot of interesting adventures along the way," he said. "At least I thought they were interesting. Maybe other people might think so too...I dunno."

At the time we were having a beer on the veranda of the marina. The day was milder than usual. The sky was pale. The Peoria skyline was as soft as a Monet painting.

"Mebee you should write a book."

"Well I—"

"Y'know, it's easy now. All ya gotta do is talk in t'yer computer, and the computer writes it for ya. That's all there is to it," he said, his hands sweeping up into the air as if a book would magically spring from them.

"I've thought about—"

"It's easy," he interjected. "The computer does it all. It's hardly any work now. Yea, you should write a book. I'd read it."

I sipped on my beer.

I sipped again.

Several empty moments fell into the wake of his monologue. Then several more. They pooled into a quietness that seemed strange. A bit eerie even. So I stole the opportunity to speak.

"Perhaps I will, Dennis...Yes...Perhaps I will."

Chapter 21

LIGHTS DIM, FADE TO CREDITS

That night I slept on the boat. There had been no gentle rocking to sleep, no lap of wave, no tug of mooring lines, none of that. The *Arja D.* was aground, high and dry on the trailer attached to my newly acquired van just north of the clubhouse.

I pulled out at dawn the next morning. There were no more goodbyes to be said. The sky was dark and murky. A few drops of rain splattered the windshield. The wiper blades smeared them away. Then came a deluge, a harsh, blinding, and relentless storm. A quarter mile out, the wipers could no longer keep up. So I pulled off the highway into the empty parking lot of the Par-a-Dice Casino.

Blustering wind and sheets of rain erased any sign of Peoria. Everything beyond the windshield of my cab vanished, my focus muddled, and my attention took refuge inward. I found disappointment there, but failure was still beyond the grasp of my acknowledgement.

Dennis's suggestion to write a book was interesting, and I admit that the idea had crossed my mind. But such a book would have no ending. Nor was any resolution in sight. I was just two days' sail from the Mississippi River. That would have been a significant milestone. I was still three thousand miles from completing the circular route I had planned for. A musician might get away with writing a baffling song about "a horse with no name"...but a book with no ending...?

The storm in Peoria was short-lived. I returned to the road within an hour and began my slow progress through Illinois and Indiana and Michigan. I was a novice at hauling a large trailer.

It took two days to reach Detroit. There I crossed the Ambassador Bridge and pulled into the customs station sometime after midnight. I was the only border crosser there, and I anticipated a squad of armed and suspicious officers to spill from their building, swarm my van and boat, and sniff through every plastic bag and recessed compartment. Both van and boat were awash with gear and supplies.

None of that happened though. In fact, they showed little interest in the contents of either vehicle. They dwelled, however, on the paperwork of importing the van and trailer, but those documents were in order and, after fifteen minutes or so, I lumbered across the border into Canada.

I was too exhausted to continue much further. So I pulled off the highway at a desolate rural crossroads. I pulled in and parked. I hoisted myself up, onto the boat and fell deeply asleep in my bunk in the cabin.

Morning brought dry weather and sun, and that cheered me considerably. Having returned to Canada boosted my spirits and made me feel as if home was "just around the corner," even though another thousand miles stretched up ahead.

Toronto's traffic ate away some of my enthusiasm though. Highway 401 was bumper to bumper and stop-and-go around noon. I worried about the thirty-three-foot mast lashed down atop my twenty-six-foot boat. In spite of the red warning colours fluttering at the ends of it, I imagined that huge spar piercing the windshield of a transit bus or tractor-trailer, and my anxiety peaked.

I made it to Montreal after dark during a stiff, blustery rain. Traffic was demanding. My windshield was fogging. I was travelling slower than most traffic, but I was I afraid I would be swept into an exit ramp I didn't want and descend into a more agonizing depth of driving hell. So I clung to a middle lane while local cars and trucks shattered the speed limit as they passed me on either side. My hands had taken a stranglehold on the steering wheel. My knuckles grew white. My thumbs cramped. Eventually, I cleared Montreal and took the road toward Quebec City. I exited into a quiet neighbourhood, pulled alongside a quiet curb, and fell soundly asleep.

New Brunswick offered a different worry and challenge. It was the only stretch of highway with mountains—two hundred miles of Appalachian Mountains—terrain in which, I had to keep trailer and boat under control to avoid jackknifing. Sudden braking, steep inclines, and wet roads were a bad combination and, under the right circumstances, nine thousand pounds of trailer and boat could easily shove the rear of the van sideways and convert an error in judgment into a tragic finale.

I passed through a few wet patches in the mountains but, except for heightened attentiveness and anxiety, the trek was without mishap. The terrain levelled out as we approached the sea and, by late afternoon, my rig clunked and rattled into Beach Point, Prince Edward Island, and home.

It would have been more artistically pleasing and dramatic to claim that the ending to this book came suddenly one night in a Gestalt flash of enlightenment, but that was not the case. It took years to accept that my cut-in-stone expectations had blinded me to the success that it had been. No, my voyage was never completed, nor would it likely be; but that had not stopped my dream from being realized.

As I said in the very beginning, my small odyssey began with a dream, the dream of a child, and the dreams of children may be many things—the reverberation of fears, the glimmer of brass rings—but my childhood dream was a bit different. It was a dream in which little happened, but it was one which stirred my emotions. It was nearly motionless, static, but those images were memorable for what they represented—romanticism, adventure, and freedom—not what I had appended to them as a young man. I had overlooked the fact that as age changes, and as experience, perception, and judgment grow, so does our understanding of old and lingering dreams.

Wiser now than I was at seven or eight, I came to understand several things. First of all, completing a circumnavigation of half the continent was not the key to fulfilling my youthful fantasy. Fulfillment existed in those qualities at the heart of that fantasy, not the route taken. Romanticism, adventure, and freedom were the qualities I sought after...and those were qualities I found.

I found romanticism in the fascinating people I met along that long watery road. Countless of them shared their joys and hopes and visions, confessed their fears, recounted misfortunes or blunders, and shared their spirits of generosity. I experienced joy and awe, humour and loneliness, friendship and fear, camaraderie and suspicion. I bathed in the beauty of rivers, lakes, and marshes, felt the power of nature and the smallness of man. And I shared a fellowship with fish and fowl, creatures great and small, who measured my curious progress through their own wild world.

And adventure? Adventure is just another word for challenge, and many of those I have already described. They need no delineation. Others remain unspoken.

Freedom, however, is more difficult to pin down. It means different things to different people at different times in their lives. For me it meant breaking away from the label of "getting older," away from routines expected or prescribed, away from ruts I had worn myself into, and doing, instead, what I *needed* to do: face new challenges. And so, as Robert Frost did, "I took the road less travelled by," and down that road I stumbled over many challenges, and did my best to face them.

Little more needs to be said.

All of this began as a child's dream, a dream built out of wooden blocks and papier mâché. Now, as I look back, I understand that that ancient dream has changed me. I have become a better person and a stronger one, and I am also wiser now, in my knowing how and why "We are such stuff as dreams are made on..."

ARJA D. BOAT LOG

2004

Date	Location	Depart	Arrive	Destination	N. Miles
23-06-04	Beach Point PE	1000	0030	Borden PE	75
24-06-04	Borden PE	1100	----	Shediac NB	38
25-06-04	Shediac NB	1000	1500	Saint-Édouard NB	24
26-06-04	Saint-Édouard-de-Kent NB	0700	1700	Tracadie NB	60
29-06-04	Tracadie-Sheila NB	0530	1900	Grande-Rivière PQ	65
30-06-04	Grande-Rivière PQ	0515	1330	Pointe-au-Renard PQ	42
01-07-04	Pointe-au-Renard PQ	0600	1450	Rivière-la-Madeleine PQ	42
02-07-04	Rivière-la-Madeleine PQ	0600	1900	Cap-Chat PQ	55
03-07-04	Cap-Chat PQ	0830	2030	Matane PQ	40
06-07-04	Matane PQ	0730	1830	Rimouski PQ	46
07-07-04	Rimouski PQ	1015	1830	Trois-Pistoles PQ	38
09-07-04	Trois-Pistoles PQ	1015	1830	Rimouski PQ	38
13-07-04	Rimouski PQ	0515	1330	Matane (Old Port) PQ	46
14-07-04	Matane PQ	0715	1830	Sainte-Anne-des-Monts PQ	43
15-07-04	Sainte-Anne-des-Monts PQ	0530	1530	Rivière-la-Madeleine PQ	46
16-07-04	Rivière-la-Madeleine PQ	0830	1700	Rivière-au-Renard PQ	42

17-07-04	Rivière-au-Renard PQ	0708	1730	Grand-Rivière PQ	42
18-07-04	Grand-Rivière PQ	0400	2000	Tracadie NB	65
19-07-04	Tracadie NB	1115	1530	Charlottetown PE	160
21-07-04	Charlottetown PE	----	----	Beach Point PE	45
				Total Mileage:	**1,010**

2005

Date	Location	Depart	Arrive	Destination	N. Miles
26-06-05	Beach Point PE	0830	1330	Wood Islands PE	19
27-06-05	Wood Islands PE	1030	----	Borden PE	46
28-06-05	Borden PE	0900	1200	Summerside PE	14
01-07-05	Summerside PE	0715	0500	Tracadie NB	100
03-07-05	Tracadie NB	0715	2030	Grand-Rivière PQ	65
04-07-05	Grand-Rivière PQ	0515	1330	Rivière-au-Renard PQ	42
05-07-05	Rivière-au-Renard PQ	0515	1400	Rivière-la-Madeleine PQ	42
06-07-05	Rivière-la-Madeleine PQ	0700	1700	Sainte-Anne-des-Monts PQ	46
07-07-05	Sainte-Anne-des-Monts PQ	0600	1500	Matane (Old Port) PQ	47
08-07-05	Matane (Old Port) PQ	0545	1500	Rimouski PQ	46
10-07-05	Rimouski PQ	1030	1945	Île aux Basques PQ	38
09-07-05	Île aux Basques PQ	1230	1630	Port de Gros-Cacouna PQ	20
12-07-05	Port de Gros-Cacouna PQ	1330	1900	Cap-à-l'Aigle PQ	30
13-07-05	Cap-à-l'Aigle PQ	1545	----	Île aux Coudres PQ	20
14-07-05	Île aux Coudres PQ	0700	1430	Saint-Michel PQ	52
15-07-05	Saint-Michel PQ	0900	1430	Neuville PQ	35
16-07-05	Neuville PQ	1130	1800	Batiscan PQ	34
17-07-05	Batiscan PQ	0530	2000	Sorel PQ	56
18-07-05	Sorel PQ	0800	2000	Montreal PQ	44
21-07-05	Longueuil PQ	1130	1830	Melocheville PQ	32
22-07-05	Melocheville PQ	1130	2000	Valleyfield PQ	18.5
23-07-05	Valleyfield PQ	0715	1500	Cornwall ON	31

24-07-05	Cornwall ON	1015	1730	Morrisburg ON	19
25-07-05	Morrisburg ON	0715	1700	Brockville ON	35
26-07-05	Brockville ON	1100	1830	Bateau Channel	32
27-07-05	Bateau Channel	0900	1400	Kingston, ON	10
28-07-05	Kingston ON	0915	----	Belleville ON	32
30-07-05	Belleville ON	0815	1930	Campbellford ON	42
31-07-05	Campbellford ON	0930	1930	Bensfort Bridge	46
01-08-05	Bensfort Bridge ON	0915	1200	Peterborough ON	14
02-08-05	Peterborough ON	0830	----	Buckhorn	41
03-08-05	Buckhorn	0700	1530	Rosedale	37
04-08-05	Rosedale ON	0630	1900	Orillia ON	30
04-08-05	Orillia ON	0830	1800	Port Severn ON	31
05-08-05	Port Severn ON	0830	1100	Midland ON	10
08-08-05	Midland ON	0545	1645	Hay Island	55
09-08-05	Hay Island	0730	1700	Wingfield Basin	35
11-08-05	Wingfield Basin	0745	1730	Killarney ON	49
12-08-05	Killarney ON	0930	1330	Little Current ON	22
13-08-05	Little Current ON	0900	1900	Meldrum Bay	54
14-08-05	Meldrum Bay	0715	1600	Detour Village MI	44
15-08-05	Detour Village MI	----	----	MacKinaw City MI	40
16-08-05	Macinaw City MI	----	1730	Charlevoix MI	48
17-08-05	Charlevois MI	0630	1730	Frankfort MI	62
20-08-05	Frankfort MI	0550	1030	Manistee MI	23
23-08-05	Manistee MI	0610	1800	Muskegon MI	69
24-08-05	Muskegon MI	0830	1800	South Haven MI	50
25-08-05	South Haven MI	0400	1730	G. Lakes Naval Sta.	70
				Total Mileage:	**1,877.5**

2006

Date	Location	Depart	Arrive	Destination	N. Miles
31-05-06	G. L. Naval Station	0915	1430	Chicago IL	27
31-05-06	Chicago IL	1430	1930	Mile 299, IL. River	27
01-06-06	Mile 299, IL. River	0730	1900	Mile 278, Big Basin Mar.	21
02-06-06	Mile 278 Big Basin Mar.	0900	1730	Mile 240, Ottawa IL	37

03-06-06	Mile 240, Ottawa IL	0700	1500	Mile 196, Henry IL	44
17-06-06	Mile 196, Henry IL	1145	1600	Mile 166, Peoria IL	30
			Total Mileage:		**186**

2008

Date	Location	Depart	Arrive	Destination	N. Miles
30-06-08	Peoria IL	0845	1155	Chillicothe IL	15
----	Chillicothe IL	1200	1420	Peoria IL	15
			Total Mileage:		**30**

Total Voyage Mileage: 3,104

ACKNOWLEDGEMENTS

I am indebted to PEI author Marion Bruce for showing interest in a partially completed draft of my journey. It is a fact that even slight encouragement will propel a writer forward. So I continued on with my venture. Three or four drafts followed before the manuscript was complete, but too much detail had swollen the text to 143,000 words. By contrast, my Webster's *New World Dictionary of the American Language* (college edition) contains a mere 142,000 entries.

I saw the writing on the wall...and there was too much of it. I also knew the consequence. Such wordiness would compel any self-respecting editor to hurl me headfirst out of his or her office and boot me soundly toward an academic career.

A lightning bolt struck. Ohmygod, I thought. I can't let that happen. So I pulled myself together.

I knew what I had to do. I headed for the garden shed, retrieved a machete, and began to hack through the jungle of words I had created. The job was tedious. It consumed six more drafts. Seventeen bushels of words were burned, but my story was all the better for it.

At 114,000 words, my fiction editor, Terrilee Bulger, read it and recommended it to Elaine McCluskey, non-fiction editor at Nimbus Publishing. Elaine uncovered the theme that I had left gasping for air in various corners of the manuscript and encouraged me to give it a chance to shine. After that it became easier to clip and trim the narrative down to 90,000-odd words.

For all of that, I thank you, Terrilee; I thank you, Elaine; and I thank your merry crew in layout, art, advertising, public relations, and proofreading at Nimbus.

My thanks as well to my wife, Brenda, for her ongoing support of my writing endeavours; to my son Finley for tech support and content suggestions; and to the countless, kind, generous, and helpful people I encountered along the waterways of Canada and the United States.